Manya Harari
Memoirs
1906 – 1969

Manya Harari
Memoirs

1906 – 1969

HARVILL PRESS
London 1972

ISBN O OO 272503 7

Made and printed in Great Britain
by William Collins Sons & Co Ltd Glasgow
for the Publishers Harvill Press Ltd
30A Pavilion Road, London SW1

Contents

Illustrations

  * *from paintings by the author, photographed by Brian Tyer*

Some Facts

Manya, the youngest daughter of Grigori Benenson, a Russian-Jewish banker with world-wide interests, was born in Baku on the 8th of April 1906. She spent her childhood in Petersburg and Redkino, a country estate, some hundred miles south of the capital.

When the First World War broke out the family were in Germany. They made a hazardous journey to England where Manya went to school at Malvern Girls' College. When she was sixteen, having matriculated, she attended London University from which she graduated with a degree in history.

In 1925 she visited Palestine for the first time. There she met Ralph Harari, then serving in the British Administration. Six months later they were married in Paris.

Her husband returned to Egypt where he was associated with various development schemes. He worked mostly in Cairo where his father, Sir Albert Harari, lived. During her time in Egypt Manya was very active in social work connected with La Providence, a Home for Jewish Orphans, La Goutte de Lait, another charity that looked after small children, and a hostel for discharged prisoners. From Egypt she often went to Palestine and in 1926 she stayed in a kibbutz where she shared the life and work of the community. The Hararis spent their holidays in England and here, in 1928, their son was born.

In 1932 Manya was received into the Catholic Church by Father Martin d'Arcy.

During the following years she was associated with the inauguration of the movement of The Sword of the Spirit, she worked with Christopher Dawson on *The Dublin Review* and then started her own periodical *The Changing World*. It ceased publication in 1942 when she entered the Political Intelligence Department of the Foreign Office, where soon her husband, who had till then been Economic Adviser to General Wavell, joined her.

In 1946 Manya founded a small publishing house, The Harvill Press. The name was derived from the first syllable of her name and that of her partner Marjorie Villiers. It specialised in translations of important books on religion, metaphysics, the arts and psychology. For some years she co-edited, with Bernard Wall, a periodical which bore the same name as its predecessor, *The Changing World*, but had a more literary character.

In 1948 she went as a reporter to Palestine during the war of liberation.

In 1954 Harvill became a subsidiary of William Collins. In 1955 Manya accompanied Billy Collins, the Chairman, to Russia to discover whether, in spite of the USSR not being a signatory of the Berne Convention, it might be possible to expand business with the State Publishing House.

In the following year she visited Russia to negotiate a book on the ballet to be illustrated by Baron.

In 1961 she went to Russia for the last time.

In May 1969 Ralph Harari died. Manya herself died four months later.

Part I
A Russian Childhood

I

My governess arrived on a winter afternoon in 1908, when I was just over two. She wore a tall black velvet hat. She was called Rikarna, short for Erika Karlovna; she was half Swede and half Finn.

My Tartar nurse had left and our maid was looking after me. Her name was Agrafena, shortened to Grusha, which meant Pear, and it was always as a juicy pear I thought of her.

Rikarna banished my elder sister Fira from the nursery which I had shared with her, put the kitchen with its cosy smells and cheerful voices out of bounds, assured me that the fairy tales Pear had told me were untrue, and was soon reading Dickens' *Bleak House* to me.

I distinctly remember, on my fourth birthday, thinking of Aunt Lisa who had given me a doll (and who, according to Rikarna, was not my aunt) 'she believes I'm still a child.'

We were living in Petersburg on the Morskaya of which I have no recollection. Fira went to high school and had a strict French governess. My eldest sister Flora was at a boarding school at Wiesbaden and my brother Yasha at the University in Freiburg. My parents believed that German education was the best.

Both came from the Jewish Pale – paradoxically Papa from Minsk and Mama from Pinsk – but my father was making a glittering career in oil, banking and real estate. I was to hear something about this in the following year when we moved to a smarter street.

The Moika, where we rented the top floor of the Volkonskys' house, was not only beautiful but very grand: Tsars had dined on the floor below. The local servants – maids, cooks, coachmen, handymen – knew the district and its aristocratic tradition. Since we clearly did not belong to it, we must be very rich, they said. As my reading widened, by the age of six, I thought of wealth weighing upon us as a tragic and evil fate.

We had settled into the Moika flat in 1909. Rikarna and I moved in first – the rest of the family were in Carlsbad. We lived in one of the front rooms facing the canal. There was hardly any furniture – the beds stood on a vast shining expanse of intricate parquet. Into these rooms with their tall uncurtained windows there burst every morning at dawn the unforgettable sound of peasants shouting, bells jingling and hooves and metal wheels clattering on cobbles, as the vegetable carts drove to the market, pulled by horses with tall, painted yokes.

When the rooms were furnished, they turned into the drawing-room with its sets of Louis XV *bergères*, man-sized Sèvres vases and tables of porphyry and malachite; the ballroom, with a painted frieze of roses high above the thicket of palm trees in buckets, arranged to hide the musicians at one end of the room; the sitting-room in maple wood and pale green satin by Maples of London, my father's study and dressing-room and my parents' bedroom – all were immense. The dining-room (tobacco-brown and mahogany) and the children's room (to which we moved when the family returned) looked out on a quiet courtyard which communicated through an archway and a smaller yard with a busy street. Across the courtyard lived a seamstress who never looked up from her work. On the left, above the stables and coach houses, was the servants' wing, and on the right another wing, furnished but unused and mysterious; in 1917 it was to shelter Fira's friends who were in hiding from the Cheka.

As far back as I can remember, revolutionary fervour was in the air. At one end of the Moika the Tsar lived in his Winter Palace, but beyond it and across the Neva, the spire of the fortress of Saints Peter and Paul needled the sky – there the revolutionaries were imprisoned – and at the other end of the Moika lay the Field of Mars to which they marched, singing, to their death. Cousins Grigori and Leopold were always in trouble for joining student strikes; they brought their radical young friends to dinner and argued through the night. The rooms in which they argued were perhaps those in which the Decembrists[1] had plotted close on a century ago, for one of the Volkonskys had taken part in the rising against Nicholas I.

Yet, radical minded though my father was himself, he had once gone to the palace as a member of a bankers' delegation and ever since had felt the charm of the sad, simple and doomed Emperor, as romantic as that of the revolutionaries themselves.

Rikarna too must have had divided feelings, conservative and obscurantist though she was. She could not have read Tolstoy, brought up the children of the nobles and the rich, and gossiped with servants and peasants, without feeling the tension of the high voltage cable stretching between the sovereign and the revolutionaries and the beggars. Besides, she had had a formative experience as a girl. In her first job she had looked after the son of a Prince Mirsky (I never discovered whether he was the one who came to England in the 1920s and returned to Soviet Russia to die). In those days she still kept up with her favourite school friend Marusya Tverskaya, now a student at Petersburg University. Marusya lived in lodgings on the 'Petersburg Side' – the left bank of the Neva – and held evening parties for students, to which Erika was invited. The subversive talk went to her heart and head, although it alarmed her. One evening, as she was getting out of the tram near Marusya's house, an inner voice warned her: 'Don't go on. Take the next tram back.' She obeyed the voice. That night the lodgings were raided and Marusya was arrested. Shaken and grieved, Erika took all the more comfort in the presence of a young man who had recently become a frequent visitor at her employer's house. She fell in love with him and her feelings seemed to be reciprocated. But one day the young man stopped coming. Opening her Bible, Erika found a note in it: 'I am not the one for whom you take me.' Ultimately she was driven to the bitter conclusion that her lover had been an agent of the Secret Police, and his visits due to her own connection with Marusya and her circle, whom perhaps she had betrayed. These events were to prey on her mind and may have upset its balance. That summer the Mirskys went as usual to their estate near Taganrog. Often at midnight Rikarna felt impelled to rise, leave the house and wade out up to her neck into the lake in the park – she was convinced that the life of the Tsar depended upon her doing this. Once, by a strange coincidence, this enabled her to save the life of her charge who had gone for a midnight bathe and swum out of his depth. When I knew her, Rikarna was looking for police agents under the beds; and when I saw her last, shortly before her death in Helsinki where she had retired, she slept at night on a trunk in the windowless lobby of her flat for fear of the death rays which Finnish, Russian and British police spies were sending from the window of the flat across the road.

II

When I was five or six, Flora came back from school. Unlike Fira who, at fourteen, had a camellia complexion, dusky ringlets and flashing eyes, Flora was tall, plump, blonde and concealed a virile mind and iron will under the prim demeanour of a German Miss. Her character had been formed in the past ten years. Before that, our home had been near the oil wells in Baku where Papa had started his ascent into the Russian business world. One day, when my two sisters were playing near the shores of the Caspian Sea and their nurse was gossiping in the shade of the pier, a caique had tied up near the beach, villainous characters had landed from it and had almost succeeded in snatching the two little girls and carrying them off to 'a fate worse than death' in their master's harem. Soon after this, and the Revolution of 1905, my parents decided to move to Petersburg.

Children bewildered them, and their one idea was to leave them in safe hands. Wiesbaden was convenient because it was on the way to Carlsbad where my mother took her yearly cure. So it was there that, when the idea first occurred to her, she took Flora to tea with Frau Braun, the headmistress of a boarding school. Flora was told to go and play with the other little girls and my mother quietly went back to her hotel. Flora's feelings may be imagined when she found herself at the age of eight abandoned in a strange house in a foreign town. She ran away. But with a heartlessness the child was never to forgive, my mother waited only a week and played the same trick on her again, taking her to tea with another headmistress, Fräulein Wolff. This time, Flora gritted her teeth and determined to see it through. For ten years she stuck it out, visited once or at most twice a year by the rest of us on our way to or from the Austrian resort.

When she returned home she was shocked by our untidy Russian ways – meals were never on time and Mama wandered about in an elegant dressing-gown until well after midday – and she shocked my mother almost as much by presenting her with a hideous pale mauve satin embroidered fire-screen of her own handywork.

The screen stood in the Maples sitting-room which luckily had an open fireplace *à l'anglaise* – most of the rooms were heated by stoves. It was a symbol of the background to which Fräulein Wolff expected her charges to return when they left her care. Perhaps as a concession to its mute demands, Flora's room was redecorated in débutante pink and white. But my strongest memory of her in Petersburg is of the sword, shield, helmet and cloak she wore to a fancy dress ball. She had left home as a mild little girl; she returned with her fire-screen and her sword.

It might be said by some psychiatrists that my mother ought never to have had children, but who am I to complain since I owe her the infinite possibilities of the life I have enjoyed in the last sixty-four years. Besides, it seemed that her ferocity was spent on her two elder daughters (there is a family legend of her buying a cow-hide whip for each and marking them with their names). She adored my brother, and me she sometimes even spoiled, according to her lights.

I remember her taking me shopping one day before Christmas (not that we were allowed a Christmas tree or any other reminder of the gentile feast). In winter in Petersburg the sun set at 3 pm. The city, shining with pale gold steeples against the darkish sky of the early afternoon, glittered with delights: the pineapples, the yellow oranges and the tangerines in silver paper in the windows of Yeliseyev Brothers, the court greengrocers – now one of the State food shops known as *Gastronoms*. And then there were candles inside the open doors of the church in the square next to the Gostiny Dvor – a double tier of shops beneath arcades, half Selfridges and half Cairo bazaar which, even today, retain for me something of their pre-1914 pre-Christmas glamour.

At home, the great stoves which took up whole walls and had small square doors opening on to fiery caverns kept the flat smelling of wood smoke. It also smelt of snow when the vent in the window had been kept open for one half hour out of the twenty-four to air the room, and, as well, there was the scent of the flowers in the vases that, before a dinner party, were scattered all about the tablecloth. The air was so warm that women rustled comfortably in their scented fashionable silk skirts and soft georgette blouses with transparent sleeves.

Scented, rustling, Mama was enveloped in sables from her neck to her toes, as, holding me by the hand, she swept down the curving stairs and out to climb into the closed carriage. We drove to Gostiny Dvor (I surreptitiously crossing myself as we passed the many churches as I had seen the servants doing), left the carriage in the square and entered the crowded shops. There, as a treat, mother allowed me to hold her enormous sable muff while she left me standing beside the counter as she went to pay for her purchases. When she came back the muff had gone. I must have put it down on a chair while I stared at the Christmas toys and it had been stolen. That muff probably cost a fortune yet my mother never spoke an angry word. She took me out through the crowd of crippled beggars in the arcades and in the coach on the way home she unwrapped her parcel and showed me what she had bought – a beautiful amethyst from the Urals in which was set an electric bell push for her sitting-room. On the same occasion I confided in her my ambition to be a ballet dancer and she calmed my fears of it being too late to start at the Maryinsky Theatre since they took pupils only at the age of eight.

This was the reassuring downy side of her nature which my mother showed me, and I was at my wits' end to understand why Flora sighed as she gloomily paced her rosebud room and Fira sobbed and hiccuped, locking herself up in the lavatory at the end of the nursery corridor.

III

Until my parents' generation the family tradition had been strongly religious; there had been miracle-working Hassids among my father's ancestors and many Rabbis on my mother's side. But father, despite his parents, had brought himself up on Darwin and the great wave of secularism and liberty had rushed him out of the ghetto. There was little to distinguish his ideas from those of many liberal Russians of his generation; like them, he admired the West and believed passionately in progress.

In our house only the great religious occasions, such as the Day of Atonement and Passover, were celebrated and only mother went occasionally to the synagogue. One of the earliest things I remember, I can't have been more than two at the time, was going into an Orthodox church with Grusha and being curious about the ikons. Rikarna was a Swedish-Finnish Lutheran who disliked the Orthodox only a little less than the Catholics. I asked her to take me to church with her but she said she wouldn't unless my parents gave her permission. So, I told them I wanted to become a Christian. When they asked me why, I said it was because I wanted to believe in angels, or to have an angel, I don't remember which. Father told me that I could, as a Jewess, believe in angels; mother said that if I became a Christian I would have to hate the Jews. She had seen the great Kishenev pogrom and that, she told me, was what Christians were taught to do to Jews. Was she in good faith? She described how the mob had advanced carrying crosses. What part did the Orthodox clergy play in the pogroms? At any rate they do not seem to have protested. And the police stood by.

In spite of this I was attracted to Christianity and retained a faith of some sort. For instance, when Rikarna went out and was late returning, I would kneel on the red carpet in the drawing-room and pray that God would keep her safe.

I even had thoughts of running away to the Troitsko-Sergievsky Lavra (monastery) and becoming a novice. I imagined the monastery as a long way down the Nevsky Prospect and one day set out for it only, of course, to be recaptured after a few hundred yards.

Later when I saw a picture of the Crucifixion in some book I tried to copy it and repeated that I wanted to be a Christian. Miss Cook, our English teacher, to whom I told this said 'Does your little heart tell you it is true?' Which I thought very cissy but thereafter such pictures and stories were removed. When I was eleven, and by then we were in England, I remember telling Rikarna that I thought everyone must share in the sacrifice of Christ, at which her Lutheran soul was horrified!

It so happened that just when I was developing ideas about Christianity, the Bayliss case made an uproar throughout Russia. A Jewish family was charged with ritual murder. For some time I could not get anyone to tell me about it, but one day the papers were full of it and I read all the details of the alleged crime. The body of a small boy had been found 'still in his blood-stained shirt'; according to the article he had been killed by Jews who had rolled him in a barrel lined with spikes in order to extract the Christian blood which they used in making the Passover bread.

I asked my governess and the maids if it were true. They brushed the question aside. Unwilling to disbelieve the papers or to believe that their employers went in for such practices, they were inclined to think that ritual murder was confined to a section of the Jews and unknown to others. My father, with whom I checked this theory, was horrified and immediately engaged a teacher to give me religious instruction. I was reassured when I learned that kosher meat had to be completely drained of blood, for I thought that if the blood of animals could not be eaten it was unlikely that human blood was used in making the matzo.

This was a real comfort to me but, even after that, I was haunted by the darkness of the child's fear and pain as described in the newspapers, by the iniquity of the crime, if indeed it had been committed by anyone, by the lie which had given it this dreadful form, by the ease with which the Russian maids had assumed that the blood guilt was in our blood and by the 'darkness'[2] of the Russian poor whom the lie was intended to incite against us.

That Christ was involved in it made the 'darkness' more intense. Fortunately, I never believed He was on the side of the Jew-hating Christians, and from now, very obscurely, I held the meaning of anti-semitism, though it was more than twenty years before I could begin to crack the shell. Somehow, the child was Christ, and Christ was also the Christians who drank His blood in one form and accused the Jews of drinking it in another. He was also the Russian poor whose 'darkness' was their poverty and who killed the Jewish poor; and He was also the poor Jews, His kinsmen, who had killed Him and who were falsely accused of killing Him by whoever needed a victim for his own killing of his God. Wherever the darkness was, there was a victim at the centre of it and the victim was always the child and always Christ.

As luck would have it that year the first and most solemn evening of Passover fell on the Orthodox Good Friday. Guests came to the ritual dinner, though fewer than in other years, and one place was left empty for the poor man who might come and who might be the Prophet Elijah. As usual, the door was left open for him, though my governess had urged my parents to have it locked on this occasion.

For the past week there had been rumours that riots would break out against the Jews. The servants had looked sulky, shuddering at the sight of the unleavened bread prepared for the feast. Not that they suspected us personally, the cook explained to me, but how could we know what was in it when we bought it at the kosher shop? When I asked her why the trouble was expected this particular night, she said awkwardly: 'Well, you see how it looks. This is the anniversary of the death of Christ and the Jews are celebrating.'

The dining-room looked out on the courtyard; the courtyard communicated through an archway with the yard that opened on to

The Moika, St Petersburg

From now onwards we included England in our winter journeys abroad, spending a month in the smokey splendour of Claridges. Here, in what is now the lounge, horse cabs clattered in and out of the fog, summoned by the whistle of the green-coated porter. Then, as a rule, we went to Nice in time for the mimosa and the *bataille des fleurs*.

Back in Petersburg, the telephone had now been installed in our flat and one year we travelled by train to a field where a crowd of many thousands watched an aeroplane rise a few feet from the ground. I remember that at this time father was breaking in Lily, a wicked English horse who rolled her eyes and one day galloped through a shop front.

On Thursdays Mr Brodsky held a dancing class and we practised the quadrille, though my sisters were secretly captivated by the tango. On other afternoons I went for walks with my governess along the granite-bordered quay which ran under the windows of the Winter Palace and passed by a hardly noticeable door at which, now and then, a carriage stopped and then galloped off carrying a muffled, mysterious man. As Rikarna was a passionate monarchist, my imagination was at the time divided between a situation in which I would rescue the Emperor (a dream vivified by going to my first matinée – Glinka's *A Life for the Tsar*[3] – at which I wept, and by watching the banners bowing to the dust before the tercentenary of the house of Romanov) and the alternative prospect of facing a firing squad for supporting the radical ideas of cousins Leopold and Grigori.

My father, swept by his Russian tastes and his love for the country, had bought a large estate called Redkino. To do this he had to evade the law against Jews owning land by registering it in the name of a non-Jewish friend. There was a lot of argument in the family as to whether this was proper or not. To me Redkino stood for happiness and had a permanent glory about it. I went there with my governess from early May till the first snow; the rest of the family came and went. When we were alone Rikarna came off her dignity and gossiped with any companion she could find. It was in this way I learned that my father was disliked and threatened. The estate had changed hands several times since the family who had originally owned it had left, more than fifty years ago, and the sugar merchant who had sold it to us had been as much a stranger as ourselves; he had, it seemed, also been a skinflint and the peasants had burned his ricks. Yet the old man who was scything the edge of the road said: 'He was a father, though he took the shirt off your back.' His present master, he admitted, was generous and easy going, yet that summer, when because of the drought a bad harvest was expected, there were rumours that he might be killed.

Father was disliked because of the agricultural machinery he had bought. The peasants believed them to be works of the devil and probably the cause of the drought, so they allowed them to rust in their sheds. He was disliked also as a stranger and a Jew. Fortunately, he was without fear.

One evening we were returning with him from a village beyond the River Luga. While the carriage was waiting for the ferry, he got out and stood with a group of peasants by the water. They were joined by others and suddenly they became a tight, sullen crowd pressing in upon him with scythes and hatchets. His expression of amused good humour never changed and evidently he talked his way out, for after a few minutes the men were pulling off their caps and laughing.

Father loved Redkino and the dark forces in it only added to his zest for life. When he was there his great pleasure was to fish the rainbow trout which lived in our little stream, shoot the rapids in a canoe made of a hollowed-out trunk, or go hunting with the local priest. In his way he understood the peasants, pitying their 'darkness' and their wretchedness, though he did little to change their lot. The estate was grand but poor and he had too many irons in the fire to do more than keep an eye on it and satisfy himself that the Agent managed it no worse, and indeed a little better, than a good many.

Violence was never far below the surface. One Sunday evening when Rikarna and I were alone the dogs began to bark loudly and we saw two men lurching past, the one supporting the other from whose arm a stream of blood was pouring. It turned out they were two friends who had gone to a fair at the neighbouring village of Sapsk; there they had quarrelled over a girl and the one had tried to chop off the other's hand with an axe. But, as soon as he realised what he had done, he repented and when we saw him he was helping his friend home.

For me, Redkino had magical places: the old vaulted kitchen hung with strings of dried apples, cluttered with barrels of mushrooms in vinegar, cucumbers in dill, and with cones of sugar, a stone or two in weight, hidden in blue wrappings, waiting to drown on a summer's afternoon in cauldrons of hissing cherry or strawberry syrup; the dairy where a maid churned butter, also there was old Prokofievna, the witch who lived by the duck pond. She had been an excellent cook and still made wonderful ices, muttering spells over the pails of cream.

Redkino, set in a great stretch of marsh and forest with a river winding through it, changed with the seasons. From June until August the valley was hot and thirsty, with naked children splashing in the stream and peasant women wading out modestly in stiff homespun shifts. The days were sweaty and sleepy, the evenings noisy with balalaikas and scented by tobacco flowers; the soft silvery marsh was filled with berries, the forests with night and mushrooms and sometimes fires blazed up which carried away whole villages in smoke.

Then on a dull October day Redkino, the house with its farm and outhouse, its old chapel with a tottering tower and its small, new, green-domed church, every wall of which was painted the same rose-red, glowed like a ripe fruit in a cloud of leafless trees, sheltered by a gentle rise of land and surrounded by monochrome distances.

Already the dusty road which cut across the park joining us to the railway station and stringing together many widely scattered villages had turned into sticky clay. Winter was coming upon us and then the impassable snow would ring each village, blanketing it with its devils, passions, charms, vodka and spleen to brew the poisons of isolation and proximity. Now we would go back to Petersburg where my imagination would be haunted by Redkino's square drawing-room with the angels on the ceiling who overlooked the buds in the cherry trees outside the windows, and by the verandah where we had our tea, sharing it with bumble bees.

Or, knowing that all now lay deep in snow and magic, I would see in my mind, our nearest village, its neat painted carvings, round the doors of the huts, proofed against the cold with frozen dung and realise that at this very moment people and animals must be sheltering together in a dark, warm fug, lit by naked rush lights.

Part II
Schooldays in England

I

On the eve of the First World War we left Russia, as it proved, for good. Our going was fortuitous. Mother, high-spirited but irrevocably devoted, had always lovingly forgiven father all his infidelities, and occasionally slapped his mistresses. With one of them he went too far; she urged him to divorce his wife and marry her. He replied with candour that he loved his wife. She vowed to revenge herself. Soon afterwards during an epidemic of acid throwing among lovers she lured him to a final meeting and splashed him with vitriol.

In danger of death or of blindness he bore his sufferings with fortitude. In the end he recovered but he remained monstrously disfigured, his face angry with scars and expressionless. Meanwhile he was very ill and mother decided that we should go to Jena where a famous professor was experimenting with plastic surgery.

This happened in May 1914. As usual the handyman was striding on his ladder, as on stilts, swinging an enormous bucket of starch as he painted the windows with a jungle of palm leaves, filling the rooms with a milky-blue radiance like the inside of an ice cube. This was done to protect them from the scorching Petersburg sun. The uncarpeted floors gleamed round the dust-sheeted furniture. The trunks, in which dresses were folded over thrice, and the hampers of linen were padlocked.

At the last minute, the unusual circumstances of the journey filled me with a disturbed sadness which I later took for a presentiment; I was not to see those rooms again for nearly half a century.

The summer drifted past in the cosy little town of Jena, with music from the bandstands and visits to the Goethe-Haus, while father, a swathed ghost in a dark room, underwent operation after operation.

On the eve of war my brother was still assuring us: 'The Socialists will prevent it,' and indeed, the streets were covered with their posters; but by next morning they had all been taken down. When, having missed our chance of going home (it was in any case uncertain whether father could have stood the journey), we followed the Professor to Bavaria. The station was full of civilians whose journeys had been

27

cancelled because of mobilisation, and in chaos. In Munich we sat silently in a café, for that morning a man who had been taken for a Frenchman had been lynched. Later we found that Russians were less hated than the French and when England entered the war she attracted to herself the full force of hostility, diverting it from her allies. The Bavarians were 'amiable but savages', said my governess, but we had little to do with them in the Nursing Home where we stayed.

At first there was news of a successful Russian advance towards Königsberg. Then the talk about the war became unbearable with the accounts of thousands of Russians drowning in the swamps.

In October, we followed the Professor to Hamburg. Only my brother was interned; the rest of us had to register twice a day at the police station, except for my father who continued to be bedridden, nursed by a woman who found it hard to look after an enemy.

Now that our absence had outrun the normal span of the summer holidays, the pale, grey city struck me with the cold of our uprooting. Twice a day we walked along the waterfront, beside the Elbe, wide and dreary, cold but never freezing; there were seagulls wheeling in the air and once a Zeppelin poised itself on the water almost filling the river from bank to bank. At other times we huddled in our rooms at the hotel, made gloomy by the trunks which towered in the corners and with only the coffee Rikarna was constantly brewing on a spirit lamp smelling of permanence and of home.

Food was getting short, bread greyer. Surely, we thought, this enemy country could not hold out much longer? Christmas with soldiers fraternising in the trenches, flashed like an awakening, but soon the cold sleep descended again.

At last we were allowed to go to Denmark. In Copenhagen, kind, windy and smelling deliciously of fresh rolls, we sorted ourselves out. Father, though not strong enough for work, was determined to go to England. So mother, taking only Fira with her, went to Russia to see to his affairs; the rest of us, braving the storms, mines and submarines of the North Sea ('so typical of your father's recklessness,' said Rikarna) crossed from Bergen to Newcastle and arrived in London on a Dickensian evening of dim-out and fog.

We stayed in a cheerful suite of rooms at the Berkeley which, in those days, overlooked the courtyard of Devonshire House, where soldiers, who from our windows looked like a toy regiment, were drilling. A canary, a kitten and fuchsias on the window sills, as well as the usual simmering coffee, lent an air of settled habitation to the room I shared with my governess. But we were not yet acclimatised. London was huge and impenetrable; the countryside improbably tight, broken-up and populous. I missed the wildness, the extremes, the ice, the fires, the rushing of the wind through forests blacker than the night.

Father soon took to going to the City, where he hatched new plans for the expansion of his Bank. Flora became a VAD at Charing Cross Hospital. I was sent to a day school but also had lessons from several governesses and worked in all my free hours. English teachers seemed to lack the certainties to which I was accustomed; in Russia, for instance, you knew that Tolstoy was the best, Dostoevsky came second, Chekhov third and so on through the literary hierarchy. Here, though Shakespeare was undoubtedly at the head of the list, and I assumed that Dickens, whom I had read since my infancy, was the runner up, the teachers were unwilling to commit themselves.

The winding up of father's business seemed to be taking an unconscionable time – or perhaps mother was not in a hurry to become an expatriate?

Then, when the 'bloodless' revolution took place, followed by Kerensky's Government, it seemed a magical fulfilment of the aspirations of the liberals and perhaps a reason for going home.

But the October Revolution exploded all such hopes and father returned alone to Petersburg to protect mother and Fira from its dangers and bring them out.

It took him a year. During this time the flat overlooking the canal was frequently searched and Fira came into her own not as a revolutionary, but graciously receiving the disorderly parties of soldiers who invaded the flat, offering them tea and shaming them into returning mother's jewellery which they had filched. Father evaded arrest by never sleeping twice in the same house. His sporting instincts were aroused by the bare chance of smuggling out some of his assets, a crime punishable by death. Even Uncle Benjamin, who had come from the Pale, caught the excitement. Though usually timid, he now drove about in cabs full of gold bars, threatening to call the militiamen if the cabby overcharged him. In the end, it came to nothing, but thanks to the help of the British, all of them eventually reached England.

Meanwhile, we had moved to a quiet Kensington flat – it seemed almost a betrayal, as though we were settling for good, but Flora had always had a longing for stability. Only the occasional air-raids and my governess's worsening delusions (she still believed that she was being hunted by the Secret Police, but now not only the Tsarist variety but the German and British were after her) lent some drama to our lives.

In the end grief wrecked our family reunion and Armistice celebrations, for my brother, still interned in Germany, died of Spanish flu. I had known him very little but he was my mother's favourite and her spirit never mended.

Now that there no longer was a choice – we could not return to Russia – I expected that our home would be replanted in England, but there was to be nothing of the sort. Although my father took to England as a fish to water (admittedly an exotic fish), it seemed that the shock of the finality of our exile had awoken the nomad in his breast. Gone was the landed proprietor, the citizen of Petersburg, he was now a citizen of the world and not the slightest concession would he make to his family's desire for domesticity.

Our fragile installation in the flat Flora had taken was quickly dismantled. We lived in hotels, our background as transportable as a tent, though a tent would in the end have had more character. The silken *portières* were always the same and always unrelated to our taste. At most, a lampshade or two chosen by Fira or myself, or a shawl draped over a sofa, with Ouida negligence, hinted at our need to impress ourselves on our surroundings.

Father never took root. Although we sometimes kept our apartment in a hotel for years, his room was not merely impersonal, in it the family trunks were stored with the suggestion that the imminence of another journey made it hardly worth while sending them down to the basement. He seemed to lack the slightest discernible distaste for these reminders of transience. A nomad's asceticism kept him in this oddly surrealist desert. It was not a taste for poverty, he continued to accumulate wealth, buying a dockyard and a skyscraper in New York. Money, for so long as father had it, was a climate, an atmosphere, a measure of his usefulness and of his impact on world affairs, a means of tirelessly spinning the invisible web which united the Urals, Wall Street and Mexico in a deliciously intricate pattern centred in his brain. In our private lives I suppose its point was that we never had to listen to the ticking of the meters as we ran up the monstrous expenses of our improbable existence.

It was true that this advantage was considerable; after all the point of having money is that you should never be aware of its existence – we were sufficiently Russian to feel this. And our Russian love of dispossession and contemptuous hatred of money as the symptoms of bourgeois narrowness and greed could equally be pacified by the ownership, and still more by the disposal, of millions. If you have either nothing or too much you can forget the niggardliness of the earth, her game of tit for tat – so much effort for so much satisfaction– and live in the illusion of a motherly bounty, disdainful of relating your merits to your needs, almost like living on heavenly manna.

Of course to father the meaning of his work, at any rate at the beginning, had been different. Money to him had been the way out of the quagmire of the ghetto, with its meanness and humiliating dangers – not that he reproached fate with having put him in the ghetto for he considered it rather as a compliment to his manliness that such obstacles had stood in the way of his taking his place in the world, there to be judged as an individual on an equal footing with others who had never been challenged in this manner. But he too, once he had proved himself and established himself on firm ground, showed the proper disregard for security, repeatedly risking all he had achieved, and spending and giving with a suitable contempt for whatever was left in his pockets.

This disposition also enabled him to accept the inevitable. At the end of his life, deprived of his wealth – and of almost everything else – he remained as impregnable as if the prizes he had chased had always been dross. And seeing him at the height of his success, in a background as impersonal as destitution, it was not against all evidence to imagine that he was already uprooted from the tangible. Though what the intangible was that absorbed him was difficult to guess.

Sometimes mother secretly reverted to the habits of Pinsk by refusing the rich hotel cuisine and treating Uncle Benjamin to suppers of chopped liver and stuffed carp, bought at Ross in the Tottenham Court Road and smuggled past the porters in a suitcase. Obscurely she felt that father's desertion of ghetto was at the back of all her misfortune.

From the moment we left Russia we became and remained foreigners. We did not strictly belong to the Russian *émigré* colony. We had left before the Revolution, our circumstances were not those of refugees and our memories and outlook were different from most of theirs.

There was the General, for instance, who dropped in or invited us to *borsch* and *bliny* at a newly opened Russian restaurant and who stood to attention every time he mentioned the Emperor. We admired his faith and the courage of the ladies who waited on us; but since our need for courage was less and there lacked between us the curtain of strangeness which released their English clients from embarrassment, we could never be at ease with them. In Russia, the mutual distrust between ourselves, as Jews, and the members of the conservative aristocracy could occasionally be overcome. Now our common condition as aliens did little to unite us; rather it emphasised the inevitable disappointment at discovering the difference in the quality of our regrets.

Later I asked myself where I would have stood in the end, if I had been in Russia and old enough to stand anywhere? Certainly not on the side of the rivers of blood or of the sacking of tangible beauty to which my memories were attached; but neither could I share the General's dream of a simple restoration.

One might think that barriers of race and religion would be largely overthrown by our common condition as expatriates, but, in fact, this did little to bring us together. In helping the less fortunate we had naturally to avoid offering more intimacy than they might have cared for in more fortunate times and even when a friendship did arise the difference in our regrets had more bitterness than the difference in our aspirations would have had at home. After all, unlike genuine Whites we had hoped for reform. I said this to one of my school friends. 'But,' she replied, 'how can you love a country which goes in for pogroms?' 'That's only the dark people,' I protested, 'but of course it is the fault of the government that they stay in their darkness.' 'What business have you as Jews to concern yourselves with the fate of Russia?' 'But we are Russian, as Russian as you are English,' I answered and from the bottom of my heart. We had a right to our patriotism: Russia had been the country of our birth, if she treated us as strangers that must be the fault of some magician, the same one who caused the wretchedness of the Russian peasants. My nostalgia for Russia was intense.

II

A day came when Rikarna was pensioned off and retired to Finland. I was given the choice of going to several schools. I chose Malvern Girls' College. It had been founded by two pioneers of higher education and was run on the pattern of a boys' public school.

At the day school I had been attending the girls had come from Jewish or cosmopolitan families, many of them from families we knew. But at Malvern Girls' College where I arrived in September 1919 and, being thirteen, joined the Middle School, the several hundred pupils were mostly daughters of lawyers, doctors, clergymen or large farmers. Only two besides myself were foreigners, one an impenetrable Swede, the other a sultry Italian; neither of them stayed long. Hardly any of the girls had ever met a Jew; Russian did ring a bell with them but it was confused with Prussian, with unlucky results for my welcome so soon after the ending of the war. Even after this mistake had been corrected they were inclined to shy off. I, for my part, was fully determined to conform to the odd conditions in which I found myself and which I believed to be those of normal English life. But when I failed, in spite of my efforts, wholly to adapt myself, my school fellows' dislike turned into enormous amusement at almost everything I did; in time I became a 'character' and possibly one endowed with unusual powers, like a dervish or a Russian village fool.

To my regret, after my first term it was arranged that I should not go to church; my attendance had been an oversight. It is true that the Abbey (to which we were taken in a crocodile, the smaller of us frenziedly pulling on our gloves and searching for our collection pennies) lacked the sumptuous ritual and emotional freedom of Orthodox churches (caverns flickering with gold and candles as I remembered them). All the same it had stirred my imagination and my piety. It was also the only place in the quickly changing little town on which the eye could rest with pleasure.

The school had been a station hotel, this building provided the classrooms and the several villas (stripped of damageable furniture and divided by countless deal partitions) which made up our living quarters were squalid in the extreme. Our hideous uniform, on the other hand, was merely a reminder of Rikarna's strictures on coquetry. We wore blue and red flannel blouses and navy blue serge tunics, deformed by a pocket in the lining of the chest in which we carried our enormous handkerchiefs. Our hair was scraped back behind the ears in a single tight pigtail. For dancing on Saturday nights (strictly among ourselves, not even brothers were allowed to be invited) we wore white dresses with high necks and long sleeves and black woollen ribbed stockings. These regulations did not disturb me except when I joined mother at the Plaza Athénée in Paris for the Christmas holidays still wearing my large mushroom navy felt hat.

After the inhuman hours I had worked at home, the lessons were child's play and my learning was regarded as prodigious. Though I was good at *broderie Anglaise*, I had never done the useful sewing and mending we were taught. I was totally unused to exercise and the games appalled me. Fortunately my housemistress, impressed by my thinness and pallor and my occasional fainting fits, arranged for me to be let off games and, in general, though I had expected school to be a trial of my toughness, I found that many exceptions were made for me. Indeed, our intelligent housemistress made me an object lesson in tolerance.

The teachers attributed the gaps in my earlier training to a background unimaginably strange and, with English delicacy, preferred leaving me with some of them rather than risking the possible unfairness of pressing me into the common mould.

Many things puzzled me. For instance, religion was never discussed, though on Sundays at Evensong in the Hall, the Headmistress addressed us on ethical themes which, by and large, moved us. Ethics were evidently a matter of considerable interest but they had nothing whatever to do with the discipline of the school. I could see, of course, that keeping silence on the stairs, or in the huge cloakroom where we changed our shoes, or in the dormitories after lights out could only be a question of expediency; but I had so far believed (in accordance with Russian tradition) that obedience was a virtue in itself, only to be set aside when the wickedness of the régime made it a duty to work for its overthrow.

Never had I visualised the cheerful warfare between rulers and ruled which was here admitted by the very fact of the occasional truce when the subjects were put 'on their honour' to obey. So disconcerted and scandalised was I at first that I considered including a monastic observance of discipline in the rules of the secret society which I founded.

The reason for the society's existence was clearer than its aims. We started it as new girls who had come to the Middle School from the outside and were the sordid proletariat of the entire school; it raised us in our self-esteem. Among this depressed class, however, there were a few individuals who were unacceptable even to itself: outcasts who for mysterious reasons of defective glands or wits were evidently doomed to permanent isolation. They were admitted to the society, at the risk of lowering its prestige, in order to correct the unfairness of nature and on the Dostoevskian principle of embracing the lepers. Another feature of the society was that it satisfied our longing for adventure which had persisted in spite of our scruffy condition and the discouragingly bracing climate.

There was little outlet for this craving except naughtiness. This was the reason, so I thought, why naughtiness was not wholly condemned but craftily encouraged by the system, outwitting the staff was a test not only of courage but also of brains which in almost everything else were at a discount.

In time, the senior girls left and the society remained in occupation of the social field, by then its secrecy was nominal, for it included the whole house, down to our enlightened housemistress who had so far won our confidence that she was made an honorary member and who used its prestige to encourage our more highbrow occupations.

It was only later that I understood the difference between the English and the Russian educational principles. The English could so far rely on law-abiding inclinations that their system injected a corrective of anarchism by making the distinction – unmistakable even to a foreigner – between clearly stated rules which you broke at your risk but without any dishonour, and which were often silly enough to goad you into questioning them, and those unwritten laws in which honour and conscience were at stake. The secrecy of the code was an important factor. Though the definition of a nobleman's honour as 'that which you owe to yourself as the son or daughter of somebody who is someone' would, if stated, have been rejected as insufferably snobbish, it was in fact the real, if unstated conviction. You were expected to be born knowing what was due to yourself as a member of your caste, or at any rate to have imbibed the knowledge with your mother's milk. Either you knew it, and then to be taught it was an insult, or you didn't know it because you didn't belong and then it was useless to try to teach you.

Other valid conventions were those which the public opinion of your school, house or private society had evolved for itself (or so it believed), and which therefore confirmed its autonomy. These you did have to be taught, but this was an initiation and therefore the more painful it was the better; the more it strained your capacity for guessing and the heavier the penalties for guessing wrong the higher the prestige of membership. The 'club' was the next best thing to caste. The club taught you the value and price of eccentricity: its right to its own eccentricity (by which it was defined) and your right to yours, provided that you paid for it or were sufficiently strong, subtle or fascinating to impose yourself on others.

Some of our rules were wholly artificial, other conventions were rooted in natural law. The gravity of the external punishment was in reverse proportion to the gravity of the crime. You were punished (if caught) for talking after dark and ostracised by your fellows for turning up the collar of your blazer without being in the Sixth. But cheating, cowardice and showing off (unless they became scandalous) carried the penalty of being ignored as impossible to believe of any member of the club. Lying was noble or base according to the circumstances, and sins against charity were mostly between you and your God.

My aura of strangeness was made visible on Speech Day when, at the Fête after the prize giving, I was put in charge of a sideshow as a gipsy fortune-teller. Needless to say, fortune-telling was regarded as a joke, it would not otherwise have been permitted. My clients, parents and teachers amongst them, came in unprecedented numbers to the tent and were abnormally expectant, and I responded by a heightened intuition which I have never since recovered. There then started a fashion for experiments in hypnotism, and I had only to glare at any of the willing subjects for these hearty fifth formers to fall into a trance. One of them I had some difficulty in arousing, which brought an end to our researches. Anyway, the role thrust on me was altogether different from the one I had hoped for after reading Angela Brazil.

At school I encountered no anti-semitism except once as slime in myself. A Russian girl came to the school and the others assumed that, like her, I was an Orthodox. I did not at once correct them and the shame of having been shown to be ashamed scorched me.

Father's cheerful disdain of anti-semitism had almost prevented it from touching our self-respect and I saw that assimilation was possible in England when Harold Solomon, Flora's husband, came to see me at the school in his Colonel's uniform. He had had a magnificent war record (which indeed he lived up to through the terrible years of his later illness, enhancing it with details of courage and understatement); he filled me with devotion but something from my love and admiration for my father must have implanted in me a small scepticism about complete assimilation. For, nostalgically as I looked back to Redkino and Petersburg and with increasing poignancy as I became attached to England (a poignancy which derived perhaps from a desire to strike roots, to make mine the landscape which I saw with a piercing freshness and intensity), I now realised that my father's capacity to pull up roots from Russia, whose local colour he had taken, was the very sign of a profound foreignness to which a part of me assented. And why not, after all? Why should there not be a people of aliens as wholly given over to the interests of the house, as ready to defend its honour as their hosts, but more conscious than they of man's permanent aloneness?

Why should I not keep the freshness and intensity of my alien gaze, knowing that this landscape, that by now was dear to me, was not the only landscape; that the beauty of the earth, while unique in any one place was also hurtfully enhanced by being fragmented, so that I could never be at once in Redkino and in Worcestershire and the beauty of each was made the more poignant for not being wholly mine and because it lacked the beauty of the other.

When I had passed my matriculation examination and been accepted by London University, I left Malvern in December 1921. I was nearly sixteen and full of blue-stocking ambitions.

Part III
The Middle East

Part III

The Middle East

Palestine

I saw Palestine for the first time in 1925; my sister Flora took me there for a holiday. We travelled on the same boat as Balfour, who was going out to inaugurate the Hebrew University, but we left his party to stay a few days in Cairo and Alexandria.

I had expected the East to be picturesque and lavish, and found it so in Cairo. After that the arrival in Palestine seemed rather disappointing. Outwardly Jerusalem had nothing of the splendour of its name. There were drab olive trees, there was soft white dust and insufficient water – I was told a drought was usual.

The Old City, it is true, had character with its narrow stone lanes scrabbling uphill, its small clattering donkeys, not to mention Jews with side curls and skull caps, monks, nuns, and besides these Arabs in robes and the occasional woman from Bethlehem, who had come in to do her shopping, wearing a blue embroidered dress and that tall coif which is a legacy from the Crusaders.

The City is capped by the Mosque of Omar with its elegant arches, terraces and cupola, placed disconcertingly over the rough rock, from which Mohammed took his flight to Heaven. I thought it looked like a casket for a jewel, but holding a pebble. Outside it, Jews were weeping by the Wailing Wall. We came downhill to the basilica of the Holy Sepulchre – Golgotha, the Tomb and the Garden of The Resurrection – all believed to be contained beneath its dome. Though I suspected its disguise, for the time being the City of Peace, on its hill of contradiction, remained unknown to me.

We visited Government House; a huge, ugly building, splendidly sited, overlooking Jerusalem on one side and on the other, the mountains of Judea galloping down to the bottom of the world and the Dead Sea.

The High Commissioner, Sir Herbert Samuel, lived in this house which, before the war, had been built by the German Emperor. He governed the country with great efficiency and a fairness so meticulous that both Arabs and Jews complained of it. Parties at Government House were enlivened by the prankish personality of Sir Ronald

41

Storrs, who in addition to being an able administrator, provided the British community with its traditional eccentric.

An extraordinary note was struck at the opening of the University. The building, as much as there was of it, stood on a hill near Government House and enjoyed the same magnificent view. The ceremony was held in the open before a great crowd which had gathered. It was bone dry and there had been services of intercession for rain. When Balfour stood up to make his speech and spread out his arms in an inaugurating gesture, the rain clouds gathered and it poured over Jerusalem for a week.

That Balfour had broken the drought did not astonish the Jews. I was told by a couple of sophisticated Polish Jews that the rain and the Balfour Declaration were of the same order of events. England, they said, had mixed herself up in the impossible and Balfour looked as though he almost understood this. Only the religious extremists would deny it, but then it was their business to give witness to the Exile at the Wailing Wall. For anyone with eyes in their head, they went on, it was evident that Balfour had ended the Exile. His document stated that the Jews in a given place, and that place was Palestine, were there as of right. The shadow of non-existence had been lifted from them and no one could have made this gesture without more than the permission of the powers of this world.

These Polish friends, who were about my age, had a dilapidated car in which we criss-crossed the country. As we drove round, the landscape came into focus for me. I recognised it. This was a remarkable experience. Since then I have met both Jews and Christians to whom it has happened. It was as though an invisible landscape, always known, suddenly became concretely visible. This was not the result of a familiarity induced by illustrations to Bible stories, for what I now saw was quite unexpected, but though unexpected intimately known. It was full of signs and contrasts: there were the hills rising swiftly to Jerusalem, falling away into the steamy precipice of Sodom, the devil-haunted desert in the south and the green and sapphire innocence of Galilee with its miraculous abundance, Nazareth hooded in a cloud of apple blossom, the small flat valleys near Armageddon and Jerusalem, the City of Peace, cresting the sky, veiled in dust on its hill and suddenly it came to me that the bare bones of Judea were *my* bones, the peace and joy of Galilee were the peace and joy *I* had been promised, the devil-haunted desert was *my* desert, struck bald for the sins for which *I* needed to atone and the City of Peace was *my* City.

One pouring day I borrowed my host's mackintosh and gum-boots and went out to post a letter. On the way I met Ralph Harari who was working at Government House and with whose parents I had lunched in Cairo. He offered me the protection of his umbrella and took me for a walk along the ramparts. We met several times before I returned to England. Six months later, in Paris, we were married. For the next ten years we lived mostly in Cairo.

The Middle East in the Twenties

In the Egypt of those days, the Jews were one of the many colonies, Western and Levantine which enjoyed the country's hospitality. Each had its own character. The British were mainly in the Administration and kept themselves mostly to themselves. The French had a corner in culture. The Greeks, who had been there since Alexandrine times, lived in marble palaces by the sea or kept pastry shops in Cairo. Some of the Syrians also were pastry cooks, while others owned great estates in their own country or in Palestine. The Copts played a brilliant part in government and in business but were being largely replaced by Turks at the one end and by Jews at the other.

Society was a paradox. Of the Egyptians, in the strictest sense, the Copts were the most Egyptian since they were descendants of the Pharaohs, but they were ceasing to be considered as Egyptians by the Moslems. This, despite the fact that many of the Moslems were themselves mainly of Coptic blood. For the Moslem desert conquerors had been few in comparison with the Christian Copts whom they vanquished and converted to Islam and with whom they intermarried.

Among the Moslems, the aristocrats, were the Turks who did not regard themselves as Egyptians and who spoke broken Arabic. But they were not wholly of Turkish blood for many of them were descendants of the Mameluks who had married Christian slaves.

Turkey, which had taken Egypt from the Arabs, who had taken it from Byzantium, had run the Middle East as a caravanserai in which foreign guests came and went. The more wealthy and gifted invested in business and helped to administrate the country but remained at the mercy of the owners' capricious tempers. The least considered of all groups was that of the native population, though within it the Moslems had a minimum of security denied to others.

In the end, the most influential of the guests, exasperated by the general inefficiency, took over the management. The British saved the Treasury from insolvency and continued building the roads and irrigation works which had been started by the French. They discouraged bribery and promoted the rule of law. With greater security, money

44

flowed into the country. The middle class grew more prosperous and the stirrings of nationalism began to be felt. But when I first saw Egypt it still had much of its pre-First World War tranquillity resting on a network of passionless relationships between the more or less foreign communities; Egypt itself, as soil and as nation, was strangely absent.

It sometimes seemed as though there were no soil. In early spring the country looked luxuriantly fertile but by May, when the scarlet and mauve blossoms of the flowering trees burst into clouds, this fertility seemed to come less from the earth than from the molten sky. By June the sky had devoured every blossom and leaf.

In the ancient city of Cairo, Jews had lived since the time of Moses for some of them, no doubt, had missed the Exodus, others had been swept in by the Greek and Roman conquests, still others had fled there after the destruction of The Temple.

In the first and second centuries, before and after Christ, the Jews of Egypt had formed part of the learned Diaspora and they had been joined by scholars from Europe in time to play their role in the mediæval flowering of Judeo-Moslem culture. Later many Jews took refuge in Egypt after their expulsion from Spain. But by the 1830s they were greatly reduced in numbers and circumstances for, though they were tolerated by the Turks, their lives were burdened and insecure, as were those of most other non-Moslem groups.

A traveller of those days describes the dank alleys of the Cairo ghetto, so narrow that two men could hardly walk abreast in them, and notes the cowed and wretched appearance of the three thousand Jews who lived there. Later, in the nineteenth century there had been a considerable influx of Jews, drawn as bees to honey by the awakening of the country under Western influence.

In my day, the ghetto still sheltered a part of the large Jewish population of Cairo, but, in the western districts of the town, a middle class had arisen and even an aristocracy. These last often appeared convincingly assimilated down to their physical features, though they dated back only to the boom of their grandparents' time.

The post-Napoleonic immigrants had come with money and a spirit of enterprise; a few had risen to high positions and adopted the fabulous manner of living of Oriental nabobs, while remaining in touch with Europe.

Civic rights went with foreign protection or the profession of Islam. Immigrants who came from the West kept their passports however long they stayed. While some of those who arrived from parts of Turkey obtained the nationality of a Western country anxious to become their patron in return for good offices. Many Jews eventually took over the ways of the country whose passport they held with an enthusiasm tempered, in the case of Britain, by the uncomprehending attitude of the native English, in whose eyes these Levantines were neither flesh, fowl nor good red herring. In the event, this insularity did not so much lower the self-esteem of the Jews as convince them of the regrettable narrowness of imperial peoples and of the advantages to civilisation of a sophistication, untinged by nationalism, which had survived Rome, Turkey, and the establishment of British rule.

Thus the Jewish colony was a strange amalgam of complex nationalities and ways of living. The poor in the ghetto were indistinguishable from the Moslem poor, but even less fortunate except for the patriarchal generosity of their richer co-religionists.

We lived in an Egypt which still had an Edwardian-Turkish air. Civilisation was European and urban, subsisting on the river mud but, in Cairo and Alexandria, sheltering in marble halls, and in panelled rooms, upholstered and furnished in mock-Gothic and Louis XVI styles. In these residences brilliant parties were given; occasionally excursions to the desert were made.

The desert lay on the edge of the towns and fields, for though it was fought back perennially by the Nile, the desert showed through in bald patches between the irrigated green and it occasionally filled the air with an angry black fog of sand. Its beauty, its immensity and its invasion of the river valley made the fertile country seem predominantly dull. You could never be a part of the desert, like a cabbage in the English countryside; it isolated you and rejected all roots. Not that it ever made you feel small, alone in it you dominated its absence. But its nothingness was a temptation; it spoke of neither life nor death, for there could be no rotting in it except of the spirit. Comforting to the Fathers of the Desert who met its challenge and to the Bedouins who lived in it, it chased the fleshpot loving citizen back to the towns.

The landscape was immemorial, the meek earth and the proud-making desert and the cities turning their backs on both. The land-bred peasants were like seed in the fields; the more land was cultivated, the more peasants there were. Such of the added wealth that went to them seemed only to increase their numbers and hardly to change their lives. They worked under their overseers in their traditional ways, whether the estate owners were Egpytians, Turks or foreigners. Meanwhile the heads of the Jewish community moved in the small circle of pashas, diplomats and financiers, combining their loyalties to their official country of origin with their obligations to Egypt, to their fellow heads of communities and to their own poor.

In Egypt under the Turks, the more alien you were the more you were secure and even privileged, provided that you held the passport of a country that protected you and, when I arrived there, this tradition was only gradually dying out. Thus the Jews of Egypt were the one Jewish community of the Diaspora whose very status as aliens protected them. The most privileged relied on protection from abroad and the passportless poor relied on the protection of the protected.

In all the thousands of years they had been in Egypt, the Jews had been divorced from the soil (except in the Biblical times of their slavery). But, this was not exceptional in Egypt where everyone was divorced from the soil, except for the *fellaheen*, who were divorced even from their fellow Moslem Egyptians.

It was unthinkable that anyone, of his own free will, should live the life of a *fellah*, scratching his own pocket handkerchief-sized plot with a stick for a plough or gathering the cotton or the sugar beet on the plantations for sixpence a day.

Permanent and changeless as the fellaheen's life was (you could recognise it on the frescoes of the tombs of the Pharaohs), and although the cities were sustained by it, this life seemed as intermittent, as shadowed by death, as the life of the plants, abundant in winter and spring and vanishing in the summer as though it had never been. Yet it continued at an extravagant cost, for only the toughest survived the dangers of infancy to face those of early manhood.

Nor were the labourers in industry much better off.

During my first weeks in Egypt I was horrified to see a little boy of four being made to crawl through a cement pipe while workmen were hammering at the outside of it. Then there were the workshops where raw cotton was cleaned, aired and pressed into cases for shipping. The first factory we came to was a big shed divided in two with an open door in the partition. One part of it was a long room with two

47

rows of frames on which the cotton was stretched. In front of each frame squatted two children between the ages of six and twelve; their work was to pick out the impurities; they stayed in front of the frames for eighteen hours a day and were kept industrious by an overseer who paced up and down the middle of the room swinging a long whip. In the other room the clean cotton was tossed into the air by young men between twenty and thirty: the work was too heavy for anyone older – many of them died of tuberculosis before reaching the age of retirement, for the cotton dust which filled the air also filled their lungs. The same dust drifted in clouds through the doorway into the children's room, and even more children died before the age of twelve.

The factory adjoined the plantations and the children were those of the peasants in the neighbourhood. Those whose parents lived too far away slept in a shed next to the factory, others went home, walking as much as an hour after leaving work. Their parents were happy to have them employed in the factory, for they earned as much as fourpence a day and this was much more than they could have earned at agricultural work.

We saw several such factories; everywhere the conditions were equally bad. They were illegal, for labour laws had recently been passed condemning them, but the vested interests not only of employers but of those who were employed made evasion easy.

We were filled with horror at what we saw and when we came back to Cairo we discussed the chances of a campaign: protesting to the Government and in the press. But we soon learned that this was out of the question: many of the owners of the factories were Egyptians and as foreigners we would not only be accused of discourtesy to our hosts but were likely to make things worse by hardening local opinion against change. By then it was already too late – if it had ever been possible – even for Britain to meddle in social conditions, for national sentiment was coming to birth with its raw susceptibilities.

So, neither as British nor as Jewish could I make the ginning factories my business. The legitimate outlet for my meddlesomeness was concern for the poor of the Jewish community and this, in all conscience, was a wide enough field. Hospitals and schools were maintained out of private contributions; in addition anyone was free to visit the ghetto choked with dust or slimy with mud, swarming with the blind and the one-eyed, where huge families lived on invisible small crafts and on the alms of the visitors.

*

Among Manya's activities were: helping with a Home for Jewish Orphans, a hostel for discharged prisoners, and later with the Goutte de Lait charity.

Zionism or Assimilation

As it was within easy reach for holidays I came to know Palestine well. In those days you took the night express in Cairo, crossed the Suez Canal at midnight, boarded another train at El Kantara, went to sleep and woke up to orange groves outside the carriage window. If it was the right season they were dark green and glossy, the oranges shining through like a gold-leaf background. In Hebrew an orange is a 'golden apple' and an orange grove is a 'paradise'. In this way they must have struck the early Zionist immigrants who came by steamer from Odessa in the 1880s. They saw the Arabs growing 'heavenly gardens' on the sandy shore and they settled down to copy them.

As they were unused to growing anything and unaccustomed to the climate, they found the going almost intolerably hard, but with time, patience and the help of Baron Edmund de Rothschild (who bought land for them and advanced money for cultivation) they prospered. By the time I saw them in the late twenties these 'Rothschild Colonies' were venerable settlements with stone-built houses, schools and synagogues, shaded by well-grown trees, and Jaffa oranges, much improved from the original stock, were the economic mainstay of the country.

Before these colonists came, the only Jewish communities in Palestine had been the ghettoes in the various towns, notably Jerusalem and Safed. Centred on the Holy Places and the ancient seats of learning, these ghettoes with their legendary past were as much part of the towns as the Bedouins were part of the desert. In the course of centuries the oldest families who claimed to have been there since before the Exile were joined by Jews from many lands (who all brought, and still keep today, their own fashions in kaftans, skull caps and fur caps), by teachers who kept up the mediæval commerce in learning, by old people who wished to kiss the blessed soil and when they died to rest in it until the call of the Messiah, and by other travellers mysteriously protected, such as the Rabbi – a great-grandfather of mine – who was said to have crossed the Mediterranean in a cockleshell of a boat; the boat split in half in a storm but he was nevertheless brought safely to Jaffa in one half of it and his wife in the other!

By and large these communities remained almost untouched by the coming of the Zionists, who were as unimaginable in the ghetto alleys as the ghetto dwellers (who lived by small trades and crafts or on alms from relatives abroad) were unthinkable in the orange groves.

Nor did the early Zionist settlers cause great changes in the habits of the country as a whole, or bring or suffer much disturbance. They used local labour and were good employers, paying the Arab villagers at slightly higher rates than had been usual. Their coming had raised the demand for labour; and if this was a disadvantage to the local employers, it was balanced by the rise in land values which the Jewish purchases occasioned. The colonists suffered from pilferers and marauders, but so did the Arab landowners, and if a traveller was occasionally ambushed on the highway, it was only to be expected in this disordered province of Turkey. These first Zionists hired Bedouin watchmen – the fiercer the better – thus avoiding conflict even with malefactors. When they visited Jaffa, they dressed as Europeans and passed the time of day with their Moslem equals, used Arabic and the accepted forms of courtesy which they took the trouble to learn.

Only in the eyes of the new Jewish pioneers who began to come at the turn of the century were they white colonials who took advantage of existing conditions to cushion themselves against the land and create a new privileged caste.

These newcomers were avid for personal contact with the soil and they dispensed with Arab labour. Their whole time was taken up with struggling against the sand or mud and in hastily putting up shacks, and they had nothing of the manners or the looks of leisured gentlemen. They discovered that the Bedouins called the Jews 'children of death' – natural murderers kept alive by the tribute which they paid the brigands whom they employed as guards – and they became prickly about Jewish honour and trained their own watchmen. Nor did they keep to the citrus growing coastal plains (where the old settlers grew crops mainly for export) but spread inland, to undeveloped areas, where they founded villages which were almost self-supporting. They were not interested in the export trade but in living as peasants. Yet these villages were unlike Arab or even European villages: they were raw pioneering settlements, having to make up with their college training for the peasant's instinctive knowledge of soil and weather, and goaded by an overwhelming haste to make the most of each day and pair of hands.

By the twenties the country was beginning to be dotted with improbable white and red roofed huts in regular patterns, and in the fields around them the tourist or the dignified robed and white-veiled passer-by could see young men and women exposing the tanned skin of their arms and legs to the blistering sun. The new peasants were as alien to the landscape, the conventions and the social structure as people from Mars.

These Zionists, like Zionism itself, had had a paradoxical history. After the emancipation of the Jews in the West, it took impetus. In the middle of the nineteenth century, only the Jews in Eastern Europe were being actively persecuted. Yet its first prophet, Herzl, was a Viennese intellectual. On his initiative and that of the Rothschilds, an attempt was made to buy Palestine from Turkey. When this failed the Western Zionists were all for considering other alternatives, such as a part of the Argentine which it appeared might be for sale, or a part of Uganda which England offered.

It was only in Hebrew, the language reserved for sacred subjects, that Palestine was called the Land of Israel. In the eyes of the religious extremists among the Jews the idea of a Return to the Holy Land under secular auspices was as blasphemous as to the Western Liberals it seemed unnecessary that a Jewish Home should be established.

But the Russian Zionists, who were the majority and who were those in pressing need of refuge, refused the bird in the hand for the sake of the bird in the burning bush and insisted on The Return or nothing.

The hope of the Return was as old as the Dispersion, for the Diaspora had always been regarded as an exile which the Holy One would some day bring to an end. The Jews were unlike the gypsies who love the road; their wanderings, they believed, were not of their own volition. Individuals migrated when they found the conditions intolerable or were attracted by better prospects somewhere else, but the ghettoes remained fixed for centuries, like fortresses – yet they were the tents and caravans of aliens whose vocation was to be ready for the journey whenever it should suit the Lord to take them home.

Every year at Passover the aspiration was reiterated: 'Next Year in

Jerusalem', and the setting out upon the homeward journey was re-
enacted, while on all other days of the year the ritual sacramentalising
of daily life reminded the faithful of the dedication and separation from
the world exacted of the people of the Promise.

Home was Palestine and this was also the Holy Land, for the
people of the God so hidden that His name could not be spoken had no
difficulty in believing that His presence dwelt in a particular way in a
particular place, a country traceable on a map. In it their fathers had
conversed with Him and there they would return, but only when the
Messiah (who according to the mystical sect of the Hassidim was
chained in Heaven for as long as His people were in exile, purging their
sins) was free to walk the earth and gather in the scattered tribes.

In the eyes of mystics, the Exile stood perhaps for the restless
wandering of the human heart until it finds its rest in the Heavenly
City, or a warning against abiding cities of any other sort, but it was
also, in the eyes of all, the actual, geographical and historical condition of the Jews. On some unpredictable day the remnant of the
people would go back to the country of its birth, which was also the
country of regeneration. But the date of this event could not be hurried
except by keeping the Law, the only ground on which they were to
stand in Exile.

Alien and apocalyptic in their own eyes, the Jews were also alien
and apocalyptic in the eyes of Christendom. There was, of course, a
measure of agreement between the expectation of Jews and Christians.
Both awaited the coming of their Lord in glory, and if the Christians
blamed the Jews for holding it up (for they believed that the conversion of the Jews was to precede it) Jewish mystics too were ready to
admit that they delayed it by their sins. But while the Jews believed
that their own faith was the one pure faith in the One God, the Gen-
tiles, in spite of the thunderings of the saints, often harried them,
veiling from them the face of Christ in the hope of hastening His
coming by force.

Even at the best of times the soil of Christendom rejected the Jews,
as though to leave no doubt of their vocation. Characteristically,
among the restrictions imposed on them in most countries were those
which kept them from the land. Pavements kept their feet from the
fruitful earth as surely as the sands of Sinai. The mystics followed the
pillars of cloud and fire; the worldly, uncomfortable in this territory

stored up worldly goods against a failure of the manna and in the hope
of protecting themselves from the harrying which they often thereby
attracted; and the letter-ridden faithful clung to every outward form
in which the symbols were enclosed, occasionally seeming to make
nonsense of their meaning. So elaborate became the daily ritual that
in the end the Orthodox, prevented by commentaries upon commentaries of the Law from doing almost anything upon the Sabbath,
could not be farmers even in the Holy Land.

Emancipation broke down the ghetto walls and weakened the
structure of tradition, scattering the Jews further afield. Secularism
affected them as it affected Christendom. Many lost their heads and
their religion together; of those who retained their beliefs, many dis-
carded what now appeared as the exaggerations of ritualism.

All at once the meaning of the Exile began to be questioned. Was it
indeed a vocation, or merely an accident of history, or an explanation
thought up to make racial and religious persecution bearable? After all,
the Christians too believed in a New Jerusalem, but this did not make
them strangers on the earth. In the new era of Liberalism could the
Jews not settle wherever they were, taking a normal part in the life of
their countries of adoption and becoming 'assimilated' – adopting,
that is to say, the ways of their countrymen in all except religion? Why
should there not be English, French, Russian, German, Palestinian
Jews, just as there were Christians of all these countries?

The movement for assimilation spread wherever liberalism gave
it a chance. It was recognised that anti-semitism had not vanished
over night, nor had the scars it had left upon the Jews. But healing and
reconciliation would be the easier because the world, it was believed,
was entering upon a century of peace, trade and science for which the
Jews had special gifts. Barred from agriculture, government and war,
they had specialised in those middle-class urban occupations to which
they had been restricted, and in these pursuits they would more than
ever prove their usefulness.

So at any rate thought the assimilationists. The Orthodox opposed
them, as they later opposed Zionism, on the grounds that the Exile
could not be ended unilaterally and that conformity with Gentile
manners threatened observance and ultimately faith itself.

By the middle of the nineteenth century assimilation was well
under way in the West. The Jews had indeed poured into the urban

middle class and Herzl was alarmed by the rising anti-semitism in France and Germany, based no longer on religious intolerance but on rivalry. In the era of capitalism, which was also the era of struggle for social justice, he blamed the Jews for taking up the most exposed positions on both sides: the successful few by their wealth and prominence and the 'mediocre intellectuals' by drifting, according to him, into Socialism: both aroused a hostility which harmed not as yet the rich minority but the masses of defenceless poor. The difficulty of assimilation was increased by the flood of immigrants from the East whose persecution was increasing and who were frankly foreign. In any case, assimilation, Herzl claimed, had failed, for whatever their mistakes or their misdeeds, they were being persecuted not as rich or poor or Socialists or foreigners, but as Jews. Western anti-semitism was as yet mild; on the other hand many Jews had renounced the Exile as a vocation that to them no longer had any meaning except injustice, and once the bearing of injustice was no longer seen as the will of God, it became dishonourable.

Herzl claimed that Judaism was not only a religion. It was also a consciousness of being a people, and this obscure awareness had only to be brought into the light of day to suggest an alternative solution to the Jewish problem. The way to peace lay in becoming a people and in 'going away' – leaving 'here' for 'over there' – and going not to a country where the immigrants would again 'bring anti-semitism in their luggage', but to a recognised homeland, wherever this might be – Palestine or Argentine or Uganda.

'Over there' the Jews would build a country and a culture. Pressed into conformity, their originality became distorted into the shady eccentricity of aliens disguised as natives; encouraged by its own climate 'over there' it would add an original culture to the culture of the world.

Yet so far was Herzl from the Jewish nationalism of today that he believed neither Palestine nor the revival of Hebrew to be necessary for this culture to develop.

This necessity was however deeply felt by the Zionists of Eastern Europe. Influenced less by the proud humanism of the West than by Tolstoyan doctrines of redemption by work and by the soil, they felt the need of refuge almost less than the need of rehabilitation.

The moral balance sheet of the Diaspora, they held, showed a greater loss than the assimilationists admitted. Persecution had resulted in martyrdoms but it had also made life in the tight little communities unbearably narrow except for those absorbed in the other world, and had put a premium on talents for buying ease and safety in a hostile climate. The Jews, they said, had only developed the gifts of middlemen and had become as withered, as barren, as the desert into which they had been forced. To continue living on these gifts, they claimed, was to live as parasites. The Jews must regain their stature, find new sources of creative life, and lose the vices of self-hatred which their disfigurement had fostered in them. This difficult regeneration would only be possible, they believed, in the land of Israel.

The Kibbutz

The first kibbutz I stayed in was called Geva. It lay in a part of the
Valley of Israel which was hidden from the Lower Emek and seemed
uninhabited, but as the car lurched between high fields of barley,
suddenly we came upon some corrugated-iron barracks. I climbed out.
A young man with a fair mop of hair and bare feet stood in the yard
watching me. I asked him in my bad Hebrew: 'Please, I want to stay a
few days in the kibbutz. Is it possible?'

He smiled, then he turned slowly away, his ugly young neck poking
out of his uncollared shirt and called: 'Roma, Roma.' A woman
answered. They talked through an open door, then he told me: 'Good,
you can stay.'

A woman came out and said, 'You want to stay in the kibbutz?
You can share my room, I have a spare bed.' I paid the driver and the
young man carried in my suitcase and the woman took me to her
room.

It was in one of the two long low huts made of corrugated-iron
which flanked the yard; each room had a door opening on to the yard
and a window looking over the valley. Inside were three iron beds
covered with coarse blankets, a wooden chair and a small table with an
oil lamp on it, and nothing else. Roma sat down on one of the beds and
motioned me to the other.

'Why did you want to come?' she asked. 'How long do you want to
stay?'

I felt embarrassed under her direct look. 'I don't know . . . Of
course, I want to pay for my board.'

She smiled suddenly. 'No, you can't do that.'

'I should like to see what it is like – and I'd like to work while I am
here.' She looked amused and friendly. I felt I had said the right thing,
but my clothes were wrong; she was barefoot, in a patched white
cotton shirt and skirt.

She said: 'Come, I have a few minutes to spare, I can show you
round.'

In the middle of the settlement was the yard; on two sides of it were

57

the sleeping rooms; at one end stood the wooden dining hall and next to it a little house with a verandah newly painted white; inside were cots covered with blue nets; babies crawled about, their little trousered behinds bumping the floor. Roma said, 'Rachel is in charge here, I help her. Other colonies have real school houses, but our children are quite small, the oldest is four.'

At the other end of the yard were the cow-sheds and the stables; all were well built in stone and had labour-saving devices. At the back there were the chicken runs and huts with showers and a laundry and a workshop. When I couldn't follow Roma's Hebrew she explained in Russian.

Her face had a nobility which fitted her improbable name. She said, 'I'm sorry, I have to go now. You had better rest if you want to work tomorrow.'

The hot yard was silent except for the children's voices; a hen tipsy with sunshine pecked lazily; from somewhere nearby came the sweet pungent smell of hay. I sat down in the shadow behind the wash-house. I felt happy; I took off my shoes and stockings and I wished I knew more Hebrew.

As the sun was setting I saw the men coming from the fields; some of them rode past barefoot in ragged trousers; their arms and faces were lit red.

With the fall of evening the yard suddenly came alive. There was a coming and going and the sound of splashing in the wash-house and of pans clattering in the kitchen.

Roma came to fetch me with another woman and a small boy. She said, 'This is Rachel and her little son. We are going for a walk now. The mothers are playing with their children. Will you come?'

We walked uphill through a eucalyptus thicket; the little boy whisked backwards and forwards like a puppy. When we came to a dark field the women stopped and looked over the slope. Rachel said, 'Here the beans are not coming up so well, on the other side they have tried the new fertiliser.' She asked me: 'You are from Russia?'

'I am English, but I was born in Russia.'

'Roma says you want to work?'

'Yes.'

'That's good. But you'll find it hard. During my first three months I felt as if my back was breaking.'

She stood wrapped up in a grey shawl. Around us the hills were salty with moonlight; the near slopes were furrowed and tangled with vineyards. Rachel called: '*Amosik, Amosik, ata hafetz lishon?*' – 'Little Amos, are you sleepy?'

Roma had come three years ago from the Ukraine, the settlement when she had joined it was two years old. Now it had over forty members; at first there had been only twelve – a dozen friends who had come from Russia together; the rest were new immigrants and mostly also from Russia, but with a sprinkling from Central Europe. I asked her why there were so many Russians.

'It's partly that so many immigrants to Palestine come from Russia. But there are settlements where the majority are Poles, or Hungarians, or Germans.'

'Why should there always be quite a large majority from any one country?'

'Well, as a rule, a settlement is founded by a group of people who know each other and it is natural that those who join them, in the early days, should have a common background with them. This kind of life depends on people getting on together, so the more they have in common at the beginning, the easier it is.'

When she had arrived the first wooden shelters had already been built and corn, vegetables and a vineyard planted, but they were still digging trenches and breaking soil.

There were obvious advantages to this communal way of life: a family on its own might have been ambushed, an individual farmer would have been at the mercy of a bad crop.

We went back and soon after we were called to dinner. We sat on benches at long tables covered with linoleum and ate a mess of rice and vegetables with brown bread. My two neighbours, Nora and a young woman with fair hair, discussed educational experiments. Farther on was a group of men. After the quick meal they lit cigarettes and sipped tea out of tin mugs. The conversation became general, I couldn't follow it. Nora said, 'That's the work meeting, we are planning tomorrow's work.'

I asked, 'Doesn't any one person direct the work?'

'No, we all discuss it and decide together, but of course we listen to what Hilik, Benjamin and Jacob have to say – they have been longest on the land.'

Gradually the conversation tailed off, and only a few words were now and then exchanged, but words and smiles appeared to me to be the surface of a secret understanding, out of which their voices rose. They seemed tired, relaxed, happy, but they looked few in the white glare of the kerosene lamp against the bare walls and the uncurtained windows, with the dark empty country stretching away outside.

Next morning I went out at dawn to weed onion beds. The green beds wheeled over the hill and two women were already there, catching the first sparks of sunshine in their white kerchiefs. At first I couldn't understand what I was meant to do; then one of them, Sara, showed me how to pull out weeds and use the hoe to break up hard roots and clumps of earth.

At seven we rested and breakfasted off luke-warm tea – it seemed a wonderful drink – and thick chunks of bread and goat's cheese. I lay back on the warm earth; my hands were scorched by the thorny weeds and my body felt weak and heavy; but after we had eaten I began again to work, easily, almost unaware of any effort.

The sun rolled over the top of the hill, the heat grew heavy; by midday the pain in my shoulders and the smarting of my hands and my grazed ankles became intolerable. The women were singing. One of them said to me: 'You shouldn't have done so much the first time, you should rest this afternoon.' At last we went back to the wash-house and undressed and soaped ourselves under the icy water. Slipping about in wooden bath clogs over the wet floor I felt light and fresh. It seemed absurd to rest, so after lunch I went back to work. But later in the afternoon it became an agony to raise the hoe and the sun seemed to stop half way over the hill as if it would never reach the rim.

Next day was still harder. Roma bandaged my torn ankles and Dora, my other room mate, lent me soft home-made slippers; but there were open blisters on my hands and I could hardly straighten up for pain.

That evening when I went back to our room I found the two women talking and laughing with a man of about thirty, Itzhak; he had a thin, dark, bearded, ascetic face. He got up at once. 'You must be sleepy, I'll go.' I pretended I wasn't. He asked me how I liked it in the kibbutz and I said it was wonderful and that I felt absolutely at home in it.

Roma told me: 'Itzhak is one of the founders of the kibbutz.'

I said, 'It seems a good life, but there must be many difficulties.'

Itzhak smiled. 'It is easier for some than for others.'

I asked, 'Isn't it difficult for many people to live so close together, without any private life?'

He thought a little, then he said: 'For some people it is impossible. It is easy not to own anything. But there are some people who can't put up with having no privacy, and again there are others who feel lonely. There are three stages in the life of the kibbutz: the stage of friendship, the stage of comradeship, and the stage which Ein Harod has reached – there are about two hundred people there – where there are so many that the solitary man or the man who wants few friends has a better chance to settle down. We are in the second stage. There are forty of us. But when we first came we were only twelve. We were like one body. Our work together did this for us. We hardly needed to speak our thoughts, they thought themselves in us.'

'You are here for good?' I asked.

'On the land? Where else?'

'And in this kibbutz?'

He got up, his slow labourer's movements contrasting with his intellectual face. 'Who knows? Well, you must be tired after your day's work. Good night.' He smiled and went out.

Dora said, 'He's a good worker and a good *kibbutznik*, but I don't believe he'll stay here long. He thinks our life has become too luxurious.'

At half past ten Roma put out the lamp, but we went on talking, sitting up in bed wrapped in our rough blankets. One of the oldest members of the kibbutz had been a school teacher. I tried to imagine her life – the Zionist clubs in Galicia, then pioneering, tents on the open hillside, months of drainage work up to the waist in mud, while across the valley Ein Harod fought off Bedouins. Dora told me about the early days. 'The whole colony would turn out before sunrise. The men's singing was wonderful. Of course it was hard; one year the cattle sickened. We ate nothing but salt fish and vegetable oil for six months and I have a weak stomach.' At last we settled down to sleep. Through the open window I could hear the distant cries of jackals and see the tops of the moonlit hills.

Next day was Friday. The women in the kitchen were working double time to prepare for the Sabbath and in the field they stooped low over the beds weeding quickly. Next to me Sara brought her hoe down cleanly between the plants – I envied her, I could still not avoid bruising them. Then she straightened up and wrinkled her eyes against the sun. 'Let's have tea now; if we don't take long over it we can finish by sunset.' We went to the edge of the field and sat down. I asked Sara what she did before she came to Palestine.

'I was a lawyer.'

'And you gave it up. Why did you? Is this all right for you, for always? For an intellectual?'

She bit off a stem of grass and spat it out and smiling she said, 'Ekh, we have been intellectuals for so long.'

Dinner was late. Some people were finishing odd jobs, others stood about looking as if they were savouring the foretaste of rest. A cart rattled by with visitors going to Ein Harod. The meal was festive. There were a few strangers – a lecturer from the Trade Union who would speak next day on irrigation, a girl with black patent leather shoes and two schoolboys. Somebody had brought a bottle of red wine; there was meat instead of rice and vegetables, and for 'pudding' lumps of butter to spread on the thick black bread. The talk grew buoyant; finally the uproar broke into song. Liquid, throaty Hebrew mixed with cockney Yiddish, Arabic and a Ukrainian lament. Then they made Itzhak fetch his guitar and for a long hour the soft, unsustained notes of a difficult melody fell from his clumsy looking fingers while the others listened silently with bent heads. Afterwards somebody shouted for the *hora*; they stacked away the benches and in the space between the tables they began to dance, shoulder to shoulder, stamping, the whole circle turning quicker and quicker. Other circles formed, broke up and formed again. There was a headiness in the dancing which unstiffened our bodies and swept away fatigue, and made it possible, after the hard week, to go on merry-making until sunrise.

On Saturday, five of us, Jacob, Roma, a young married couple – David and Simha – and I, went on a picnic. A rattling cart took us down the bumpy road, shaking my sore bones, to a field separated from the rest of Geva's land. It was used as pasture for sheep, and an odd character, Haim, lived there in a shanty and looked after the flock. He was a Tolstoyan, the others told me; he did not strictly belong to the spirit of the settlement, for he loved solitude; but everyone liked him, so they allowed him to stay on and respected his tastes: once a week he welcomed visitors.

In the sunny stillness of the long afternoon we lay on the grass and slept or talked. It was Haim who answered my question: what was it that made the life of the settlement a happy one in spite of the harsh conditions? He said it was friendship, work and poverty. That he included poverty astonished me, though the settlers were indeed poor.

Geva, like all such villages, had received its land from the National Fund – as much land as its members were able to work without employing hirelings. The Settlement Fund had given it credits for tools, animals and seeds. These two Funds were kept going by donations from Jews all over the world. The quicker a village developed its land, the less it spent on itself the sooner it could, out of its earnings, pay rent and repay its creditors. Then more villages could be set up, more immigrants could be brought in and more land could be 'redeemed'. These were the outward circumstances which laid poverty as a duty on the settlers.

But there was an inward impulse as well, I thought, which drove them to dispossess themselves. Their socialist theories rationalised it, but they did not altogether explain it.

So unbridled was this impulse in those days in villages such as Geva that you could really say the villagers did not own a single thing that they used. Certainly not their land – you were always being told that the landowners were neither the farmers nor the settlement. If the land belonged to anyone it was to those thousands of poor people who kept money boxes marked with the Shield of David in their homes and gave their pennies to the National Fund. It was on these that the Fund relied, more than on important donations from the rich. As for the villagers, all they had was the use of the land – as many acres of it as they could use by tilling it with their own hands, and for as long as they would use it in this way.

Even their clothes were neither chosen nor owned by them. On Friday Roma had fetched a clean dress and set of linen in exchange for the dress and linen she had worn that week, but they were no more hers than the mug she used at meals, any other woman of about her size would fetch them from the laundry and wear them the week after. When all the women had worn their dresses to shreds a meeting would be held and someone would be sent to town with enough money to buy a roll of cheap cotton; and whoever was on duty in the sewing-room would run it up.

I asked about books. Haim answered: 'We have a few books. One day we'll have a library. And the Histadruth – that's our trade union – has a circulating library and lends us books. It does a lot of things like that, sends us lecturers and occasionally even films. And it runs the school in Ein Harod to which our children will go when they're big enough, and the hospital – and other schools and hospitals in other *kibbutzim* . . . But about books – if it's something I want only for my amusement I might still get it, but I'd have to buy it out of my pocket money.'

'I didn't know you had any.'

'It isn't much. It depends on the year. At present it's usually a pound or two a year per head. Most of what we earn goes into the land or to pay our debts or for our keep, but if we make a little extra some of it is kept back and shared out in cash. So if I wanted a book I couldn't get in the library, I could send for it. As for holidays, everyone is entitled to a fortnight a year – though it's a job getting them to take it. But if there was a special reason for a journey, it might be decided to send you at the community's expense. Of course if anyone goes on the community's business, that's always paid for. But it's understood that a member might have some special personal need – say he has a sick relative he has to go and see. And look at Judith – her parents were in Poland in very poor circumstances – well, the community paid their journey out and now of course it keeps them. They're too old to do much work, though they do what they can.'

'Tell me more about poverty,' I asked Haim. 'Why does it make people happy?'

He smoked a few moments in silence. 'Well, you live among rich people – are they or their children happier? Our people are happy because they don't care for money or for what it gets. Of course a time may come when they'll begin to care how much the community has, and then even if they have nothing of their own, they will be beset with dangers. But at the moment they care for nothing but the land and the good life. That makes them happy and it's good for them. It's even good for the Jews abroad who give money so that these people can give their work.'

And yet even this did not quite satisfy me; it still seemed to me that poverty was also being sought for its own sake. I suggested this to Haim.

'Well, there's something in that too,' he answered. 'Poverty is a freedom. And we needed to be set free, not only from the servitude to masters, but also from the servitude to fear which makes people chase after wealth. And it's a purification if you like, as any passing from a lesser to a greater freedom usually is. After all, we're a religious people, though these boys and girls think they're irreligious.'

Jacob disagreed: 'I don't think we are religious in that way,' he said. 'All that's your Tolstoyanism, it's Christian influence.'

I asked Haim: 'Were you poor before you came here?' It turned out that he was the son of a rich manufacturer in Poland and Jacob had been a professor of mathematics in Vienna. 'Do you really prefer manual work?' I asked him.

He shrugged his shoulders. 'Someone has to do it. The country has to be built.'

'But not necessarily by professors of mathematics.'

'No, I agree. It's not only that. We Jews have been too abstract for too long. Mathematics, that's typical. Always at a distance from concrete reality, always translating reality into abstract terms. Of course, if I'd been Einstein, I daresay I'd have gone on doing mathematics but I wasn't Einstein and we have plenty of mathematicians, we have some craftsmen too and some factory workers, though not enough – our greatest need is for peasants.'

'Why is it so important to have more peasants?' I asked.

'Because the soil gives people something that nothing else can give them. Working on the land is different from any other kind of work. You can work hard, you can give your whole strength to the soil, but you can't impose your will on it as you can on a machine. You sow the seed and you water it but can't pull at the shoots to make them grow. You have to be patient. You have to wait on the seasons, on the weather. The land has a will of its own, you have to win it over and this is good for you. It makes you know that it's nature that creates – or God if you like – and all you can do is to help it by your work. It's a living relationship. You need the land, the land needs you. The land wants to give of its abundance but it can't unless you help it. Israel became a desert – and why – because we weren't there. Its state of dereliction was just as much poison to it as the Exile was for us.

'Of course everyone doesn't have to be a peasant. We won't stop having mathematicians, perhaps in future we'll have better ones and almost certainly, we'll have better writers and artists. But before we can have our own culture some of us must get our feet on the ground, and bend our backs and our wills to it. Haim says: "Poverty makes people happy." Manual work, and particularly work on the land, is a kind of poverty. Your ideas you can possess, even what you make you can possess because you've made it. But what comes out of the soil is not just the fruit of your mind or of your hands. It's the fruit of a marriage. Of course there are many Jews who think all this is a waste. They are proud of our being an intellectual people, they are afraid of our losing our mental agility, our way of being always wide awake. That's being like a man who is afraid of going to sleep. Sleep refreshes the mind – re-creates it by revivifying its unconscious springs, with water from the subsoil. In the same way people are refreshed by returning to the land. For centuries we have been wide awake – we had to be, we always had to be on the look out. Now we must give our consciousness a rest.'

'Isn't it very difficult for some people?'

'For some it is hard, for others impossible. I'm not speaking of myself. I think I must have been meant to be a peasant – it comes so easily, so happily to me. But there are women to whom it means sacrifice, and from whom it demands heroism. Deliberately they give up the children of their mind, offer them like Abraham did Isaac. To such people this kind of life involves going down into the unknown, overcoming their fears. It isn't always good for them.'

Again I asked Haim: 'Tell me more about why you think that poverty is good for people?'

'Jacob's right, poverty is a freedom,' he answered. 'We need to re-establish a suitable relationship to things. Because we were chased from pillar to post we grabbed at possessions – particularly possessions that we could carry with us. It was difficult for us to be trustful. The richer we were the safer we felt – not that it always worked out that way, often it only gave us an illusion of safety. It is a funny thing but people don't as a rule get rich by handling material things directly. For instance there is nothing more abstract than big business, which depends directly on a capacity for making abstract patterns, translating real things into figures. This proves that there is a way of living in abstraction and yet being a materialist and it is the opposite of poverty.

'Of course I don't mean that poverty which is imposed on you is good for you. You're no better just because you are poor. You can worry about material things as much if you are poor as if you are rich. Not knowing where your next day's breakfast is coming from can be as bad for you or as good as gambling on the stock exchange. The kind of poverty I am talking about has to be chosen or accepted and it doesn't consist in not worrying about where your next day's food is coming from. What's good for you, what makes you happy, is to give. Real poverty means giving oneself and one's work all the time – giving up even anxiety. Everyone has this need. It takes different people in different ways. With some people it's quite unconscious and very successful just because of that. Take Sara for instance – she's been working in the kitchen lately. When she stirs a big pot of soup – she's stirring it for her forty children. She's married and has two children of her own, but all the others are her children too. She'd hate having to stir a smaller pot, and if she had only herself to do it for, she wouldn't bother. She doesn't feel she's giving anything – all she knows is she'd be miserable without her big family. But take Vera – she's different. She's a virgin. Perhaps even if she marries she'll always be a virgin in her heart. Hers is a different kind of heart to Sara's, one that does not give itself easily. It's a hard little shut-up heart just as her body is a hard body. But every time she hears a sick child cry, she is moved – not because it's her child but because it's the cry of every helpless thing in the world. That's why the settlement suits her. It suits Sara because it gives her a huge family, it suits Vera because if she weren't living so close to forty people who don't belong to her she might never have recognised that she needs to give. It's hard for her, because it gets at her by way of pain. For Sara it's an easy and a cheerful life, for Vera it's hard, but all the same it gives her joy. Joy comes from poverty and nothing is any good without it.'

'Is that why people sing and dance?' I asked.

'Yes, but mind you, the movement that has created this kind of life may not last, even if collective settlements go on being set up. It's a very rare thing. The last thing of its kind that happened in the life of the Jewish people was the Hassidic movement. And the two have something in common, though peasants you see around you wouldn't recognise it. They think they're not religious. They think they don't believe in God, or they don't know if they believe in Him. And all the time He doesn't care a fig what they think. He accepts their service,

67

because they give it joyfully, though they don't know why. In fact the joy *is* the service.'

'You said there were three things – poverty, work and friendship. What about friendship?'

'They're all related. If you give of yourself you give to friends. If you give yourself I mean, not just give what you have. That's what the friendship in a settlement rests on. That's why they can be so many different people, with different temperaments, living together peacefully and happily. Of course it isn't only that. There's the other kind of friendship based on preference – people who are meant to be friends because they naturally suit each other. And a small settlement like this is a compromise between the two. Once a settlement gets much bigger – like Ein Harod for instance – they have to break up into groups – inevitably some people are closer to each other than to the others. But in a relatively small settlement like this, there can still be a strong common friendship. It's a strain – it isn't cosy like a small clique, it means a big effort on the part of everyone, but it can still be done.'

'And yet,' said Jacob, 'people can be very lonely in a settlement.'

'Yes. In a way everyone is lonely in a settlement. You can't lean back and let yourself go as you do with one or two friends or within a family if it's a happy one. You can't go to sleep. You aren't coddled. Your essential aloneness isn't taken from you and there isn't even a pretence that it is. Forty people can only meet on the level of giving. As soon as you want to take you're up against it – nobody belongs to you exclusively – not even your wife or your child. They all have ties with all the others, duties to all the others. There again, some people find it much easier than others. There are people for whom companionship satisfies almost all their needs. And others for whom the constant presence of all the others is a heavy burden.'

'It's evidently that for you, Haim,' Jacob said smiling.

'Yes, that's one kind of poverty I couldn't put up with. Never being by myself, that's my idea of hell. I haven't the vocation for it.'

It is now more than thirty years since I stayed in Geva and had these conversations. The reason I remember them in such detail is because all the time I was there I was filled with a sharp sense of expectancy, as though I were on the edge of an important discovery, also, of course, I had kept notes.

I came back to Cairo with sore fingers from the blisters I had got weeding the onions.

In my mind Palestine stood for the opposite of Egypt. Egypt stood for no rebirth, only for continuation. A country of sex and death and magic. Very heartless and very corrupt. There was too the contrast of the little boy in the cement pipe and the marble halls and bridge parties.

I began to be interested in Zionism, in the getting together of a committee, the funds it raised to be split between the Palestine Settlements and the local baby centre we founded in the Jewish quarter. I addressed a few meetings, once I remember I started my speech with a piece from the Hassidim: 'A disciple asked a holy man where God was, and the holy man opened a window and showed him the street and the country and the sky and the people and said: "He is all these things." '

At that time I believed that the Jews would settle in Palestine, and that eventually they would perhaps intermarry to some extent with the Arabs, and revive the mediæval Arab-Hebrew culture. I thought it was right that Palestine should not belong to them. The point of Zionism, as I saw it, was rebirth, not ownership. Poverty.

In 1934 I went again to Palestine, this time I stayed at Jerusalem in the King David Hotel. I thought it incongruous and later recognised it as a true Osbert Lancaster hotel. By then I was a Catholic and I saw the paradox of the City of Peace, always at war, the fountain of living water built so high that every summer there was a drought. I saw the holy places, the quarrelling sects and all the rest girded with the Passion. I felt that to be a Christian Jew in Palestine was most fitting. I thought the link between the Jews and Palestine sacramental.

I went there once more in 1948. What drew me to Jerusalem under siege? Was the barbed wire across the town the crown of thorns . . .??

This Year in Jerusalem

With the story of her visit to Geva the draft Manya made for her auto-biography ends. She was too weak to continue writing. The basic material she would have used had she been able to go on remains. There are articles, reviews, broadcasts and besides these travel diaries. One of them describes her visit to the Middle East in 1948 when she went there as a journalist. Since she refers to this journey in the last sentence of the previous chapter it seems justifiable to insert it here, even though this is done at the expense of chronology and it is in an unpolished form.

The fourteen years that separate these two visits had been times of great turmoil. Owing to Hitler's persecution of the Jews, immigration had greatly increased and had alarmed the Arab population with the result that a state of lawlessness developed. Britain as the mandatory power set a figure of 75,000 immigrants to be allowed into the country over a period of five years. Jews arriving in Palestine over and above that number were transferred to Cyprus and after the war one ship-load was returned to Germany. All this inevitably caused great tension between the Jews and the British. As an alternative the Jews were for partition.

In 1947 the General Assembly of United Nations drew up a plan for Palestine by which it was to become a bi-national State with Jerusalem as an international city. The Jews accepted the proposal but the Arabs rejected it.

The British now agreed to end the mandate and to withdraw their forces. Jordanian, Iraqi, Syrian and Egyptian troops began to in-filtrate into Palestine.

On the 14th of May 1948 British troops left Jerusalem and on the same day the Council of Jews assembled in Tel Aviv proclaimed the establishment of the State of Israel. By then the Old City of Jerusalem was under siege by Arab forces. On the 11th of June a representative of the Security Council negotiated a truce which was to last for a month. Hostilities broke out on the 9th of July and lasted for ten days after which a further truce was negotiated but constantly broken. Manya arrived in Israel on the 27th of July.

27th July
Amsterdam

I am sitting in the local Groppi[1] with a view on to a canal and the wet street. In this light colours are intense. A girl in a red coat comes out of a Dutch picture. It is a scene with a lot of green in it; green chairs, hanging baskets of plants, greenish shadows and reflections in the window-panes which bring out the scarlet of the girl's coat and the greyish pink of the houses, and one guesses at the green water. There is a church across the way which rings the quarters and a little complicated tune in a gentle, gay, elderly voice. It was ringing last night when the Communists marched by.

I have just been to church. I meant to dedicate myself and my journey. But I was restless and distracted. The church had no obvious entrance and was, I think, part of some Catholic Action Centre – a lot seemed to be going on in the back of the building – the congregation looked hardbitten and reverent; there was a young devout priest and a lot of plain chant in which the laity joined. I was conscious of an extraordinary sense of continuity, of the past continued into a robust present and even into the ornaments and shapes of the vestments. All this suggests that people are busy working for the faith now in much the same way as at any other time. I have also an impression of great unworldliness emphasised by the complete absence of glamour or fashion. There is a curious air of innocence about the faces of the young and of the old men; perhaps it is easier for them to look like that because of their blunt traditional features. The women wear no make-up; a pity we can't go back to that, there is something touching about their pale lips and their faces have more character. The old ladies look pretty tough with their yellow skins and black clothes and their unbecoming, heavy, vaguely modern, but unmodish, hats which resemble coifs. Splendid to hear the familiar Latin when you don't understand the language of the country.

In the plane between Amsterdam and Marseilles
An old gentleman with a bushy black beard and a skull cap reading the *New York Herald* flicked his head sideways like a bird and asked me:
'You go to Haifa?'
'Yes.'
'Why?'

71

'I am a reporter.'

He looked pleased.

'So am I. Look, I have a press card.'

I wish I had one too, perhaps they will give me one at Haifa.

There were five other passengers, three young men who look more like real reporters than the Rabbi and myself, and two Amsterdam merchants.

While we were passing through the customs in Marseilles the Rabbi told me he was returning from the United States where he had been with a delegation of Orthodox Jews but had broken his journey in Amsterdam to avoid travelling on the Sabbath.

Here we are joined by several more passengers, one man comes up and says he knows me and also knew my father in Russia. This makes me feel better. I had been thinking that if I were a real reporter I should, by now, be on good terms with everyone on the plane.

We walk up and down the lawn of the Marseilles aerodrome, smelling the extraordinary sweet, southern night air.

My companion is worried about what is going to happen to Haifa, where he lives, when, in a few days' time, the British leave. He says that because of its strategic importance it may become very unsafe. I ask whether the Jews are not all the same pleased at the evacuation? He says, 'Yes, pleased but very worried.'

The Hagana² is such a small force, and it has too few officers and arms. He thinks the terrorists (Irgun and Stern) could have been fine boys too but they are 'spoiled by the feel of a gun. A lost generation'.

After Rome I slept and woke up to Attic sunshine over a purple sea edged with turquoise shoals. From the air Greece looked quite burnt out, but when we landed a cool light breeze lessened the heat. We straggled towards the buildings at the end of the airfield, but an official stopped us and made a speech. We were travelling to a country at war; the Greek Government wished to remain strictly neutral; so the company must ask us not to leave the vicinity of the plane and to take our seats in it as soon as it had refuelled.

It grew hotter with a haze over the pink earth. We stood drinking lemonade under the wings of the plane; then re-embarked and suddenly there is only one more hour to Haifa.

I have never before come to Palestine except by the night train from Cairo. That meant the wait at Suez, with talk in many languages in the dark, then the crossing by ferry; at Kantara I once saw an immigrant kissing the earth.

In the late afternoon light the coast was ochre and dark green, and above it, the soft clouds were ochre bellied. We came down near the oil installation which from the air looked like tops and tin counters. Two young men in khaki shirts and shorts collected our passports and a neat competent woman conducted us to the airport office. An American correspondent and myself stood on the verandah hugging our typewriters and bags. Nothing happened for a long time then a large young man pushed through the crowd and handed me a letter from a friend in Tel Aviv. She wrote asking me to come and stay with her. All the hotels were full but I could have a sofa in her room. The young man who brought the letter was a taxi driver and would bring me to her.

It was growing darker. Along the edge of the airfield I saw a row of British army huts with little gardens in front and soldiers wandering in and out. Suddenly there was a hustle. Our passports were returned to us, we filled in medical forms; there was a friendly argument between the customs officer who thought I had too many cigarettes and the taxi driver who considered this meddlesome of him. Inside the shed a family of immigrants was in difficulties. The passport officer had found some irregularity in their papers. 'They're forged, aren't they?' he said, smiling. The mother, a worn looking woman in her fifties, insisted they were genuine.

'But Mama,' said her son. 'Why bother? We have arrived. We can tell the truth.' She gazed at him in terror. The official stamped their papers and waved them on cheerfully.

An hour later I was sharing the taxi with four people and on my way to Tel Aviv. As the road left the town the driver took a large homemade-looking revolver out of a compartment in the dashboard and put it on his knees.

'Road not safe?' I ask.

He grunts, 'Safe enough now but better be careful. There was a little sniping last night.'

He tells us that we shall make a detour.

'How long,' I ask, 'will that add to the journey?'

'About half an hour. It was quite quiet last week, but now they've started up again at Tira, so the Hagana have imposed a curfew on a bit of the road.'

Leaving the big shadow of Carmel on our right, we climb a little hill road. I feel drowsy and excited. The bumpy hillside and the earth-smelling breeze seem good after the abstractions of the sky.

'Was there much fighting around here before the truce?' I ask.

'Yes, some of the settlements had a bad time. You see that place?' and he points to a clump of mud-brick houses. 'That's an Arab village. They were all right but some Iraqis got in among them. They raided a kibbutz and killed forty of our men and girls. They paid for it! Our own Arabs were keeping quiet. It is a pity so many left.'

I look with faint horror at the desolate village.

'When did they leave?'

'After Haifa was occupied. Since then the road has been fairly quiet, but a couple of my pals were ambushed along this stretch.'

'What happened?'

'Their car was shot up but they managed to get out.' He grins at me. 'It's really all right now. I know every inch of the road. My pals and I kept it open all the time. We've a co-operative of taxi drivers and we saw to it that communications with the airport didn't break down.'

The hills open out. There is a feeling of big empty country falling away to our left.

We pass another settlement and see three boys with rifles and a lantern on guard on the road.

Then another deserted village.

My mind running on horrors, I ask, 'What *did* make the Arabs leave?'

The driver thinks for a little, then he says: 'The Iraqis and their leaders. Of course we weren't going to let the Iraqis stay and since last winter there were more and more of them about the place. It was they who made the trouble. But that was no reason for our Arabs to go. We weren't going to ill-treat them. Mind you, I don't say that they weren't frightened by what happened at Der Yassin.[3] That was a bad show. Those Irgun boys are fools. Though they had a lot of provocation. Some are good and some are wicked but both kinds are foreigners here.'

We pass a military camp evacuated by the British and now used for training the Hagana.[4]

Then we pass through beautiful country with rounded hills. I ask one of our passengers who has come from South Africa, where she has been collecting money for WIZO,[5] about the immigrants.

She told me that when they arrive in Israel they first go to a camp and continue training. Then they are given £40 to £50 to look for work and start up. When a job is found they are given one room for a family, till the Council builds them a house, which costs about £450. The young people go on the land but this is too hard for the old.

We pass a small town with a rather untidy blackout.

It was too late to see anything of Tel Aviv that night, but next morning I had a look round. It never was a handsome town and after my ten years' absence, I thought it uglier than ever. The only time I had seen any charm in it was during my first visit in 1925, when there was little more of it than a few villas and the newly built school standing on the sand dunes. The houses were ugly, but I had found them a little touching, for each one seemed the embodiment of some pathetic middle-class dream transported from Minsk or Warsaw, absurdly unsuitable to the climate, but evidently delighting its owners.

I remembered an evening I spent in one of them with some friends from Russia. After dinner we went for a walk to the beach, making our way along the unpaved sandy roads and arriving suddenly at the empty shore. The emptiness and the starlight went to our heads and one young man started to dance by the edge of the water, the rest of us clapping and singing, with not a soul or a house in sight except for the dark silhouette of an open-air café closed for the night.

By 1948 Tel Aviv had become a big sunny city of concrete blocks with a holiday beach lined with hotels and the wreck of a ship standing out in the harbour. This was a ship which had arrived a week ago loaded with immigrants and arms from America. It had caused a scandal. The Irgun had tried to collect the arms for its own use. The Government, whether mindful of its truce obligations or afraid of strengthening the Irgun, had refused permission to unload the arms. When the terrorists insisted, they ordered the ship to be sunk by the shore batteries. Meanwhile the immigrants had landed in a state of the utmost confusion, most of them, coming from America, were ignorant of the quarrel between the Irgun and the Hagana. On landing the young men were asked if they wished to become soldiers. Most of them had come for this purpose and were drafted into the Hagana. The Irgun leaders were enraged at losing both men and arms.

I returned to Haifa late in the evening and went at once to the Lion Hotel to see the press officer and meet a young journalist from *Time Life*. He told me the defence of Haifa was going to be a big problem as preparations were impossible because, until the British evacuation had been completed, people were still liable to be arrested for carrying arms. The city was obviously at the mercy of invaders but the Jews were completely determined to hold it.

I reached my hotel tired and dishevelled and had a long wait for the PRO who gave me a pass. I talked to other journalists who told me that three British tanks had been stolen during the previous night. General Stockwell had made no comment but had refused an invitation to a banquet at which the Mayor was to be present. He was respected and said by all to be 'really neutral'.

After dinner I went for a walk up town. Haifa was beautiful – ochre colour under the dusty blue star-strewn sky and the hills looming at its back.

On the eve of the British evacuation the town has an outwardly normal air. The streets with their brightly lit shops, cinemas and cafés and dangerously driven trucks, buses and taxis are filled with the usual crowd of young men in khaki shirts and shorts, young women in print dresses or 'ATS' military uniforms and older people whose lapses into Yiddish break in on the stream of Hebrew talk. There is a spate of rumour: will the Arabs attack? Will all the British leave? Who stole the three tanks from the airfield? The British Military Authorities for their part are prepared for trouble: will the Jewish hotheads, hungrily eyeing the final disposal of priceless military equipment, resist the temptation to interfere?

In the event everything goes off in an almost unnatural calm.

By six o'clock on Wednesday morning the embarkation began. It would be hard to convey the impression produced by the enormous, unhurried strength; hour after hour, as the warm grey dawn sharpened into glaring sunlight, unit after unit tramped the long quay to be swallowed up in the yawning hulls, together with a mountain of equipment; the formidable paraphernalia of modern war was handled lightly in a perfectly timed ritual, until finally came the sudden dispersal of the British fleet.

By arrangement with the Jewish Authorities the harbour was taken over by the British-trained Jewish military police. Then the docks were closed until the ceremony of the hoisting of the Jewish flag had taken place at six o'clock. By five-thirty some two thousand men, women and children were jostling excitedly in the tiny square behind the sheds and the adjoining harbour block house. The Prime Minister, the two chief Rabbis and the Mayor and notables of the town took their places on a raised platform. Two sides of the square were lined with military police, a detachment of the Hagana, and the newly inaugurated Marines who were impressively smart in their brand new uniforms. The crowd pressed all around and small boys perched on the steep, sloping roofs of the surrounding sheds.

With a flourish of trumpets the blue Israeli flag was hoisted over the port. The National Anthem was sung, the small boys scrambled precariously upright. Then the army and the Marines marched off to the music of the voluntary fire brigade band and the civilians crowded to the waterfront. The Israeli fleet, consisting of some battered immigrant boats, three corvettes and, pirouetting round them, three harbour tugs, all gaily beflagged, was deployed in the harbour.

Up in the town everything was calm though a little breathless. The fact that there was no immediate breaking of the truce relieved the tension, and by Friday people were talking hopefully of its continuation. The country was living consciously under threat and was prepared if necessary to resume the fighting. But there was a kind of cosiness about those few days, as though they were a promise of a peaceful future.

The more moderate papers spoke tentatively of a possible turn in the relations between the British and the Jews who had co-operated for so many years in a creative enterprise. But on the whole the people were wary.

The last moments of the embarkation moved me oddly, but I was aware of this only in the back of my mind. What was the significance of all this business? The British lion off in a huff? Or humiliated? At the time I thought that, in spite of everything, there might be some generous significance to it, if only we could see it. After all, it was the British lion who had fathered this roaring cub of Judah and, sooner or later, the Mandate would have been given up anyway. It might have happened in less tragic circumstances, but today so far as the State of Israel is set up it is firmly on its feet and, after all, the explicit purpose of the Mandate was to set up a National Home for the Jewish people. Now let's hope that Israel sticks to its own past and treats 'our Arabs' well.

After the fleet left nothing happened and there were no disturbances in the town, except that people were walking about in places where, until the evacuation had been completed, they had not been allowed to go.

I went with the *Time Life* correspondent to see the damage to the Central Station where British troops had been billeted. Just before leaving the soldiers went berserk and smashed everything; not a window-pane, not an electric light bulb was left whole. Wash basins were smashed, mattresses ripped up, shelves were ripped out and cupboards turned out, even the ticket machine was broken to pieces. Finally they had started a fire. Outside, the cement walls had huge ink-stains on them, quarts of ink must have been used. I felt miserable. A couple of old people were shaking their heads saying: 'What it means to us – our best station.' Beside them children were playing hopscotch unconcernedly.

I wanted to return to Tel Aviv.

A Hagana boy who spoke good English agreed to drive me to the civilian airfield where I had landed. The flight took twenty minutes: then with some difficulty I booked a room at a hotel.

In the morning I visited a synagogue, it was untidy with household goods and a child's bed in the women's gallery. I asked a tailor from Poland about this. He told me that refugees from the Jaffa district were still living there. Many people, he said, were religious. Some, including young people, went to the synagogue twice a day. All had religious instruction at school. I had noticed that many people said to me: 'I am not religious but something mysterious is going on.' Some even said: 'We are not fighting for the State of Israel but for the Jerusalem of the Torah.'

As I walked down Allenby Street, the main thoroughfare of Tel Aviv, an alert sounded. Only a few planes were overhead but the police ordered everyone to take shelter and I found myself crowded into a shop with an enormous plate-glass window, feeling much more nervous than I would have been outside. The crowd looked exhilarated, as people looked in London in 1940. They obeyed the police with a self-conscious pride in discipline and it would have been unkind to point out that the shelters at their disposal – shops and flimsy office buildings – were about as useful against bombs as opening an umbrella.

When the raid ended I was told that the only damage had been to a school, and that fortunately none of the children had been hurt as they were at lunch in the canteen some distance from the school building. My friend Iris was at that moment helping to transfer them to a temporary schoolhouse and so I went to join her. The children were assembled in a classroom and a teacher was keeping them amused. I spoke to one of them, a small fair girl of ten with Gretchen pigtails. She had been brought from Germany a month ago and evidently the air-raid was nothing by comparison to her wartime experiences for she had hardly noticed it. Almost all the children were new arrivals and almost all were orphans. Their expressions were impassive, neither frightened nor excited by the air-raid or the move.

This visit made me curious to see more children so Iris took me to a school in the country which catered for about a hundred, half native and half immigrants. The Headmaster and his wife looked kind and experienced. The children were quite different from those I saw in town; they had arrived a year ago and seemed healthy and gay, with little on the surface to distinguish the newcomers from those who had been born in Palestine. The mixture was good for the immigrants, the Headmistress told me. The natives were so 'normal' – it helped the others to settle down. Of course, there were hard cases among the orphans. She told me the stories of two of them.

There was Peter who was nine years old and who came from Poland. When he was two his parents, knowing that they were to be deported, left him with a Polish couple who undertook to hide him from the Germans. But soon the couple realised in what a dangerous position they had placed themselves, and were so frightened of Peter being discovered and of all of them suffering some terrible punishment that they kept him throughout the occupation underneath their bed, feeding him there like a puppy and never letting him out – at five he had almost lost the use of his legs. But he was intelligent and when one day he heard his foster parents discussing whether it would not be better, after all, to hand him over, for their situation was becoming desperate, this five-year-old blackmailed them by threatening to attract the Germans' attention so that they would all be killed. Thus he terrorised them until at last the town was liberated and he was taken first to Germany and then to Palestine. His parents were never found. Physically he had quite recovered but his face bore a closed, stony expression which hardly ever melted. For a whole year, the Head-mistress told me, she could not get him to take an interest in anything, but recently she noticed he listened attentively to the Bible stories which were told in class and he liked looking after animals.

Then there was Katie, a gentle-faced girl of sixteen. Her father had been deported and had not been heard of since. Later the Gestapo came for Katie and her mother. They were taken to a concentration camp in Germany. The mother was pregnant but she concealed this and, thanks to the help of other prisoners, she gave birth in secret and kept the baby hidden. Soon after this she died. Katie took charge of her small brother and succeeded in keeping both of them alive. Today she was another awkward child, without Peter's difficulty in communicating with the outside world but exhausted by her too heavy burden of responsibility.

'All these immigrant children,' the Headmaster told me, 'are survivors. Their capacity to become normal often depends on the reason why they survived. Those who have survived through some-body's kindness and have therefore kept their faith in human nature are the quickest to settle down. The hardest cases are those who have survived only through their own toughness.'

I am quite determined to go to Jerusalem and have made arrangements to do so. The convoy forms up outside Tel Aviv, at its head a car flying the blue flag of the Truce Commission, then the taxi I am sharing and behind us about twenty trucks. There are only a few days of the truce left and we discuss the chances of its being prolonged. Here and there we pass a house ripped open by an explosion, or deserted huts. At one time the road was under constant threat from sniping and ambush. The Iraqis had infiltrated the Arab settlements and established strong posts. In some places the local Arabs had objected. At Nes Ziona, for instance, where Arabs had lived together with Jews for over half a century, the Arabs had tried to evict the 'foreigners', and when they failed, had entrusted the keys of their houses to the Jews.

So far we have been passing through orange groves; they look neglected now. We enter Judea and the red earth changes to white. The dust turns our hair into periwigs and covers the olive and pine trees with a white film that looks like snow; we stop before the Arab post at Latrun. The UN officials get out as the road is closed by barbed wire. Behind the wire stand Bedouin sentries, smiling and immovable. One is armed with a tommy-gun, a grenade and a short sword; the other holds a rifle. The Arabs can't understand the UN official and one goes off to find his superior officer while the other, bland and good-tempered, stands beside our cab. Eventually the officer comes up and lets us through. We pass a bend where anti-tank and machine-guns are levelled at us from a strong point. Our taxi driver grumbles that they are a better model than those of the Hagana.

The road climbs into the hills. We pass burnt out trucks and a car. This, I am told, is where a convoy of nurses and doctors, on their way to the Hadassah Hospital, were kept under fire for hours. We arrive at a road block, an Arab officer looks in at the window of the taxi, examines our passes and the barbed wire is rolled up.

A few miles farther down the road we drive into a Jewish village and are stopped by men of the Hagana. Here we pick up a girl holding a towel, who says she has come from another village to have a bath.

A little farther on, in a dip on the right, is a peaceful scene – an Arab village threshing its millet, children and black goats on the road and an old man in a *tarbush* trading with two Jewish settlers.

The first sight of Jerusalem is infinitely moving and I know this is where I had to come. It remains beautiful until we reach the new city. This reminds me of London after an air-raid; broken windows, chips out of walls, a lot of debris and glass crunching under one's feet as we get out of the taxi. I am told that all the shops are open and some cinemas are giving shows for the troops, but that all restaurants are closed.

I stay at the Eden which is pretty empty. The porter tells me that during the siege it was the only place that had food. The guests seem to be marooned Americans and university professors.

Water is now rationed. Three slices of bread and four grams of lentils are given out. Sardines can be bought, but are very expensive.

Paraffin, usually fourteen shillings a tin, now costs £16 or £20, or it can be paid for with sixteen packets of cigarettes. Weiss, the Public Relations Officer arrives and promises to show me the battlefields. He adds that our walk may be dangerous as there is still some firing. I look more closely at the damage at Ben Jehuda: four buildings, two of which were hotels and one an ex-soldiers' club were blown up. The place is known as Bevin Corner; the Palestine Post building is also badly damaged. Weiss says this was done by the British Police with Arab support.

We have some difficulty and parleys at various posts, then we visit the Russian enclave – a white birthday cake church with monks and nuns still there.

Later, as we approach Notre Dame, we hug the walls as if to shelter from rain, but it is because the crossroads are particularly exposed to snipers' fire. The Arab houses in front of Notre Dame are heavily damaged but their inhabitants had left before they were shelled.

We enter the improbable, studious but homely convent library and find the books still there and also a statue of St Augustine. Beyond it are devastated passages and rooms and huge shell holes.

Suddenly we hear loud shouts and some mortar fire. I see two nuns scurrying, with flapping coifs, about the courtyard where a family of Arabs is squatting. I go down and one of the nuns takes me to the Reverend Mother. She tells me two Irgun boys came first, were polite and went away. Next day the Arabs tried to come in with arms but she prevented them from entering. Finally the Hagana arrived and said the doors must be opened or they would be blown. She replied that she was deaf and couldn't hear what they said. This was followed by shelling from both sides. Then the doors were blown and the Hagana occupied the building. I love the Reverend Mother and want to go on talking with her but my escort is obviously getting very impatient. We climb up a ladder, go through a vestry with a huge shell hole, visit the chapel and look through the glassless windows and over the sandbags at the view. No permit is going to get me into the Old City so I gaze at the warren of roofs crowding up to the domes of the churches. The City of Peace, terribly vulnerable – and peaceful.

Mortar fire starts up and we keep out of the line of the windows.

When I get back I ask a Welfare Worker about the siege. Its events are difficult to visualise. The Jewish families of the Old City had lived there since time immemorial, though there was also a sprinkling of first, second and third generation immigrants who had come to live near the Wailing Wall and the ancient synagogue. The relative newcomers belonged to a particularly strict orthodox section which at first opposed Zionism, believing the return to the Promised Land must be the work of the Messiah. Only recently have they changed their attitude and allowed their young men to enlist in the Hagana. Some were extreme pacifists, but prepared also for extremes of endurance; others provided some of the most fanatical warriors.

The Welfare Worker told me that during the hour of prayer she had seen young men, a rifle in one hand and prayer tablets in the other, manning the long stairs under a hail of bullets. Books of religious commentaries lay on the steps where the elders held discussions, and during lulls in the firing a crowd would gather to debate some particularly interesting point. Whether out of affection for their age-old homes or devotion to their place of worship, these people clung to their district; some even insisted on trying to return to it if they happened to have been absent at the beginning of the siege. Meanwhile the Hagana fought desperately to break through, hampered by its shortage of arms. One Area Commander was heard telephoning to another a request for the immediate despatch of 'the' Spandau.

I got up at six, meaning to go to Mass. It was cool, barely light and there was a dry wind. The front door was locked and the french windows of the lounge (they were riddled with bullet holes) led only to a garden full of rubble. Eventually the porter came down and let me out. I walked eastwards but found every road blocked. I passed a couple of Protestant religious institutions which were clearly occupied, either wholly or in part. By eight, having failed in my purpose, I returned to breakfast and asked the hall porter if he could tell me where I could go to Mass. He directed me to the Fathers of Ratisbonne.

For the first time since my arrival in the Holy Land I went into a church. The Father Superior appeared; he had a black beard and bright Oriental eyes. At first he expressed the utmost distrust of journalists but eventually became more confiding. At the beginning of the war he had given refuge to both sides – Jews from the Arab quarter and Arabs from the Jewish quarter – but after having had one of his guests kidnapped by the Irgun the situation had become too complicated. I left to attend the blessing and presentation of the colours of the Jerusalem Area Command. I walked in the blazing sun to the playground of a girls' school where five hundred soldiers were on parade. They looked quite smart in their khaki uniforms and brown berets, with their bren-guns and two inch mortars. All were tanned to the same colour whatever the improbable variety of their origin. Descendants of old Palestine families, born in the colonies founded by early immigrants, or immigrants from every country in Europe and even America and Africa. These are the Hagana. (The crack regiment is the Palmach, whose cadres were trained by Wingate. Many of the men had served in the British Army during the war.) The Hagana is the force that the Jews rely on for their safety. The Irgun, which is believed to be numerically small, is now again, as under the Mandate, practising 'underground' tactics. It is deeply distrusted by most people, not only for its fanatical behaviour but also for its supposedly Fascist tendency; the smaller but equally distrusted Stern group has recently declared itself Communist.

The Area Commander and two officers and the two chief Rabbis rise to their feet. The Colour party marches up. Rabbi Hertzog makes a longish speech. The man next to me says: 'He is praying for peace, but it seems very unlikely; that is why he looks so sad.' The Colours are blessed and presented. Then the banners are dipped for the prayer for those who have fallen in the battle for Jerusalem; it was beautifully chanted by the Rabbi. After this the little, frivolous band which had previously been playing nondescript tunes, plays the National Anthem with dignity. The troops, the military police, the fire fighters, the radio operators and the, slightly self-conscious, 'ATS' march away.

A young Polish PRO takes me home, and as we walk tells me his version of the battle. Firing started in early December; after a time the Old City was virtually cut off, but, by arrangement with the British, convoys were allowed through after being checked by the Arabs. Then serious fighting broke out in dominating positions in the north and the south from which the Arabs fired at the town. The Jews occupied Sheikh Jarrah in the north but had to give it up just before the British left as they said it interfered with their evacuation route. They then moved on to Katamon in the south-west which enabled them to regain several colonies occupied by the Arab Legion. The Legion had

Easter eggs painted by Manya

been brought in by the British as part of the British Army and was supposed to leave when they did, but failed to do so.

The Pole also told me more about the attack on the convoy of doctors and nurses which was on the way to the Hadassah Hospital. They were under fire from ten till three, covered by a detachment of the Hagana. When these could no longer resist the Arabs came up and set the trucks on fire.[6] All this happened a few hundred yards from a British post. The Pole said that the officer in charge was a decent fellow but couldn't risk his men. He sent for artillery which didn't arrive. Individual British officers went to the rescue.

After lunch I went to see a WIZO shop which sold objects made by immigrants. The aim is to find a market for the things these people know how to make and also to teach them to make other objects. This will help the women to supplement their husbands' wages. It is also hoped that it will keep the local crafts alive: e.g. silver filigree, weaving, embroidery.

I said I would like to see a Home which had been evacuated from the Old City to Katamon. We set off in a taxi and after passing many heavily damaged houses, came upon a row that were fairly intact. At the Home, two young Sabra (the name given to Jews born in the country) nurses explained how they ran the place and showed me Arich, a minute and pitch-black-haired infant who was born on the last day of the siege. His mother was dying and handed him, done up as a parcel, to a neighbour to take away. Arich now looks well and is very hungry. We see more babies in cots, others in pens. Then we go into the Girls' School.

The refugees from the Old City had been, some for twenty-four, some for thirty-six hours, without food or water before being released. By the time they arrived here, kitchen premises, clothes and food had been prepared for six hundred children; also a hospital and a home for the aged. It was a remarkable piece of improvised organisation; the only thing that went wrong was that they did not have enough water.

The sewing mistress told me they had to go slow on the first day because the little girls' hands shook and they couldn't focus. Those between twelve and fourteen had run messages for the soldiers and some knew how to shoot. The boys, I was told, had gone to the Irgun HQ and were 'out of hand'.

At four o'clock I went back to see the Father Superior of Ratisbonne. He told me both sides are equally to blame for the damage done to Notre Dame. At five o'clock I went off on an expedition with a Jewish UN liaison officer. We passed several colonies, an evacuated Arab village and a police station captured by the Palmach, whose signature was chalked up on a wall.

Finally I was dropped at a church. Père Alexandre came out and took me to the chapel, then, as I was very thirsty, he drew exquisite water from a well. There was once a Roman bath here built by the Tenth Legion. The Crusaders called it The Spring of Emmaus and built the church. Afterwards it became a hospice for travellers going to Jerusalem and was run by the Knights Hospitallers. At one time, in the eighteenth century, it was abandoned but rediscovered in the nineteenth century. It was then ceded by the Turks to the Christians and occupied by Franciscans. In the interval the village had been captured by the robber chief Sid Abu Ghosh who levied tribute on it and was murdered, but his descendants had continued to rule the place. Lady Hester Stanhope and Chateaubriand both received hospitality here. During the bad times the Franciscans would be held up to ransom and send letters to their Superior in Jerusalem saying they were 'in the bread oven' – in fact a big room with a bread oven in one corner. Père Alexandre has been here for many years. He liked the British rule but thinks he can be happy under the Jews. He said only the richest of the Arab families had left for fear of reprisals or of being shelled by their own people.

I left after having a little glass of strong, sticky orange liqueur brewed by Père Alexandre.

I walked up to the high road with urchins clinging to me, gaping at my sunglasses, asking to be photographed and to have their picture at once, also begging for cigarettes; it was almost Egypt, but the children looked jollier and more healthy.

Back at the hotel I shared a table with two journalists who had spent the day crawling and dodging bullets along the front line. In a dug-out they came across an inscription: 'I, Moses Bernstein, have come from Belsen and am still alive.'

I managed to get to Mass at the Ratisbonne. There were three bearded priests there, and one Arab woman. I had so longed for Mass but was as distracted as ever. All the same, it is simple to ask God's will to make things all right.

Afterwards I joined other journalists who wanted to get to Ramat Rahel. We had already asked for permission to go there but on account of intermittent shelling it had been refused. Now again we were told it was impossible because it was so near to the end of the truce and the perimeter was getting nasty.

So instead I asked if I could get in touch with Buber. No one seemed to know where he was living since he left his house in the Arab quarter near the University. While waiting I was invited to lunch at the soldiers' canteen. It was very clean, and had the best food I had met with so far: a good soup, meat and cucumbers and a cherry compote. Everyone looked jolly.

I am sad to think that soon I must leave Jerusalem; for one thing I have run out of money. The hotel is hideously expensive and the banks won't cash travellers' cheques. But before I do so, having at last succeeded in finding out how to contact Buber, I go to his house and am let in to a cluttered-up, darkish parlour, shuttered against the afternoon blaze. Here Buber sits, looking inquiring, in a small, stiff chair. We talk about his party, the Ihud, a small, academic group led by Dr Magnes. It has always interested me because of its support for a bi-national State. Buber says: 'What we wanted was not the thing the Arabs mean by a Unitary State. We hoped to bring the two nations together as in Switzerland and Canada.'

I ask whether a *rapprochement* with the Arabs will not be much more difficult now. He replies: 'More difficult certainly. Yet is not war a kind of ventilation of passions? Perhaps a way of understanding will be given us. After all, we have one thing in common – the Arabs want a great Palestine and we want great things to happen in Palestine.'

'Does the young generation of Jews take account of the problem?'

'Many of them have a real desire to understand the Arabs. Many learn Arabic seriously. In the settlements they often achieve excellent relations. The Arabs and the Jewish elements cannot merge, but they can co-operate and stimulate one another. The Jews could give much to the Arabs, and the Arabs have a kind of primitiveness – I have great feeling and understanding for it – which could become creative through the stimulation of the Jewish spirit.'

'What is coming out of Israel?' I ask at last. 'Have the young people in the settlements any real link with the Jewish religious tradition?'

He thinks this over. 'If you ask them you will not get a satisfactory answer because the answer will come out of their conscious minds. I think that all this work in Palestine comes much more out of unconscious than out of conscious intentions. Unconsciously it is based on traditional ideals. Zionism is the secularisation of a religious ideal. It has been born out of traditional hopes. The young people come out of a background in which the tradition has degenerated. They don't know its roots and they react against it. But living the life of the settlements they feel the lack of something which they don't know. They are groping for it. They don't know that religion renews itself. There are times when a religion hides its meaning, its renewal is not yet manifest. But I believe in this power of renewal.' He looks past me with a mildly prophetic air, and then goes on. 'Of course, it is difficult for people like myself to be patient, to know that today must be lived as it is – we cannot put in its place a more glorious day. We live in the days of the Hidden God. We must be patient with all these people who do not know the religious goodness of what they are doing here. They are trying to live together in justice.'

'Might not this be a purely secular ideal?' I ask.

'Do you know in history of a purely secular ideal which has produced such results? No, this goes back to the Hassidim and to the Prophets.'

'But is there a necessary connection between the life they want to live and the soil of Palestine?'

'Of course. The Promise has always been bound to Palestine.'

'Might not this have been a symbol?'

'A true symbol is always concrete. Without a concrete form it is only an idea, not a symbol. The Spirit needs corporal form to manifest itself. Without it, it does not exist on earth.'

'Then you believe that a true symbol is a sacrament?'

'Certainly . . . Of course, it remains to be seen what will come out of all this. Will the community be faithful to the Jewish ideal of justice? A community is necessary; you cannot practise social justice in a purely individual life. And a State has this importance, that justice is not only what its members have between them themselves, but what States have with one another.'

'Do you think Jerusalem should be part of the Jewish State?'

'No. I have always wanted Jerusalem to be international. I have great hopes for Jerusalem. It should become a great centre of co-operation, not only between Jews and Arabs but between peoples generally – a symbol of the beginning of real co-operation between human beings.'

As he saw me out, mortars, and machine-guns spurted with re-newed venom from the east of the City.

The military convoy is to leave at six and I am to go with it. I wish Jerusalem didn't tug at one's entrails. It is heart-breaking to leave these people and these stones at this time.

In the last few moments left the PRO takes me to a café. I find I am beginning to cry and feel awful about it. He asks 'What is all this about? Jerusalem? Or is something else the matter?'

I gulp out 'Jerusalem' and ask for black coffee to come quickly. While drinking it I try hard to think of a way of staying on, but I have no money and I realise that it would be a great nuisance to all con-cerned to get me out once the fighting has started up again. Also, I ought to send off my article. Anyhow, I am quite determined to come back if I can find a way of getting in and out on my own.

We have a long wait till our numbers are called, after which we climb into the trucks. People sit on their luggage and two or three stand. Next to me is a pretty little boy with pink cheeks and clear, black eyes. He is travelling alone to an outlying colony. When we come to the turning off to it he says he is all right and will take a taxi but others are also getting out here and they look after him and say he is to spend the night with them and will be put on to a bus tomorrow. I feel relieved.

In the middle of the truck sits a Biblical figure, a woman with a face of great character, nursing a small, fair, sleepy child. We are stopped half a dozen times and our 'movement orders' checked by Hagana boys who climb up the side of the truck, balance precariously and collect the papers, which are handed out with jokes, though there is some grumbling and even refusals.

We reach the Burma Road and the truck jumps about unmerci-fully. The man next to me inquires if I am all right. It is wonderful how 'all right' I am, and always have been, except when I get distracted and no longer keep my certainty in mind. Nothing tires me; I seem to need no food and hardly any rest and I do not even mind the heat except during moments of distraction.

The road is hideously vulnerable. There is no cover and we can't go fast; finally we get stuck while climbing up a particularly bad stretch. Two trucks are jammed. After a while, a little breakdown van appears and zig-zags its way down to us but, in the end, the truck has to be left behind, at least it has been got off the road so the rest of the convoy can get by.

We go on for what seems like hours until we emerge on the old Jaffa road. It is dark and cool with a lot of stars. We stop at the Agricultural Experimental Station and are given good apple cakes. We reach Tel Aviv at 11.30 pm; the streets are crowded. I haven't got a room but Iris puts me up.

Next day there is an alert at around midday but nothing happens, except that the wardens tell people it is forbidden to walk about the streets, and buses and taxis stop. I have a touch of the sun, finish my article on Jerusalem and later go to a hotel on the beach, sit on the verandah and listen to the heavenly sound of the sea. Then I make for a café. Suddenly there is another alert followed by the sound of an explosion; people go quickly but cheerfully into a shelter. The street is deserted. I wait for a while then go out and have a look round. The street is still emptyish but is looking more normal, with military trucks rushing by. I try to buy sandals in a little shop with a big glass window. The proprietors and the sales girl don't even look out and apparently feel safe.

At the Public Information Office I am told that six bombs have been dropped, one hit a Children's Home. Two children have been killed, the rest have been taken to a big hall. I go there. They are sitting in rows while their names are being called out by a girl in khaki. They are all aged between twelve and sixteen. A handsome little boy with fair hair, dark eyes and a nervous expression tells me that he was born in Germany, went to Russia, then back to Germany where he was in a camp. After that he went to France, Italy and Cyprus. His parents are still in Germany but hope to join him. Another big Tartar-looking boy says he came from Poland. During the war his family fled and ended up in Siberia. I ask him how he got here all the way from there. He shrugs his shoulders, spreads out his hands, laughs and says: 'Like everybody nowadays.' Apparently his is not an unusual story. A stout girl of fourteen with fiery black eyes comes from Greece. The teacher says that a good many of the children come from there as anti-semitism is active.

I talk to Hannah, sixteen, who was in a camp in Berlin during the war. I ask her about today's incident and she replies, 'It wasn't too good.' I then hear she had been playing with the two children who were killed when the bomb fell. However she looks quite cheerful and asks to have her photo taken. She says she wants to go 'home', i.e. to the blitzed house and adds, 'I have always been a refugee – I want to sleep in my own bed.'

At six o'clock I am collected by car and, with other journalists, set out along the Jaffa road. We turn off it to Rishon Le Zion, the most human-looking of the colonies I've yet seen, quite old, and somehow it has not turned into a progressive town; it still has its plain little flat-roofed houses and there is a big synagogue looking over the square.

Before Ramleh we stop when we see other reporters at their antics. A young man in a tarbush is sitting on the fender of a car, talking merrily. He is the son of the Mayor and last night he walked two hours between mines to negotiate a truce.

A sergeant gives him a drink. We start off again, having been told to stick to the road on account of mines, but soon we get turned back and told to go to Lydda airport which was captured last Saturday. I sit on the verge of the road and over a pink lavender bush see smoke rising from a faraway village where fighting is going on.

Now we follow a dusty road between millet fields. All this part has been fought over. There are destroyed houses that have settled in on themselves, in the funny way they do after being blown up. We pass a village captured on Friday, it makes an arc round the airfield.

At first the airport looks intact; the runway is undamaged but, on nearer inspection, the main buildings are fairly messed up. We see an Air France plane laden with grapes. There are soldiers everywhere. We are taken to the Operation Room. The instruments are dusty and many are missing. A soldier tells me the Jews removed a lot before they left; then the Arabs packed up what pleased them but did not dismantle systematically.

I go to Ras el Gin, which has just been captured. There are Roman ruins on a hill and, a little beyond, a tiny village built round the power station for the Jerusalem water supply. There was hard fighting for the hills above but finally the Arabs drew out and the village was taken without the loss of a life. An officer comes along and tells us that the capture of the hills took place at night. They were held by a mixed force of Egyptians, Iraqis and Arab Legionaries, the last much the best but believed unkeen to fight here without their British officers. He took us to the power station which was undamaged but mined. (The Arabs were surprised and had no time to blow it up.)

I asked the officer where he came from. He replied that he was a Sabra, by profession a PT instructor – and he said that he hoped to go back to civilian life after the war. I inquired about language difficulties in the army. He said that orders are given in Hebrew, then translated into Yiddish and sometimes into English. We handed round cigarettes and went away. Again I was impressed by the friendliness shown to British reporters.

The driver of the taxi grinned all the time. I asked why he was so happy? 'To be driving on a newly opened road.'

I am left at a big place on a hill with long, low houses and a large Home. Here I am escorted by a guide called David, he is from Vilna and talks a mixture of Russian, German and Yiddish. We enter the dining hall. It has windows on both sides. Those on the right are sandbagged. Firing is going on all the time; when it gets very bad I am advised to sit near the sandbags. Afterwards we go out, but I am not shown round because of the shooting and I end by having to sit at the back of the house to be out of the way of the bullets.

On my return to Tel Aviv I went to see a friend who could tell me about education. She lived at the top of a house near the sea; it had a huge heap of sandbags in front of the doorway. The door was blown in during a raid.

Firing echoes across the town and now and again the tail light of a plane moves across the sky. My hostess tells me that Hebrew was first adopted in the Rishon school fifty-two years ago. Before that Yiddish was the spoken language but Hebrew was used for writing. Modern

Hebrew is pretty different from Biblical Hebrew but she says that the Bible is taught, loved and constantly quoted and that people make many excursions to places mentioned in it. She tells me it is intended that the kindergarten schools should take children from three to six; after that they will go to elementary schools and stay there till fourteen, then on to secondary schools for four years and finally to technical schools. I ask about religious teaching; she said that about five per cent of the schools are secular but nevertheless respectful of religion; of the rest a proportion are very strictly Orthodox and here the Torah and the Talmud are taught at the expense of other subjects – the rest of the schools are anti-religious.

Next day, with some Israelis, I visited a hospital. I was not taken into the ward where the heavily wounded from Jerusalem were being cared for, but to an annexe. Here I talked to an English boy who had been a sergeant in the British Army. He said, 'I'll get seven years if I go home.'

I asked him, 'What made you do this?'

He replied, 'I don't like what we are doing; I think the Jews are right. I wanted to help them. Quite a few English, Canadians, and South Africans felt that way. Mind you, I don't like the religious Jews. They're lazy. They go about with side locks and won't fight. If I'm good enough to fight for them they can fight for themselves.' The boy had been wounded two days before. He and his Jewish sergeant had gone to get more dynamite. They were caught by mortar fire. The sergeant was killed and the boy hurt. In the next bed was a very good-looking young man from a well-known Tel Aviv family; he begged me not to tell his anxious parents what had happened to him.

I then drove on past ghastly evidence of devastation and looting, all of it covered with what looked like plague-stricken dust. This was the result of hand-to-hand fighting and its aftermath.

We passed a bus full of Arabs who had been arrested; then a large mass of rubble where the Irgun had blown up the Town Hall in re-taliation for the blowing up of Ben Jehuda Street. Our party was dis-gustingly tough – or perhaps making up for feeling uncomfortable about it.

During the night there was an air-raid, rather noisy with heavy Ack-Ack. Eventually I dropped off to sleep but woke up to screams and shots above my head. I went into the passage where I saw a man in pyjamas showing people into their rooms and then darting off into his. I went up to the roof where I found three women scolding at the top of their astonishingly loud voices, and a man in pants with a revolver. It seemed that one of them lit 'only a little candle' to inspect the cistern on the roof which is apt to overflow. This, added to the generally poor black-out (the landing windows have no curtains), caused indignation among the neighbours, so the man in the pants followed her up to the roof and shouted: 'I've come to shoot you.'

She replied, 'Go on then', and he shot twice into the air!

During the day I went with friends to Rishon; when we arrived there was an alert. The chauffeur tried to get us into the shelter. This was a garage full of cans which we believed to be filled with petrol, also startling noises were coming from it – so I went for a walk. People were taking various precautions; many were standing under the awnings of shops. Some were reading their papers in an old garden with an alley of palms. They objected to our walking about, presumably fearing that a moving target might attract machine-gun fire.

We returned to Tel Aviv; another alert went off while I was going out to dinner with some fellow reporters but we reached our little restaurant where I ate borsch, stuffed fish and a lovely water melon, sitting in a narrow passage outside the building, having pointed out that this was safer than inside under the unstripped window. The danger is pretty small anyway, but I feel people are rather nervous; of course, they will get used to it if the raids go on.

Suddenly a bomb hit the top floor of our restaurant and damaged it. It was said to be a 25-pounder dropped by a Spitfire. Cement debris fell all around us.

One of the journalists asked a Sabra: 'Why do women have to fight?'

He is told: 'The new type of woman, who has taken an equal share in building up the colonies from the beginning, wishes to take all the risks the men face.' I suggest it is good to share danger but not good for women to kill. Not a proper role for women. But perhaps the country has not yet reached the stage when they can have a proper life.

There are more alerts. Something falls near the Public Information Office where there is a commotion as reporters drop on to the floor or rush out with cameras. It is known that a bomb fell on the deck of a ship but no one can find it.

Later I go to Garona where, after a short wait, the Minister of Police receives me. A magistrate is with him. We have Turkish coffee – like in Egypt – and watch a plane which seems to be chasing a ship that is zig-zagging out to sea. Hearing sharp noises we at first take them for bombs but then recognise they come from Ack-Ack. The magistrate wishes to go home to see his son who is just going to the front. A smart ADC holds open the door of his car for him, but my taxi driver refuses to move as he is afraid of losing his permit for six months for driving during a raid. Eventually the 'all clear' sounds and I get home.

My next expedition is, with other journalists, to the Negev. We go through orange groves which look rather sad and arrive at a clearing. Camouflaged arms are hidden under trees. I see a truck with soldiers, one looks about fifteen. We sit in a crowd in the shade, waiting. A couple of trucks go by with grinning soldiers back from battle. An officer comes and says the road to the Negev is dangerous but instead he has a scoop for us. Dayan is here. He passes by us. Then we divide into two groups, and in spite of the officer's discouragement, start for the Negev. We pass out into the open road. A mortar shell zigs by: then more of them come over. We get out of the car and keep our heads to the ground.

I find I am not frightened; on the contrary, I shall remember this moment gladly. So, what do I feel about danger? Admittedly, this is nothing compared with the big raids on London but people had told me that being actually aimed at is much worse than bombing. I don't think it is danger in general that I enjoy, but here it seems appropriate to share it . . . I felt this with anguish in Jerusalem. A shell bursts close to the right . . .

We return to Tel Aviv and I am taken to visit the 'ATS' station. We sit at the officers' table in a big room; there is a vase of gladioli on the table; bread, oranges and packets of chocolate are set out. There are all sorts of faces to be seen. Opposite there is a small child with Asiatic eyes and fair plaits. I am told she was in the Underground. The girls spend a week here learning drill and the use of arms. They are then sent off to put their knowledge into practice; some are nurses, others cooks, clerks or drivers. A girl with a lovely grave voice chants the blessing; all bow their heads. Then another reads psalms (the radio broadcasts a chapter from the Bible every day). Finally the CO says 'Good appetite' and we start eating. I talk with a pretty, dark girl, her black hair piled up high on her head. She came alone from Tunis; her family disapproved but she looks radiant. Afterwards we go to a Rest Room, furnished with hideous padded furniture and rugs from Jaffa. The girl who sang the blessing now sings songs of the Negev very beautifully. In civilian life she is an office worker but also learns singing. Finally, the girls march past, rather badly; they are an extraordinary mixture, a black girl marching beside a goose-stepping immigrant from Germany.

A nasty raid. An Old People's Home was hit as well as other buildings; six people were killed and some wounded.

To my great satisfaction I have now organised my return to Jerusalem. We go two-thirds of the way along the Burma Road in clouds of dust. Then at a turning we find a lorry and a jeep stopped. Machine-gunning is going on so we turn left. The officer and driver of the jeep come up to us. They say reconnoitring is taking place but they will try to sit it out. Flourishing my pass I climb into their jeep. We come back to the place where the firing was going on. The officer looks through his glasses and gives an order. We put our heads down and go ahead hell for leather. It reminds me of a run-away horse.

There is an awful bump and we nearly overturn but we have reached 'a safe stretch' and can now go slower. Funny that I feel no fear, only the need to pray. This surely means that I am doing the right thing.

The road climbs higher and higher. We see smoke rising not so far off, and pass a devastated village and then a party of workers, one wearing the remains of a shell on his head; he is eating a bunch of grapes. We stop by a vineyard. The officer gets out and I imagine he is looking for mines or snipers but in fact he is only after grapes. We join the old road and pick up two boys at Abu Ghosh where everything looks peaceful.

We arrive in Jerusalem. I find it much changed; more sandbags, fewer people. At the Public Information Office I am told there had been a two-hour truce to evacuate the Hadassah Hospital.

They tell me that when the shooting started up it was not at first very bad but it increased and there was an air-raid on Wednesday. Thursday night was calm but a thousand shells came over on Friday. Casualties are however less bad now because people have learned to take precautions and keep their windows shuttered. There had been, besides other fighting, an attack on the New Gate, the wall was blown up. I try to get a taxi to Ein Kerem which has been taken this morning but all agencies are closed as most taxis have been requisitioned and there is no petrol. Mortar and shell fire go on all the time. I make my way to the Fathers of Ratisbonne, go to the chapel and later meet the Father Superior. He says they have had some incendiaries in the garden which is full of pink laurel and bougainvillea and looks lovely. Also a shell chipped the chapel window; that is all, but he believes that most churches and convents in the New City must have received some damage. He had been out when I arrived, burying a child who died at St Joseph's because there was no ambulance or car to remove the body.

I went back to the Public Information Office and found that a shell had damaged the teleprinter. I was told that there was firing going on from behind the Dormition and near the Church of the Nativity. I took a walk and was filled with the improbable feeling of peace that Jerusalem gives me – even now when it is the very paradox of peace.

Sunday I went to Mass and then succeeded in getting to Ein Kerem. The drive was incredibly beautiful. Little pink hills encircling the long buildings in the valley which are deep pink or white among their cypresses. When I arrived a very civilised young officer took me to the Church of St John the Baptist where we met a cheerful Franciscan, polite and delightful looking. He showed me the chapel at St John's birthplace. Then I walked up the narrow street to a deserted Russian Mission, surrounded by dark pink laurels and on to the convent of French nuns of Our Lady of Sion who have been here since 1860. The Reverend Mother says they have had no trouble except noise from the fighting on the heights all round and sometimes a few bombs dropped their way 'by mistake'. She asks the officer who accompanied me to ensure that there would be no shooting from the convent since this would draw fire and she inquires about 'Sister Elizabeth's little axe for chopping firewood' which had been borrowed by the Hagana. The officer replies courteously.

Back in Jerusalem I am obliged to arrange for my return to Tel

Aviv. An officer suggests that I board a truck going to a place where I may find transport for the rest of the way, but nothing seems to be going to Tel Aviv and I become rather worried. Then a little unshaven man comes up and says he hears I need transport and he knows of someone who is going part of the way. He tells me he came here from Austria, via Switzerland, ten years ago, and puts me into a truck, driven by a nice red-haired Roumanian who tells me to sit near the cabin; this has (blessedly) blankets on the seat but the door won't shut and there is no roof over my head. We bump along the Burma Road past groups of soldiers wearing Canadian slouch hats and dressed in anything from blue pants to battle dress.

The Roumanian tells me he 'did' the road by day as well as by night during the fighting. He says he likes books. I ask which? Shakespeare, Dante, Dostoevsky – anything!

After a while I transfer to another truck and sit in the cabin between a Russian intellectual and a ferocious looking Hungarian with a shawl over his head and a lot of black stubble on his chin. His revolver sticks uncomfortably into my thigh-bone. We stop at Hulda and transfer to a car. But this is borrowed from us by a doctor who has to dash to a camp where a hundred and twenty immigrants have just arrived. We wait for an hour and then set off. There are big olive gardens but there has been no time to water them and the earth around them is not worked so they look thirsty.

After many miles we stop and acquire a new driver who wears a tarbush. Finally we reach a place where I am able to hire a taxi and eventually reach Tel Aviv very late.

My last day in Israel! I pack up and try to reach Nazareth but everything seems to be against it so instead I visit an institution where about a hundred and twenty girls are taught agriculture and domestic science. They arrive at the age of fourteen and stay a couple of years. I have lunch there – porridge, bread, eggs, a salad of tomatoes, horseradish and sour cream; there are also home-grown grapefruit of which they are proud.

Afterwards, quite determined to get to Nazareth, I share a car and drive through country already fertile with pines, cypress and eucalyptus trees, but we are stopped at a road block where I am found to be the only one with a pass. So we go back to a police station, eventually we are allowed to go forward; an officer escorts us. We reach Terra Santa. A Christian Arab shows us in and tells us the Father is resting but he is sure he will come down later. He does, and is affable; everything is obviously peaceful and unharmed, but the Father tells our officer that he has found cartridges in the garden where there was an arms dump and would he please take them away now? The officer says 'Yes', and we wait while a parcel is done up.

Then we go on to the Edinburgh Mission Hospital, where we see the doctor, the Matron and the nurses who are having tea in a chintzy drawing-room. The doctor, who has been here for thirty years, is most welcoming. He tells us that the majority of the Arabs in Nazareth are Christians and pretty civilised; the children mostly attend the Mission School. Previously, the Government had offered teachers for the Moslems if they provided a house, but they did not do so. The Jews always occupied most of the administrative posts here so he thinks that, after a time, no one is going to notice much difference.

When the war broke out every man got a gun but this seemed to the doctor chiefly a reversion to the traditional outfit: 'They don't feel they are anybody unless they have a cartridge belt!' No one wanted to fight but there was firing all day as the young men showed off their guns by shooting birds. A few scraps took place, but nothing serious happened.

A couple of truckfuls of foreign soldiers – the doctor believed they were Syrians – were brought in, but when the surrounding heights were taken by the Israelis they moved out. The population, unlike that of Haifa, did not move out with them and soon the Jewish military police were rushed in with strict orders to prevent incidents. They imposed a curfew. During the whole 'war' only two people were killed here and a few chickens stolen. The Arab nurses were very friendly as they showed us around.

Next we went on to Geva, where I had stayed so long ago. I recognised the view but everything else had changed. Now there is a great well-proportioned dining-room with netted windows, lots of tables with places for about eight at each. We ate their home-made bread, famous for its quality, and jam; but still, I see, there is no butter, in spite of the kibbutz possessing a hundred and twenty cows. We visited an improbable kitchen, run on electricity and kerosene, complete with a stainless steel outfit and various gadgets. The old people have their own kitchen and lunch on their own; the other meals they share with the rest.

We were taken up to the kitchen garden, to see the building they used as a dining-room for fifteen years; now it is the sewing-room; adjoining is a laundry and a drying-room with pigeon holes with the names of the owners of the clothes stuffed into them.

Next we crossed the garden which now has lawns and thick palm trees for shade. I saw the room I slept in with two others; then the only furniture consisted of three truckle beds and one chair; today it contains a double bed with a pretty cover, an armchair, a cupboard, a bookshelf and a rug. I heard the sound of a harmonica and soon a teacher appeared playing it, she was followed by a straggle of children. We were shown houses for babies in cots and others for children of various ages. Children from another kibbutz which is very exposed were staying at Geva; they were camping downstairs. The stairs were sandbagged.

I was shown the quarters of a young married couple; a bed under each window, with striped spreads, a round table with a bowl of flowers on it, an armchair, a rug and the usual Dostoevsky etc. library on the shelves. Next door, in a small room, was a little old lady. On, past the Recreation Room with radio and more books, to the cowshed, where the first electric milkers were being tried out.

In the vegetable pantry I heard someone call out, 'Roma'. I look up and see that she is changed, yet so unchanged. In 1926 she was beautiful; now she has a different, toughened nobility. She is preparing vegetables. Roma has not married. I have the feeling that life in a kibbutz is a religious vocation – otherwise how could they stand it?

We go on to the Hotel Sion at Haifa and arrive in the middle of an alert. I was supposed to have plenty of time to catch my plane but am now told I must rush and, indeed, when I arrive find it waiting, but am then informed that permission to take off has been refused. So I go back to the hotel, take a room, and have a, for me, hideously expensive meal; after which I stay on in the dining-room which is the only place properly blacked out, and talk to the waiter who is laying breakfast. He speaks about the British, says they were 'good guys' and behaved quite well. The Police got tough before the war but were checked by Commissioners. (There is an extraordinary difference between reactions in Haïfa and in Jerusalem where people are very bitter.)

It is too late to be worth while trying to sleep, so I go out through the verandah, past the sleeping porter, into the streets which are bright in the moonlight; the sky is almost green. A truck passes by full of men and women singing. At 3 am I leave again for the airport where we have a two-hour wait as the police are searching for someone. I feel very depressed at leaving; it has taken me so long to get around and I could have used a few more days profitably, but I have no more money left and, anyway, perhaps Ralph and Michael would worry unduly if I put off my return, though they don't know that at one moment I was reported killed and someone was sent out to identify my body.

Part IV
Retour aux Sources

Manya left no account of the war years, when she worked in the Foreign Office, nor of the founding of the Harvill Press or of her activities as a publisher and translator; these are briefly referred to in the Note on the Author at the end of the book. There are however three detailed diaries of the visits she made to Russia; two were directly related to publishing projects. Her first journey with Billy Collins, the Chairman of William Collins, was made for the purpose of discovering whether, in spite of the fact that the USSR was not a signatory to the Berne Copyright Convention, it might be possible to expand business relations between the two countries.

She had left Russia as a child and it was a moving experience for her to return after forty years.

*

There are many references to prices quoted in roubles in this Section. Since there were a number of different rates of exchange: tourist exchange, business exchange, international exchange, etc. – it is difficult to relate the rouble to the pound, but 4 roubles were at the time considered by British officials as a reasonable rate.

First Journey to Russia
Autumn 1955

Stalin had died in March 1953. The celebrated 'Thaw', which made it possible for Manya to re-visit Russia had been inaugurated by the Malenkov[1] government and was symbolised by the publication of Ehrenburg's novel *The Thaw*. Beria,[2] the evil police-chief, had been arrested in the summer of 1953 and then, or later, shot – together with some of his more notorious subordinates. There was a large-scale amnesty of political prisoners; many who had been unjustly sentenced to the camps were rehabilitated – all too often posthumously.

Towards the end of 1953, the bolder poets, novelists and dramatists were finding their voices and appealing for sincerity and vision in the arts as they began to break out of the shame and corruption engendered by the Stalinist Terror. But past evils were still being blamed on Beria, rather than Stalin, whose 'closest colleagues' still ran the country. After Malenkov's forced resignation as premier early in 1955 the Thaw was temporarily checked as Khrushchev fought for ascendancy. Soon he had emerged as the dominant figure, though by no means unchallenged, and, although nobody realised this at the time, the way was being prepared for the more radical reforms which followed the denunciation of Stalin early in the following year and for the subsequent reduction of the most prominent die-hard Stalinists, Molotov[3] and Kaganovich[4].

When Manya at last found herself in Russia the new direction was far from clear. The shadow of Stalin still lay heavily over the land. The people were still afraid; life was very hard; the secret police were active. It called for quite remarkable courage for Manya to venture, as she did, alone, from the beaten track, where she could see for herself aspects of life as lived by the mass of ordinary Russians which had been hidden from foreigners for so long – which, indeed, from all but a handful, remain so hidden to this day.

We landed at Helsinki which is handsome with its 'Big Square', low on three sides and a tall, stage-set church in the fashion of the eighteenth century but built in the nineteenth, on the fourth. Flowers were still being sold in the market square by the harbour. Most of the town is new, post war, sober. The shore with its sprinkling of low houses, the light, the granite and the meagre trees reminded me of Petersburg.

After a short wait we returned to the aerodrome to catch our flight for Leningrad and then Moscow. The little plane we climbed into started its propellers with the door open; there was no air hostess; the seat belts were pinned up and evidently not for use. There were a few Russians in front and a Swedish boy carrying the diplomatic bag on our right.

The Finnish landscape looked poor: silver birches and pines, stones, lakes, distant smoke and clouds. The Swede told us when we crossed the frontier but I could at first see no difference. We flew low, between scudding clouds, over a sheen of water, and the dark earth showed red-brown and black-green, and the moon was at the tip of our wing, scurrying along beside us. Then the clouds turned into a mist, invading the space between us and the earth with the softest cold pale blue above, and still the moon. Eventually the mist blew past, leaving the earth darker and more desolate, with the water invisible except when it reflected the moon. At moments I could still see forests, strip fields or larger square fields which I supposed belonged to the collective farms, and occasionally I saw what seemed to be new villages beside the big barns of what must have been an old manor. Suddenly a patch of thin snow spread quickly to the horizon under the dark sky. The farms were bigger now, closer together; the Swedish boy pointed out the broad winding Neva and the outskirts of Leningrad. I couldn't see the city, only a new factory suburb with spreading smoke. We landed in a Norfolk landscape of grey sky and dark earth, with a broad straight avenue bordered by neat beds of shrubs leading to the airport in front of us.

We strolled up to the mammoth building, then through a marble panelled entrance to a huge drawing-room – carpets, brown plush draperies and pelmets, plush covers on round tables and Repin-style[5] pictures of sea and forest in gilt frames. We signed forms declaring that we were not bringing in forbidden objects. Customs are passed *in absentia*. Our passports are taken from us. Then we made for dinner – up a country-house staircase, with a faint smell of cabbage, through an empty dining-room with more drapes and an old style bar – 'buffet', to the special dining-room reserved for travellers; here the goats and sheep are seated at different tables (the Russian passengers at one, we and the Swedish boy at another). The food was disappointing – a dull cucumber and beetroot salad, solid fish which we mistook for meat, and a glass of apples in syrup.

Soon we were called to the plane. On it was a hostess in a shabby black leather jerkin who offered us tea and papers. I read *The Workwoman*, undated, which featured a 'True Story' by Mark Twain, of cruelty to slaves, another of a mother whose son's engagement makes her remember how her own was thwarted by her fiancé's rich Cossack family, a photo of the trial of a Vietnamese landowner, and an article on decorating one's room – too much embroidery and china pigs with gilded ears were discouraged, but the illustration showed a Victorian sideboard, tablecloth and drapes.

MOSCOW

At Moscow airport we entered another palatial waiting-room, only a little smaller than the one in Leningrad, with a picture of Stalin gazing dreamily at fields and tractors, and hideous walls panelled in dark wood with steel medallions picturing wings.

Now the Russian passengers trooped in, suddenly sinister, like Dostoevsky characters, in their long black coats and fur hats; some were met by an oldish woman in a black shawl with a thin red nose. The scene was quickly reverting to my childhood and was completed by a procession of *dvorniki*[6] in boots, caps and aprons, carrying the luggage, and an official in a *gorodovoi's*[7] long grey coat. A vague Intourist official asked politely what our business was and then shepherded us to a large 'Zim'.

Slowly and silently we 'coasted' down the broad straight road and round the wide bends of the avenue that approaches Moscow. The first building we saw in the distance was the University, enchanting like a Christmas tree with red lights on its turrets and all its windows lit. We drove past it through the university suburb where a lot of new buildings were going up; they were prettily lit with rows of bulbs along the tops of their unfinished walls. Then we entered the new wide streets of the city, dim, bare, with groups of dark-clothed people. Billy noticed a woman quarrelling with a man and using her fists. The old streets and squares we drove along were even wider, with the red stars of the Kremlin shining out of the dark; we followed a river bordered by Regency houses, crossed a wide bridge, and the Red Square, to the Manège Square and stopped at the National Hotel. The polite receptionist ('administrator') took our passports, and the chauffeur and the lift boy, wearing a cap, took us up with our luggage to our quarters overlooking the Manège Square. Here we found that our rooms were huge; they had the usual deep carpets, brown curtains, brown-draped alcoves with beds in them and discouraging bathrooms with hot water but no soap or basin plugs and only small slithery bath towels. I unpacked and then joined Billy and we walked down the great shallow stairs, with portraits of Lenin on each landing (and also over the floor-girl's desk), to the dining-room where we had tea. Back in my room, the maid asked me if we would be there for the October celebrations – we would, she said, see them excellently from our windows. A slight frost followed my answer to her inquiry as to why I spoke Russian, but she looked cosy, so did the sly waiter who later brought us two beers costing 12r 50k.

I stared out of the window at the huge empty square and across it to the Red Square and St Basil's, then I experimented with the *fortochka*[8] which let either too much or too little cold air into the over-heated room; finally, in spite of the noisy gurgling bathroom pipes went to sleep under the light, comfortable eiderdown.

Following my instructions I was awoken by telephone punctually at 6 am, dressed and went down. I wanted to leave the letters I had been given for the Swedish and the Austrian Ambassadors and asked the porter the addresses of their Embassies. He didn't know them and there were no telephone books or street directories, but the polite 'administrator' found out where the Swedish Embassy was and suggested that I should ask there for the Austrian Embassy. I waited for a trolley-bus, failed to board the first as the doors clanged to within seconds, but I caught the next. The conductress told me where to get off, but in spite of hurrying I again missed the opening of the doors and had to stay on till the following stop. The buses were full but not overcrowded – the passengers were wearing shabby, but not tattered, clothes, the women mostly wrapped in shawls, were quiet and businesslike. Twice I asked the way and was given precise directions. As I didn't know the number of the house I did not realise I was actually there when I asked two militia-men, who were standing outside a private entrance, where the Swedish Embassy was? They inquired, 'Who are you?', 'Where are you from?', 'What do you want?' I showed them my letter, pointed out that it was for the Ambassador and again asked where the Embassy was; finally they admitted reluctantly, 'Here . . . But you won't get in, not at this hour . . . Well, you can try. Go in through the door and press the button.' (They must have been confused by my Russian – a year before no Russian would have been allowed in.) I didn't see a bell and waited, presently I heard footsteps and out came a young woman in riding clothes. I called to her in French and she took my letter and looked up the address of the Austrian Embassy. Then I walked along a busy street to the Arbat, past government buildings and two *stolovaya*,[9] asking my way of passers-by and of a militiaman who politely touched his cap. By now I was getting late for breakfast, so I inquired 'Can I get a taxi?' – 'Well, there are some round that corner though it's illegal' I was told. There I found a car, not strictly identifiable as a taxi, and said to the driver that I wanted to go first to the Austrian Embassy, then to the National Hotel. The man, who was brushing the rugs on the seats, told me to wait for a taxi. Another car drew up behind him and the chauffeur came out and asked where I wanted to go. This time I told him the name of the street and we started off but when I said 'I want the Austrian Embassy' the chauffeur looked worried. 'I won't take you to an Embassy. It's forbidden.' 'Well then leave me at the corner of the street.' 'No, I won't go anywhere near it.' I gave in and told him to drive to the National. He was relieved but still sulky and didn't talk.

After breakfast we rang up Mezhkniga, the State Agency which handles contacts with foreign publishers. Utenkov (the head of the export department) hoped we had had a good journey and said the

President was not yet there, he'd ring back when the President had arrived. He did so at ten, saying the President would see us at two. We asked if, as our time was short, we couldn't have a preliminary talk with someone that morning. This needed further consideration but eventually Utenkov said we could come and see him at 11.30 am. We filled in the time by walking across the Red Square to St Basil's, but found it closed until eleven, so went on to GUM, the store which takes up almost the whole side of the Square opposite the Kremlin. Inside are many shops joined by passages and stairs covered by a glass roof. There is a fountain at the centre. The milling crowd was composed mainly of shabbily dressed women in shawls, whom Billy took for country women up for a Saturday morning's shopping. The wares were shoddy and dear. There was a huge queue on the first floor where a woman was advertising goods through a loudspeaker. We came out at eleven, and asked a militiaman whether, if we went to St Basil's we should find a taxi when we came out; he said he'd stop one for us. A queue was forming outside the Mausoleum and a smaller crowd outside St Basil's. We waited with them, outside the Spassky Gate of the Kremlin from which, every now and then, cars drove out preceded by the ringing of an electric bell. Billy wondered at the shabbiness and glumness of the crowd and said, 'You notice if anybody smiles. Fancy this place keeping Europe on its toes for years.' He was cheered when a woman talked to me as we entered the twiggy little garden on the way to St Basil's, but in fact she was asking me whether we had seen the execution place in the Red Square! St Basil's is a lovely toy with bright painted cupolas and towers. We went into a gallery which showed earlier views of the Red Square, then up to the first floor, where fairytale chapels under each tower are joined by vaulted passages flowing with painted patterns. When we came out the militiaman kept his promise and stopped a taxi, but even so we were going to be late.

The Mezhkniga is housed in a skyscraper belonging to the MID[10] and the Ministry of Foreign Trade – it is itself part of the Ministry of Foreign Trade. We were met, just inside the door, by a polite girl, Korovina, who was to be our guide. (Only on my last visit to the building did I realise that without a guide we would have needed passes, as in war time.) She took us up in the lift and along a wide passage to Utenkov's office, which is medium size for Moscow, large for London, and contained a boardroom table as well as a big desk. The head of the export department, Utenkov, is a pale, apologetic young man. I explained who Billy was and what kind of books we wanted. The London representative of Mezhkniga had taken down a list of subjects we were interested in, and had promised that all would be ready when we arrived in Moscow, but the only thing certain was that we were expected. We said we would like to see books on medicine, and were offered text books and a pamphlet in English on cancer; we suggested popular science as a possibility? Did we mean school text books or pamphlets like the one on cancer? Well, what about sport? – Utenkov put his head on one side and smiled mockingly (or apologetically?) . . .

'Our athletes do not write books.'

We said, 'Our readers are interested in ballet' – one book with grey illustrations was produced.

'Travel?'

'You mean for children?'

'No.'

'But nowadays the whole country has been explored, so why should people want books on travel?'

We were exasperated by the lack of preparation, yet Utenkov seemed sorry and Korovina leapt up to get more and more unsuitable, dreary booklets. Finally I dictated my list of novelists and the titles of books on archæology in which we might be interested; they were delighted. We left crossly, agreeing to come back to see the President, Zmeul, at two. Our complaint about the difficulty of getting a taxi produced an MID car.

At the hotel we tried to hurry through our meal, but this was impossible as service, though amiable, was endless. Anyway, there seemed no reason to be on time for Zmeul. We arrived late and found Korovina patiently waiting. The President's office had an ante-room and was much bigger than Utenkov's, with a larger desk and board-table. Masses of unsuitable books had been put out for us. I reminded Zmeul of his London representative's invitation to us and his offer to give Billy first choice of books with a view to larger scale business developing between English and Russian publishers than has taken place so far. Zmeul, in his forties or fifties, was a big, square-headed, intelligent-looking man, with a paternal manner. He said he was willing to back such a project thoroughly (rather as though he had only just heard of it but approved). The same pamphlet on cancer was trotted out, and a pile of hopeless children's travel books. They suggested we should take some with us to read, and promised to have those we asked for ready on Monday. I told Zmeul of Billy's wish, as a publisher of ballet books, to see the Moscow Ballet School (a visit which the Intourist office at the hotel seemed unlikely to arrange). He suggested we should visit the one in Leningrad from which, he said, most of the best Moscow ballerinas come, but I insisted on our seeing the Moscow school, knowing by now that nothing is arranged from one town to another and that everything needs more time than we shall have in our one afternoon in Leningrad. Zmeul spent a half hour on the telephone tackling ballet authorities, in spite of which we left without any assurance that the visit would be arranged.

The most profitable information we got from Zmeul was that we must visit individual publishing houses – those which do art books, foreign books (translations into Russian), novels etc. From the hotel I rang up Mrs Ehrenburg (her husband[11] was away for a week) and asked her to receive us before Billy left. She agreed though she said she knew nothing about her husband's books.

We had dinner – lunch and dinner being interchangeable and eaten at all hours. Then we went to the Puppet Theatre. It was small and crowded and the audience was as shabbily dressed as the people in the street. As everywhere (except, as I found later, at the cinema) outer clothes had to be left in the cloakroom, and this caused an endless wait when the show finished, while group after group collected its coats and the rest waited motionless in an utter patience which surprised Billy. During the interval there was a lecture on puppets in the foyer, which served as a puppet museum. The crowd was quiet but obviously enjoying itself. The story, based on an Italian Renaissance play, was called 'King Deer'.

Before dinner I had asked the blasé but otherwise now friendly chit at the Intourist Office where the Catholic church was; she answered with amiable surprise that she had no idea. Thinking I might fail to discover it, I asked the 'administrator' where there was an Orthodox church in use. She said there were several, best go to the Yelokhovsky Cathedral; she knew the way but not the times of the services, had never been there. A man in a good brown suit sitting by her desk and talking with her, said: 'I know – ten o'clock,' and then turning to her added, 'I know for the good reason that I am going there myself tomorrow.' 'Going to make up for your sins?' she giggled. He laughed: 'No, that's the difference between me and other people, I haven't any sins to make up for, but I go all the same.' I wondered if he was MVD[12] (I also wondered about the other vague personages who hung around the ground floor and floor desks) and if this were an act: if so what was its purpose? Is the present line not only that there is freedom of religion but that people are religious?

I had myself woken early and came down about seven. Only the two porters and a cleaning woman were visible. I asked the porters for the Catholic church, they said: 'Do you want the Polish one?' as though there were several. I said the Polish one would do very well. They didn't know where it was but appeared anxious to be helpful and asked the lift man. He looked startled but eager and said: 'I can find out in a minute,' popped up and down in the lift and then told me it was in the Malaya Lubyanka and also how to get there.

It was a lovely day and there were already quite a lot of people about. Dressed in their cotton frocks, and wadded three-quarter jackets, galoshes and shawls, women were cleaning the streets with besoms. I went up a small street with a fine building at the corner but it turned quickly into a slum – with peeling sordid façades and untidy yards. Two old women were walking purposefully in my direction, one helping the other, who was lame. I asked them where the church was: 'We're going there,' they said, so I slowed down and walked with them. They remarked welcomingly: 'It's the first time you're going?' (Are there converts, I wondered?) I said I had just come to Moscow from England. The lame woman looked interested and asked if I spoke Polish and if there were many Poles in England. After a few moments we arrived at a rather pleasant, small, white church, Western-looking and newly done-up (later I was told it had been repainted for Adenauer's visit). We turned into the yard where there were three smartish cars (diplomatic?), and entered through a little side door. The church was dark and fairly dull, most of the congregation were elderly or middle-aged women (but women look so much older here than in England that it is difficult to tell their age) and old men; there were also some young men and women and a few children with their mothers. Mass had already started. It had a painfully moving beauty, and the faces of the congregation expressed suffering. But before I had time to notice much I burst into tears – for this was the first *living* thing I had seen since I arrived. I felt the urgent need to pray for Russia – for these people. There were many communicants and most people looked like staying on after Mass but I left, as by now it was getting late and I had to get back to the hotel and go with Billy to the ballet school which, miraculously, we had received permission to visit. We were met by Korovina. She was of the same type as the Intourist girls but more businesslike, less flashy, perhaps also more tentative: she wore a hat with felt wings which got on Billy's nerves. We walked across a yard to a back entrance and were taken up dark stairs by a young man belonging to the school. (Somehow here, with people darting past, the air was more alive and the place felt neither plush-draped nor sordid.) Then down a corridor lined with photographs of dancers which led to the study of the Directrice, Ella Victorovna. Here there was a little plush and a bronze writing set on the ornate desk, but only looking as though they were part of a well used old-fashioned study.

Ella Victorovna was middle-aged and charming, she could speak French but preferred not to. Sitting at her desk, with Billy and me opposite and Korovina on the sofa, she gave us an introductory talk. The school provides an eight year course consisting of ordinary lessons, special studies and dancing. All the pupils learn music as well as classical, national, historical and duo dancing. The children start at ten, never earlier as it would be too strenuous for them. Ella Victorovna said that, judging from the questions people put to her, they must start younger abroad (but perhaps they were only impressed by legends of Imperial ballerinas starting in the cradle?). The Moscow school, founded in 1773, though the daughter of the Leningrad Ballet School, is now the more important. It supplies ninety per cent of the dancers for the Bolshoi, which gets first choice. There are eleven other ballet schools in Leningrad and various provincial towns. Billy asked if there were foreign pupils. Ella Victorovna said 'Yes', meaning ones from Iron Curtain countries – then she realised the limitation and went on, with a nice smile to Billy, to say she hoped one day it would be really international with pupils from everywhere. She then suggested we should watch one of the classes so we went back along the long corridors to the fifth form, and came upon a typical Dégas scene. A big square room with a gentle, cold light, barres against three walls, a floor of bare boards, a piano in one corner and chairs against the remaining wall. A dozen adolescent girls in pale pink tunics (not tutus) were doing exercises. There was something oddly moving and enchanting about them. Perhaps the crossing in time of the ancient ageless dance form and this fragile moment in the life of these girls? We were introduced to the teacher who then went back to her class, and we sat down.

Ella Victorovna is an artist with manners universal to civilisation, but she is also very Russian, though French tinted, like Petersburg. When Billy said he would send her his ballet books she pressed his hand with a charming, warm, open gesture. At first the girls were beautiful as a group but soon the beauty was concentrated; first in two, dancing a duo, then in one, Lena, with a thin, as yet sexless, body, so perfectly controlled that it became the form of the dance.

Ella Victorovna continued explaining things to us in a low voice. Most of the girls at this school are from Moscow – there is no hostel, which makes it difficult for provincial pupils. When they finish all of them get jobs at once, the best in Moscow, the others in the provinces. The passing out exam is a tremendous occasion to which all important theatre managers come.

'Do some who start in the provinces ever return to Moscow?' I asked.

'Not often; but that is not a disappointment to them because each troupe is a collective with an excellent spirit.' (I wonder?) Each year there are some five hundred applications for the thirty vacancies. (And at this moment I remembered myself at the age of seven dreaming of the ballet, walking on my toes, and asking mother how to become a ballerina and her saying it was too early for me to think of it. That was the day Mother had taken me shopping and had brought back a little electric bell, made of some mauve transparent stone, to put on a table, and an ash tray with a bronze monkey, both seemed wonderful to me. But more grandly wonderful, with echoes of dedication, was the thought of the ballet school.)

Lena should be one of the lucky ones; Ella Victorovna says she will go far. At the end of the class Lena sprinkled the floor, doing a ballet-bird trip across it with a water-can, perfect and natural as though she lived dancing. Ella Victorovna called her up and asked her her age. She was fourteen, younger than the rest. She stood before us with her bare limbs in utter un-selfconsciousness, her body not her own.

Another teacher came in, quite unlike anyone we had yet seen in Moscow. She was fortyish, dark, with an intelligent, beautiful monkey face, and wore a brilliantly thought-out yellow dress such as her kind anywhere would be proud of. She looked as if she might burst into vivacious conversation with us, but in fact only said 'how do you do', and started teaching vigorously.

Each class begins with exercises at the barre and we were told that this continues throughout a ballerina's life. Even a prima ballerina will come in before a performance and do exercises under one of the school teachers. I asked the name of the 'teacher' in the yellow dress. Ella Victorovna smilingly corrected me.

'She is one of our best "pedagogues", Vassilieva.' The 'pedagogues' are themselves ballerinas, still dancing part-time or retired. Other artists come in from time to time to give special lessons or advice.

The amount of time given to dancing is at first only an hour, but it goes up to four, and even to six hours in the highest forms. Not all of that time is however devoted to practice. From early on the children are allowed to dance in ballets, with a cast of pupils, that are put on at the Bolshoi. As they grow older they perform more often; this is what makes their lives so strenuous and so exciting.

Classical dancing is still the basis of their training but national and historical dancing is important too, also acting which all learn. The school is inspired by Stanislavsky's theories. For a time after the girls leave they are obliged to go on doing all the different kinds of dancing, though even while at the school they tend to specialise. Pure classical dancing tends to become dead; the dramatic ballets are more popular with the public and with the dancers and even classical ballets are dramatised to some extent. The school is anxious to absorb elements from folk dancing in order to bring ballet closer to the people.

Ella Victorovna now took us to see the top form. The same kind of room but the girls had less charm, though some were obviously excellent. E.V. told us, in a whisper, which of the pupils seem to her the most talented; one she had great hopes of was a well-developed, fair, full-bosomed girl. Most of them were in fact of a different type from the sexless, stylised creatures one associated with Diaghilev, and somehow their fair, blooming youth was disenchanting.

This we were told was the fateful year for the girls for at the end of it is the 'concert' at which they will dance to an audience of the greatest connoisseurs who will decide their future. Parents are not invited, but they come to a tremendous party when it's over.

We went on to the boys' class. (Over a third of the school's pupils are boys.) At this stage they are very charmless and loutish: robust village lads they looked to be and certainly they could not be less pansyish. Their teacher was a thickset elderly man. Ella Victorovna said he was once her teacher, and that he had written a book on the ballet. She too had written a monograph, in collaboration with another artist. I mentioned Billy's interest in a book on the school. She said the staff would love it, and would probably like to help with it. When I asked the best way to get a book project accepted she suggested we should approach the Minister of Culture, N. A. Mikhailov, or his Deputy, E. V. Kaftanov. If the Ministry gave the green light then the book could be done.

We went on to the girls' third form class. More charmers. The obvious star was a small, fair, sturdy, uglyish, splendid child, with a funny, tip-tilted face. Another, her partner in a *pas de deux*, was a dark elf. Some looked overgrown. The teacher appeared to bully them but they seemed to love it.

E.V. talked of the difficulty of selection. How they choose the thirty lucky ones from the five hundred applicants. Some dropped out in the first three years because they proved to be unsuitable or grew too tall. Some were taken on as late as thirteen because they had only just been spotted at their schools.

At the end of the class the teacher demonstrated selection tests. The first requirement is physical fitness, straight legs, a musical sense. The small clown was put before us, her gauze tunic tucked into the top of her pants (at the selection test they wear only pants). She was un-selfconsciously delighted at being shown off. To qualify the child must be able to stand with straight legs and feet turned out in a straight line (second position), bend her knees flat out – the clown did it astonishingly well, like a flat dummy, with flat straight back; spring high and straight into the air, do a high-kick and then do the nearest thing to the splits. The teacher showed us how high her leg could be stretched up. The clown, and others, demonstrated the difference between the right and the wrong way of doing the exercises.

It was now almost twelve, at which time we were due at the Bolshoi to see *The Fountain of Bakhchisarai*. So we said goodbye to Ella Victorovna. I told her I hoped to see her again when I came back to Moscow after we'd been to Leningrad and she was welcoming. I regretted leaving this Petersburg and Rive Gauche atmosphere. In spite of the few slogans in E.V.'s conversation (e.g. about the happy collectives) the attitude of all the staff to their work made the place feel alive. It must have been much like this in its Imperial hey-day, in spite of the conventionality and the intrigues then (though didn't the real hey-day come perhaps abroad with Diaghilev, with as many intrigues but more genuine bohemianism?). On the way out we were shown the bad photos of artistes that hung in the corridor; E.V. was proud of them, but they reminded me of the photos of ex-Heads at Bedford College.

Korovina, who had followed us about meekly and wordlessly, took us to the Bolshoi. She still had an apologetic, though jaunty, air. There was no time for lunch at the hotel; but she said we could lunch at the theatre canteen. Unfortunately I had run out of Russian money. Korovina pressed fifty roubles on me; as we were to see her the next day, I accepted the loan.

The Bolshoi is immense. We showed our tickets and tried to avoid leaving our coats, but the ticket woman said 'our position' made it impossible – I suppose she meant our good seats. We reached them just before the bell. The enormous theatre is Covent Garden plus, a riot of red and gold, with great, handsome lustres hanging from the ornate ceiling. The audience was stuffy, shabby, possibly white-collared but more likely, I thought, prize-winning workmen and their wives. Some men walked into the Imperial box and I asked my neighbour who they were. He said that among them were two members of the Supreme Soviet.

We had been told that *The Fountain* was one of the best ballets and the Prima Ballerina, Kondratieva, the most outstanding dancer of all. The ballet dates from '34. With *Romeo and Juliet*, *The Bronze Horseman* and *The Flame of Paris*, it is one of the dancers' favourites.

Though the stage is vast, the realistic Polish nobleman's country house took up too much of it, flattening and crowding the garden in front. The long first act works up to the battle scene with 'real' flames shooting out of the windows. During the interval we went down to the crowded restaurant, a waitress took our order and brought caviar rolls and opened a bottle of nastyish apple-juice; for this we were asked sixteen roubles (fourteen when I questioned the bill). Then we wandered through hideous halls, used I think for rehearsals, with monstrous pictures of dancers and producers hanging on the walls, very depressing. Billy was impressed by the difference between this and the London ballet public, and every time he noticed a group of reasonably well dressed or intellectual looking people they turned out to be foreigners.

The second act takes place in the harem, the second ballerina who acts the sultan's wife seemed good in an older, harder way than Kondratieva, who was very good but had an ugly jaw. Again there were huge crowds of dancers and the scenery was overdone. The last act was mostly mimed.

After the ballet we were going to see Mrs Ehrenburg and I wanted to take her some flowers, but we were told there was only one shop where we might buy some. On the way to it we saw what looked a bright flower-stall, however when I got out and went up to it it turned out to have nothing but paper flowers, very cheerful and realistic but not suitable to present to Mrs Ehrenburg, and the flower shop, when we reached it, had only large, expensive, beribboned baskets and a few bunches of brownish-white chrysanthemums. I gave up, feeling frustrated and that it was unnatural that bringing flowers to people should be made impossible.

The Ehrenburgs live in Gorky Street, a big road with brightly lit shops; but to reach the house you go in through a shabby yard. A maid opened the door and Mrs Ehrenburg came out. She was dark, fortyish, with an intelligent Jewish face which suggested a lot of character. She took us into the living-room, its walls hung with pictures and we sat at the usual, small, round table covered with a fancy cloth. A theme for conversation was provided by the fat white Scottie. The Ehrenburgs had had three of them, but one had died and another was so bad-tempered that they had sent it to a trainer who has had it for months but it still bites him. He told Mrs Ehrenburg the only way to stop the dog biting would be to put it into a collar with an electric battery which would give it mild shocks when it misbehaved but Mrs Ehrenburg wouldn't hear of it. We all, of course, agreed with her. I asked if it was the dog in *The Thaw*, she said all the characters, including that of the dog were mixtures. We talked about her husband's books, of which she disclaimed all knowledge, but she offered to show us some translations and fetched the Italian edition of *The Thaw* in its handsome Cézanne wrapper. After a while, with an air of admitting us to a little further intimacy, she gave us cognac and we took courage to ask about some of the works of art in the room. The bold tapestry on the wall behind us was modern Polish; the stone sculpture in the corner Byzantine, it had been found some years ago by workmen digging up tram lines. On the wall at the other end of the room were three Picasso drawings from the series reproduced in *Verve*, all inscribed to the Ehrenburgs. More Picassos on other walls, a Braque, I think, and two small pictures which might have been of the same family but were by contemporary Russian artists. On little shelves were bits of pottery and objects in carved and painted wood, peasant work but more archaic looking than anything I had seen. Mrs Ehrenburg collects them. Next she took us to her husband's study, a smallish room at the end of the passage, comfortably cluttered up with a big desk, a sofa, an armchair and bookshelves. Hanging from the lamp over the desk was a pretty mobile, made of straw, looking like a fantastic cage with tassels – this was another piece of peasant craft. 'A good room to work in,' I said, but Mrs Ehrenburg replied that her husband couldn't work in Moscow, he was kept so busy and the telephone rang all the time: there was his work as a Deputy and for the Peace Movement and all the rest. They lived mostly in the country, where he was able to work, but when he was abroad she came to town. A bookshelf which covered the whole of one wall was full of translations of Ehrenburg's books. We asked diffidently about the Chagalls.

'You really want to see them?' 'Yes' we did. They were in Mrs Ehrenburg's bedroom where many pictures were stacked on the floor. Showing the Chagalls to us and talking of the French Exhibition which was soon to be held in Moscow, Mrs Ehrenburg said the Impressionists were no longer considered dangerous. I remarked on what a nice flat it was to which she replied 'No', it was too small, but 'they' were building them another. By then it was time to go.

At the hotel, in Billy's blue and gold salon, I tried to get drinks but the bell didn't work. I knew there was only vodka or tea and tackled the maid on the landing who said, 'The Comrade "Officiant" doesn't seem to be out, perhaps he is in his own quarters'. I went in search, discovered him in his pantry and explained that we were in a hurry. He assured me he would bring our order at once but twenty minutes later he still hadn't given any sign of life.

We dined at The Prague – an extraordinary place. It takes up the whole of a big building, which looks rather modern from outside. A bewhiskered, old-style porter bowed us into a marble and mirrored hall-cloakroom; then we climbed up broad marble stairs to a huge saloon with 'vermicelli' on the walls and the usual drapes and crystal chandeliers. It was one of an endless *enfilade*. To the left was a room with Egyptian decorations and on the right the rooms opened one out of the other; in the end one, very far off, an orchestra was playing, its noise loudly amplified at our end. The menu was long and expensive, the food bad and the service amiable but slow as ever. I offered our Intourist coupons, but they were not accepted. I looked eagerly for *styliagi* among the public of smart young men (they are rather like Teddy boys but mostly from the upper classes, not necessarily bad but individualistic and reacting against the dress and hair style of their parents' generation). I saw only one, an intellectual-looking boy. Across the room was a bourgeois family and behind me a table full of youngish people. All decently, but not well, dressed. Later a row developed at the family table as two young men came up and stood drunkenly beside it, they were shouted at by what seemed to be the mother of the family: 'Go back to your table, go back.' For a long time they didn't move, then they wandered away looking offended. Nobody paid any attention.

As I sat there I began to think how much I wanted to go to Redkino and decided I would tell Intourist to arrange it. Later I asked an Englishman we met if he thought they would do so. 'If you ask you won't go,' he replied, 'and if you just go to the station you may be stopped. The one thing certain is that whatever one does has to be done openly and simply. Actually there is no law against people travelling if they are not diplomats.'

I had forgotten the time of Mass and arrived early. The doors were still shut but there were a lot of little old women waiting in the porch. I got into conversation with one group. When I said I came from England they looked excited and asked me if there were a lot of Poles there and when I said 'Yes' inquired anxiously how they were getting on. Then a woman drew me aside and made more worried inquiries about the fate of Poles. I reassured her as best I could and asked how long she had lived in Russia; she said since 1905. Then she whispered fervently: 'You know that we only live and pray for the liberation of our country.'

At that moment a verger came along with the keys and the woman who had been talking to me drew aside and signed to me not to say anything.

It was still half an hour before Mass would start. I couldn't settle down to pray so I came out into the yard and sat on a bench and smoked. It was cold – two degrees of frost. Suddenly there was a scene from my childhood – the wooden fence and behind it the leafless garden, people muffled in dark coats and fur caps, or shawls, going past along the alley to work; children playing, and the sharp bright air.

There were fewer people at Mass than on Sunday. Mostly women between forty and fifty, though I sat next to a girl. Again I had the impression of stillness, and of alive suffering. But I was distressed by wanting to know more about all these people.

On my way back to the hotel I stopped, as if struck by lightning, at the sweet stall in Derzhinsky Square: there were the 'crab necks', the sweets with a pink sugar-coating and brown stuffing, in paper wrappers with a crab on them, that had so enchanted me when I was small. I bought two with an expectation either of the miraculous or of disappointment. The first taste brought me back outside the grocer's in the Moika, next to the little shops with paper transfers and the cut-outs of angels in long pink and pale blue robes which my governess gave up buying for me after the row with mother about religion; but the second taste was synthetic, with that sickly scent one doesn't mind in childhood; all the same, it was worth it. The morning was lovely, cold and light. Everyone was wearing snow boots and warm coats (though not of fur); only the street cleaners were still in their cotton clothes underneath their padded jackets.

Billy had been woken up by music broadcast in the square and had watched the cars dashing round the corner through the crowds, like a knife through butter. The music was part of the rehearsals for the 7th of November celebration. We had an appointment with Iskusstvo, the Art publishers, at ten. For once, the Intourist car was late and couldn't find its way, but at last we discovered Korovina, still in her winged hat, outside the office. Here were publishers' offices like anywhere else. The Chairman stood in the middle behind his desk, supported by a youngish, dark, sturdy man, and three others, paler, less upstanding, looking more bookish. The desk was piled high with learned books on the history of art, no glamour – big and heavy they were, with ugly blue or brown bindings, and grey illustrations. But the publishers were not only co-operative but also human and interested in their books. Obviously we should have stayed at least four hours to please them. Unfortunately we had hardly an hour to spare.

As we drove to our next appointment, at the Foreign publishers, the view of the Kremlin across the river was like a fairy tale with its sunlit silver and gold domes against the blue sky. Billy took photographs, while I crouched out of the way looking at the scene. Very gay it was, with the red, turreted walls, the yellow Regency style building and the three glittering domed churches. This and the inside of St Basil and the ballet are all, richly, exuberantly gay, with a hit or miss wealth which comes off perfectly in the traditional buildings. All this on one side and the drab crowds on the other, but at this moment they were invisible to us and I could lose myself in the gold, silver and blue, and forget them and also my uneasiness at mismanaging Billy's business. The business side was not looking like much and I wished that at least he had had an interpreter and made his own impact on all these committees instead of having me bully them in Russian, often forgetting to translate the backchat.

The journey to the Foreign publishers' office was endless. We passed several churches, one pretty round red one, and I asked the cross-looking chauffeur if it were in use, he said a lot were but not that one. At close on two we were still driving, now through a suburb of board or log houses, with trees between and a familiar, half-country look. Many of the houses had good traditional proportions but no carvings, some were painted a not unpleasant green.

How difficult it must be for the Russians to develop a style: the good houses of the past are like these, or chaotic *kremlins*,[13] only the Western eighteenth century makes some sort of link with the present – but then not with the past. At last, we stopped in front of a huge new building.

We were very late, but there seemed no need to apologise to the unsurprised committee, which was bigger than the one at Iskusstvo. Here the Chairman was stockier, more robust than the usual run. He explained the 'set-up' to us. This was the office of the section of the State publishers which dealt with translations, and it had eighteen departments for different subjects and the 'Creative Art' publishers brought out foreign as well as Russian classics. New foreign fiction was done by Foreign Literature but the head of that department was not then there though he came in later. Scientific and technical books and history interested them most. The head of the history department mentioned English books they had published – on Crete, on the pre-history of Europe, Zulus, on Wyatt's rebellion. We suggested that Bryant's books might suit them and showed them Collins' catalogue; they said they had it, and assured us they received all the English publishers' catalogues. Tea and chocolates were brought in. We looked settled for the afternoon.

We spoke of books about the war, *The Wooden Horse* for instance; they had turned it down, this puzzled us. What about modern novels we asked? They talked about Galsworthy. Careless by now, I said everybody we met so far had mentioned him, but that his novels did not describe contemporary life. They were surprised and the Chairman sent for the fiction editor and asked him about contemporary English fiction. He at once mentioned Galsworthy. We all laughed and some-one told him what we had said. Next they consulted a list of their recent translations. Sean O'Casey, Ogilvie, Jane Walsh, Jack Lindsay, Doris Lessing, Catherine Susanna Pritchard, Dick Scott . . . We promised to send lists and books. They were grateful and it seemed to me that they thanked us in a really hungry way.

Finally, late as it was, we left, with a wrench, to lunch at the National where people were eating as at any other hour. I ordered vodka, caviar, borsch, cutlets and ice cream. But as we were starting on the borsch, and before Billy had even tasted the vodka, I was called to the telephone and told that one of the Deputies at the Ministry of Culture, Nazarov, could see us at once but had only twenty minutes to give us. We agreed this was the one call we must make. I asked for a car which seemed to take an endless time to arrive.

At the Ministry we noticed a different climate from that of the other offices. A man met us outside the door; he must have waited a long time but his temper had not suffered and he spoke resolutely in good English. Deputy Minister Nazarov, made an excellent impression. He is a big, squarish man with a strong, intelligent face. The room was large and ornamentally Edwardian but looked, like the study at the ballet school, well used. Instead of sitting behind his desk at a distance from us as the other publishers had done, Nazarov walked about and settled us round a little table with the interpreter between himself and

Billy. With relief, I subsided, on the Russian pattern, into the attitude of being Billy's shadow-attendant. Here, at last, he could make his own impact, and he certainly did. A curiously representative pair he and Nazarov made, the Russian squat and rock-like, Billy leaning back with elegant English ease, but their expressions were similar – bright, kind, humorous, reserved, the reserve a jokingly sly understanding of one another's national bluff, but the kindness quite luminous, creating an intimate contact between them. Nazarov's manner was tremendously deliberate, under the kindness and the humour, giving each word its full value, as though it were a symbol! And Billy's manner assumed something of the same quality, though less ponderously. No doubt, they were both having fun. Nazarov gave his blessing to the Collins' project. Billy should send books and explain the type he wanted and Nazarov would encourage the heads of the various institutions to produce them. Billy suggested he would be interested in a book on the Hermitage and mentioned the one he had seen on the Impressionists, Nazarov replied that such a book would have to be brought up to date to include the present day contents of the galleries. Next they spoke of a book on the ballet, commissioned and with English help. Nazarov said it would have his approval. Then he described the size of editions in the USSR – children's books were done by the 300,000 etc., afterwards he asked Billy how many volumes Collins averaged a year. Here the interpreter made his one and only mistake; he translated Billy's reply: 'About fifteen million' as fifty million. I kept quiet: what difference could it make? We left after an hour.

The interview had been worth while; Billy had made his mark at the level at which it mattered. And now there were to be no more business appointments until he left, the darkening afternoon felt fresher.

We had tickets for the Kremlin and drove there. The chauffeur was evidently not used to such visits for he went back and forth looking for the right entrance, finally he left us at the gate to the gardens which run in front of the walls, and he told us to follow the people who were going in. There were groups drifting around looking strangely democratic and peaceful. Our tickets were checked at the entrance to the Armoury. There was no guide book. Inside we were overwhelmed by the richness of the treasure, first armour, then a crushing profusion of gold and silver vessels, crystal and ikons stream-

ing with pearls. Most of the objects were Russian, the others were gifts
from foreign courts. There was much that was spectacular but little
that was beautiful – or perhaps we should have noticed beautiful
things if there had been time, endless time, to sort it all out. We however had to rush. The attendant was distressed to see us leave so soon.

Outside, we followed the crowd to the square with the three
churches, their domes shining in the darkening air. They were lovely
inside with many-coloured frescoes, each a packed story; all gave the
same impression of overcrowding – small spaces, thick walls, gold and
scarlet vaulted ceilings, a profusion of gay colours thrown together
anyhow but settling into garlanded patterns. In one of the churches
people in rows were staring at the unadorned tombs of Tsars, they did
not look at anything else. Outside, the evening was beautiful, deep
blue around the white walls, and the gold and silver cupolas. We
walked to a big square, where the great bell of St John stood on the
ground and dark buildings loomed in the distance, then we went on to
the Spassky Gate. Here busy civilians with portfolios were hurrying in
and out of a small side door, and the electric bell rang at intervals to let
a car out through the main gate.

'Oughtn't we to see the Metro?' asked Billy. Certainly we should
and so we hurried through the Red Square and the Manège Square,
stopping to look in at the entrance of the huge, new, hideous Moskva
Hotel, where a Lyons buffet seemed to be set up in the hall leading to
the Okhotny Ryad Metro Station. Swept with the evening crowd and
disappointed at first, because this station is not part of the new, palatial
network, we travelled to the Komsomolsky Station where the mag-
nificence began. There you had your money's worth – immense spaces,
chandeliers, marble and mosaics, 'just like in the pictures' only more
impressive. Spotlessly clean too, and practical, without jams or hold-
ups at the rush hour. I was deeply impressed. These Versailles halls
seemed to me a genuine reward for toil, a glittering, comfortable
interlude between the office and the home. A touching attempt to put
forgotten splendours at the disposal of the masses. Uselessly rich, and
out of touch with Western forms of luxury, but functionalism would
not have given the illusion of a future fairy tale – or was the impression
rather, that of the crowds streaming through Versailles in 1789 and
were the workers who were returning to a hovel angry?

Almost equally impressive, but more charmingly funny, was

Billy's determination to bring us back to Okhotny Ryad through the maze of turnings, stairs, passages and changes, without once asking the way. A considerable achievement. In the train he told me about Mr Smith, now Collins's chief editor, who, as a young man, coming from Glasgow to be interviewed by Billy's uncle had found his way back from a walk to Trafalgar Square by means of chalk signs. That story and Billy's track-finding talent were comforting, a reminder of British common sense and training which would stand a man in good stead even if he were playing Pimpernel in a huge grey, anonymous world.

In the hotel dining-room we were offered the remains of our lunch left uneaten several hours earlier. We ordered new plates of soup and just managed to finish our cutlets in time to set off to the Stanislavsky Theatre, and sit down in the third row of the stalls, as the last echo of the last bell died out. Billy was justifiably triumphant at his timing. The theatre is smaller and cosier than the Bolshoi.

They were giving *Swan Lake* and we had been told that many people liked the Stanislavsky production better than the one at the Bolshoi. I could not remember the ballet except for the lake scene. Here even the scenery was realistic, the spacing and the colours ill thought out, the corps de ballet perfect and the audience enthusiastic. During the interval we went to the smoking room where groups of intellectuals, looking like intellectuals, wrapped in clouds of smoke, sat talking or reading at a big round table. The general impression was more alive than at the Bolshoi. The next act opened with real water and almost real swans swimming across it; the audience clapped. A very sinister wizard with huge wings mimed his part. There was less crowding than in *The Fountain*, and the dance of the four swans was beautiful. In the third act the 'brides' came in with their mothers in *kokoshniki*[14] and *sarafany*,[15] stepping out as in a Russian folk dance and incidentally illustrating Ella Victorovna's point about livening up classical ballet with elements of the traditional and national dances. Rather nice I thought it, but the colours and the clothes were unpleasantly jumbled. At the close of each act the young people crowded up to the stage and clapped; and at the end of the ballet there was an ovation, and most touching little bunches of paper chrysanthemums – like the ones I had rejected when going to see Mrs Ehrenburg – were thrown at the prima ballerina who picked them up and clutched them to her breast with all the delight Kseshinskaya[16] might have shown at the great baskets clustered at her feet. After this the audience and the dancers stood clapping at one another and it seemed as though they would never stop. It was nice to end up on this note of genuine spontaneous gaiety. We were both exhausted after our enormous day, still there was a satisfaction in knowing that we could not possibly have got in anything else.

LENINGRAD

I have only a vague memory of packing and breakfasting in the dark and half asleep. We had been told to start at eight for our plane to Leningrad but it seemed to be taken for granted that we would not start till quarter to nine. The usual silent limousine took us to the airport, but this time we could see the road and the flat landscape under the pale sky. We passed wooden houses and one old estate with a big yellow, porticoed house and a few cottages round it; the chauffeur said it was now a sanatorium.

In the plane, I sat glued to the window watching the monotonous view. Forests, rivers, villages, occasionally an old manor house or a church, mist was drifting over them; then, suddenly, the ground was covered with snow which spread quickly to the horizon, lighting up the earth against the grey sky.

We landed and from the airport a Zim, less leisurely than those of Moscow, took us the short distance into the town. Passing through the suburbs we noticed that the style of the new houses was different from those built in Moscow – here were classical façades, an attempt no doubt to fit in with the old buildings; there were no sky-scrapers. The effect was absurdly ornamental but I liked it.

The sky looked menacing but there was no snow. I was afraid of finding Leningrad as alien as Moscow, but, all at once, there was the Fontanka canal and then the St Isaac's Cathedral; we drove round it and arrived at the Astoria. I vaguely remembered passing in front of it, walking with Rikarna, and recalled the stories about father and Uncle Benjamin staying there during the Revolution and hiding gold bars in their chest of drawers, also the very sound of the name Astoria suggested stories, heard very long ago, connected with Petersburg glamour, parties, luxury, good food.

When we arrived I was happy to see it had an elderly elegance that was lacking at the National. The hall looked more or less like the hall of a hotel, and the spaces and the stairs were not so mammoth or so marbled as in Moscow, even the Intourist bureau were more civilised.

Our rooms seemed charming to me; the whole place was smaller, and the velvet curtains were at least a dark blue. There were the same alcoves for the beds but the bathrooms were more attractive. And outside the windows was the view on to St Isaac's Square – grey, sober, urban Petersburg.

At about three o'clock we lunched, badly – worse even than in Moscow and served as slowly – in a cold glass-roofed dining-room which must have been a lounge. When we came out, our guide, Leontina, a middle-aged Jewess, and a former schoolmistress, put on her gloves and led us to the car. By then it was darkish and snowing a little. We drove into the Winter Palace Square. The Palace was now a greyish-green and the curve opposite Regency yellow, the column stood in the middle and the whole impression given by the dignified proportions was vast, restful. Then we went past the Admiralty to the quay. I had asked our guide to arrange this so that we could have a glimpse of the Neva – stone, water, space, muted greys and the faint gold that shines before a snowstorm.

When we reached the museum poor Leontina was appalled as I explained that we could only spend one hour there. She had just told us of the dozens of Rembrandts, 'all of them originals', and obviously intended to show us round, school by school, choosing the best examples of each, and making our introductory tour last until closing time at seven. As it was, we rushed from room to room, Billy looking at what pleased him and I looking hardly at all except out of the windows. The view over the river grew more and more beautiful, then all at once, it vanished in a flurry of snow. On the other side, the tall narrow windows looked on to a courtyard with snow-powdered trees. Billy was anxious to see the Impressionists, and this was the first thing I had told Leontina, but she had seemed flustered and said we had better make the usual tour. I think she hoped we would give up our intention of seeing the Impressionists, evidently something about it was difficult; indeed, when I insisted and she asked one of the attendants the way, this elderly woman sitting at an entrance like a *tricoteuse*, said the modern French galleries were under repair and closed to the public. I went on insisting and Leontina began to look desperate; finally she said we must visit the Scythian treasure first, after that somebody in authority might let us see the Impressionists. Down we went to the basement, where I had to leave my bag with the cloak-room attendant. A youngish, scholarly girl met us and showed us into the vaults. They were like Aladdin's cave – their walls covered with showcases full of ornaments that looked like glittering gold leaves. Here one would have needed a week to take all of it in, and I only kept a memory of necklaces of golden flowers rather like the ones that came from Ur. The youngish curator was less disapproving than Leontina of our wish to see the Impressionists. She took us up a lot of stairs to three rooms full of pictures by Picasso, Matisse, Braque and the rest – these had been brought up from the cellars to replace the thirty or so modern French pictures that had gone to Moscow where there was to be an exhibition. After this we saw the rooms of Dutch paintings and the two Van Goghs. On the way Leontina confided the cause of her distress to me: at first the tour had proceeded normally, she had shown us the Primitives, but after that it had gone wrong. I tried to console her – in one afternoon it was impossible to get more than a fleeting impression, the main thing was that Billy should see what he wanted to see – and get an overall impression that would make him want to come back. This convinced Leontina that Billy must be an art expert, who knew what he wanted to see and understood what he saw, and so had to be indulged, which made it easier for her.

I was walking on air: before seeing the treasure, as we passed from one part of the gallery to the next, I had looked out of the window on the right and seen the 'Bridge of Sighs' which joins the Marble Palace to the Hermitage across the canal. There it was in front of me, as charming as I had remembered it, and beyond it the Moika and our house! I grabbed Billy's arm and showed him the view. He said when we came out we must go and see the house. The extraordinary thing was that the view itself was so familiar, so exactly right – the snow, the grey, the water and the stones – dank, grandiose Petersburg, the Venetian tang and the mould; and there I was, down below, in brown velvet and proud of my new fur collar and muff, walking with Rikarna along the canal, expecting with a frightened fascination to meet Dostoevsky's Double or Gogol's Nose; or I was passing into the long ballroom with the windows on to the Moika, the intricate parquet, a row of gilded chairs and the tall mirror in a carved gilded frame; or, there I was, practising the piano which stood surrounded by a clump of palm trees, or I was curtseying before the shadowy mirror, playing at being a princess. It was as if the curtain had gone up.

When we came out it had stopped snowing and the view was transformed by the whiteness on the road and the granite parapet and the light on the water. It must have been just about here that Rikarna and I once came on a glittering chapel being built of ice and snow, for Twelfth Night, on the frozen river. But now it was all pale, soft greys with a black tug pulling a barge, it was unbelievably beautiful. Standing in the covered drive, we stared at it, Billy as transfixed as I; then we drove along the river to the right and went to the Field of Mars. This I did not recognise, I think I had only been there once, and then it had been an open parade ground, the classical buildings round it had been barracks, and it had had an air of open waste and an association with the song that had always moved me (to Rikarna's distaste): 'We are falling as martyrs in the fatal struggle,' said to have been sung by revolutionaries on the way to execution. Now it has a neat garden planted all over it in honour of the martyrs and the buildings too are neat and yellow. We went on along what used to be called the Millionnaya and along the Moika, stopping opposite the Hermitage bridge; here I got out. It was almost dark now, cold with slushy snow, and the houses loomed huge, neglected and grey. At this angle, made by the Moika canal and the other smaller canal running under the Venetian bridge to the still glimmering Neva, flowing between the tall houses, we were in the stony heart of the city. Here the buildings had not been repainted and their grandeur was morose, silent, inward looking. Perhaps, in the dark and slush outside, they had always looked like this, while behind the drawn curtains the fire burned in the 'English' fireplace and the tea cups tinkled, and, in the dining-room beyond, the napkins were being folded into marvellous shapes and the silver was spraying up from the white cloth scattered with roses and violets.

Poor Billy had obviously overdone it so, when we got back to the hotel, I sent him off to bed with tea and a hot water bottle and I had chicken broth sent up to his room. The ballet did not start till eight-thirty and by then he insisted on going to it though I thought he

Manya

and with her governess Rikarna

wasn't well enough, but he certainly has astonishing stamina. We went to the small Maryinsky Theatre and, although in Moscow I had given up changing and the audience here was likely to be as shabbily dressed as there, I felt obliged to put on silk and scent. Not that when I lived here I had ever been to evening shows – only to two matinées, but the Maryinsky had compelling associations of elegance.

There was chaos in the cloakrooms where, together with two other women who had come at the last moment, we tried to get rid of our coats to attendant after attendant who refused to accept them, shouting crossly that they had no 'numbers' left. Finally we managed to leave them and collapsed into our seats.

In spite of the shabby audience, the theatre bore out my expectations – it is a dream of a traditional theatre, smallish, well proportioned, with the light from the pretty crystal chandeliers falling on dull velvet and pale silvery gold. The ballet was unbearable, endless, intricate, ideological, with real fire and someone riding in on a horse, and a crescent moon rising with a ballerina, wrapped in gauze, cradled in its curve. The setting was the Caucasus, complete with crags, villages, palaces and ruins and at intervals the 'Seven Beauties' danced in Oriental *négligés* with a curious Victorian obscenity. My two neighbours were delighted; untouched, either by the ideology or by the scenic effects, they basked in the spirited Caucasian tunes. During the interval, in the crowded main foyer on the first floor, we looked from the window on to a magic scene: out of the deep, obliterating darkness above, snow was flurrying into the lamplight and had already thickly covered the garden in the square; a little boy was trying his skis and a few other small dark figures of children could be seen darting in and out of the trees.

Before we went to the theatre we had been told that Billy's plane would leave in the morning. He asked me if I didn't want to return with him. Was I sure I wanted to stay on? He begged me, with touching concern, not to go to Redkino and even offered, if I must go, to stay on and go with me. By now I felt that Leningrad offered so much that perhaps I didn't need to go to Redkino; and the weather, though pretty from the windows, was appalling when one was out in it – cold, slushy, dank. What would it be like out in the country?

All the same, when in the morning the smooth Intourist man from the airport turned up to drive Billy off, I changed my mind about going with him to the airfield. It would have taken the whole morning and I could not resist the chance of making my way to the Baltic station to see if Moloskovitsy (the station for Redkino) still existed and if the journey were possible – even though I wasn't going to make it. The night before I had felt rather lost and frightened at the thought of staying on alone. But now, as I put on my snow boots, thick gloves and a black woollen shawl on my head, and came out into the cold bright morning, I had a new uprush of adventurous impulse.

On the way to Leningrad we had passed the Warsaw station and the chauffeur had said that the Baltic station was next to it. That must be the one, I thought, and asked a passer-by the way there. Was it my imagination or did he direct me in a more personal human manner than people did in Moscow? 'Trolleybus No. 10.' I took it and watched the other passengers. After all, except that my boots were fleece lined (and you wouldn't notice that at first glance), my shawl too thin and my camel hair coat too ample and not sufficiently padded at the shoulders, I did not look very different from the Leningraders. I had put on very little make-up and the varnish had come off my nails. I tried talking to the woman opposite, saying that I came from England and asking what the different streets and buildings were, but I had chosen badly, she looked closed, uncurious, suspicious; the streets seemed generally familiar, but not in detail for they were outside the normal radius of Rikarna's walks. The Baltic station was the terminus of the trolleybus. I walked in and took my time looking for a list of stations. I found it by a ticket office: Moloskovitsy was there all right, so clearly marked that I could hardly believe my eyes – here it was taken for granted – while to me it was fabulous. But the list gave only the fares (14r 80k), there was no timetable. I came out and discovered an inquiry office near the entrance. The woman clerk said I had just missed the 9.50 direct; but I could go at 23.00 hours, changing at Gatchina, 'If they give you a ticket'. That was that, I thought, only just bothering to scribble down the time and wondering why I might not get a ticket to Gatchina? I was sure that the clerk did not take me for a foreigner, but would there be a little man at my elbow as I had been told there might be? At the hotel I asked if I could put off going to Moscow till Friday and abroad until the day after the holidays and was told, 'yes, probably.'

I said to myself that I would use my time in Leningrad, looking at the town and making a few literary contacts. I asked the operator for the telephone numbers of the Secretary of the Writers' Union and of the novelist, Panova.[17] There was no directory, of course, and I was told that Panova had no telephone, but they would try to get the Secretary of the Writers' Union.

I sat down at the desk, put on the table lamp and wrote up my notes. Outside the big window with the net curtain, which I had looped aside, was St Isaac's and the snowy square. The room closed round me, warm, velvety, old-fashioned, dark, except for the weak light from the window and the shaded lamp. I thought it would be a nice place to work in, I felt at home, the old threads tying up.

After a time I again rang the Intourist bureau about my call. They sounded hurt – they had been trying to get the Secretary of the Union but he had not yet come in, they offered me the number. I rang the Union; the Secretary would be there at twelve. I said I would drop in and then went out. As I walked towards the Admiralty two women asked me the way so evidently I passed for a Leningrader. Or were they 'shadows'? I had been warned that 'tails' used this device for pointing out their quarry to their successor when they went off duty. I walked through what had been the Alexandrovsky Garden but without recognising it; I had thought of it as leading to the Bronze Horseman but I could not see him, and from here the splendid yellow façade of the Admiralty overshadowed the garden. I cannot have noticed it in my childhood, though my first distinct impression of beauty was of the Admiralty Arch. Small muffled children were tumbling on skis and pulling sledges. They were familiar sights. I walked with a feeling of lightness and beauty all round me. The Winter Palace Square opened in front of me, as satisfying as the day before. There were no longer any cobbles, and the horse-drawn trams had been replaced by trolleys. Women were sweeping away the snow. Apart from buses, there was hardly any traffic except for two big military-looking trucks. The palace was a little spoiled by the slogans and portraits of leaders put up for the holiday. I knew exactly where to go, along the beautiful little street and over the canal and then left along the Moika. My breath was caught with all its beauty, I had no conscious memory it was like this – the lovely proportions of the streets and the classical façades, and the enchanting light, the contrast between the snow and the dark stone stressing the details, and the bronze water in the canals. I felt my child-hood ennobled.

Now, I could have a proper look at No. 16. It was huge. I counted the windows and identified the rooms: from left to right, one for father's dressing-room, two for his square study with the leather arm-chairs I wasn't to bounce on and the pattern of the inlay in the furniture carried over on the walls (hideous that must have been); two for the end wall of the ballroom and the four for the drawing-room with its huge malachite table, ivory vitrines and the patterned red carpet that covered up the parquet; one for mother's sitting-room which had seemed to me so beautiful with its maple and pale green, two for her bedroom. The rest of the rooms had looked out on the yard, with a frightening corridor running through the middle of the flat and a staircase from it to the two cosy light attics. The maids' room and the kitchen (fascinating, with the smell of black bread and the lights before the ikons), had run along the left side of the yard; the right wing did not belong to us, but it had a special mystery attached to it because I had been inside it once before it was shut off, never to be seen again by us.

The front door looked infinitely shabby, and the hall inside smaller than I remembered it, but there was the glass roof the porter had fallen through. I climbed slowly up and sat down outside our door and smoked a cigarette. Up a few more steps on the right was the door of the mysterious 'other' flat. Behind me was the curious wood and glass partition which had turned part of the landing into an entrance lobby, it had been hung with dark tapestries of woodland scenes, and the coats people left in it had smelled of snow. It had opened, absurdly, into the ballroom.

A girl, poorly dressed in a dark coat and grey shawl, came upstairs passed me incuriously and walked into the flat. I followed her; the door was open. The lobby was bare; the ballroom blocked, both on the right where the windows had been, and on the left, where the door to the dining-room had been – that had now disappeared. It was a dark entrance, painted an official green; only the remains of the pattern of the parquet still stood out through the dirt. The huge light room drumming to the gallop at the end of the mazurkas detached itself from this scene. The dark opening of the corridor was still opposite the entrance, and half way down it there remained one of the ornate, panelled double doors. But there were five other doors, shabby, like the doors of tenement flats. A woman came out of one; I told her my story and asked if I might come in. She refused, half crossly, half apologetically. There were many little flats here now, she said, I might try one of the others. I tried the one next door but had no luck. 'Try that one,' the woman said, pointing to the door at the end of the passage, 'ours are little ones.' But the rooms at the end could only be what had been mother's and our bathrooms, so I knocked across the way. Yet another woman came out; I told my story again, now with desperation. She hadn't finished cleaning; no, I really couldn't come in; but finally, as I crazily stood my ground, 'Well, if it really is *so* important to you!' I was already inside the tiny, cluttered warren of partitions. The two squalid cubicles must have been made out of some corner of the drawing-room, but nothing remained except a window on to the Moika.

Well, that was that, but I couldn't feel quite finished with it yet, so, going out into the street, I looked up again. The windows on this side no longer meant anything to me. But I went through the entrance to the yard, and there everything was unchanged; even the logs were stacked up on the right where they had always been, and they were covered with snow, and the same children were playing round them. Our windows on this side were still the windows of our rooms, and the one across the yard was the one belonging to a woman who used always to be sewing.

It was close on twelve, time to go to the Writers' Union. The shop with transfers and angels had gone, in its place was a food shop with a lot of people in it, and none of the mint smell or the sugar 'hats' in blue paper wrapping. The river was as lovely as ever with its wide expanse and the buildings on the other shore and the palaces along the quay. An old Petersburgian directed me, stumbling over the new name of the Trinity Bridge (as a child I had never understood about the Trinity and thought it had something to do with the lamp posts with three lamps – they were still there).

Strange that I did not feel more sad about the dingy warren in our home. I had walked out of it crying, but now it was no longer real, and yet my childhood was again about me, enriched by all the beauty of Petersburg.

As I was nearing the Liteiny Bridge a crocodile of little boys crossed over to my side. An urchin, perhaps six years old, turned back and called to me: 'Styliaga'. So now I knew my clothes were not quite right but also not impossible. I walked on laughing. Close to the bridge a policeman stood inside a glass cage on a tall pedestal. I reached up to him to ask the way and he opened the cage door to answer me. The Writers' House was round the corner. I mistook the door and went up a slummy staircase to the 'Literary Fund' but two writers, very obviously in search of funds, sent me back to the front door. The Secretary's office was on the first floor, a big front room with a girl secretary in it. I asked for Mikhailov, the Secretary. He was not expected in. I explained my business in full (I had already explained it over the telephone). The girl said the Assistant Secretary was not there either but she could ring him, and did so. There was a foreigner in the office, she said, who spoke Russian, what was she to do with her? Finally, she told me the Assistant Secretary, Prokofiev, would come in at one and I could wait. I said I would also like to get in touch with Panova, could she be rung up. No, said the girl, she thought Panova was ill. I asked where I could have lunch while I was waiting; there was a restaurant in the building, she said, I could go there now. But when I went downstairs, the woman in the porter's lodge told me the restaurant did not open until 12.45 pm. Had I come to see Mikhailov? He had been and gone. Had he indeed, for I had been told by the girl that he had not been and was not expected. The woman let me sit outside her lodge. We talked a little. She was interested in my boots. They were lined, were they, and made of suède? Theirs were not like that. Then she shut herself up in her glass cage. I went out again and walked for a little while and suddenly along the side street to the quay, the water gurgling down the drain pipes, the drops falling from the cornices – the sunshine and the thaw were forty years earlier.

When I came back Prokofiev had arrived and I was taken to his office. He was a stocky, middle-aged man. I explained my business. As usual, he too asked anxiously why I spoke Russian. I realised at once that in trying to establish publishing relations here I was doing something more difficult than in Moscow: for one thing I had no letters of introduction, no evidence of official backing; I mentioned Zmeul, Nazarov, everyone I thought could help, and of course our publishing *The Thaw*. He seemed to take my word for it; but it was not until I said how beautiful I found Leningrad that I felt I was accepted; there was no doubt he had a proper pride in his city. I spent an hour with him talking about publishing and he arranged for me to go to the Dom Knigi where, it seemed, a dozen publishers were housed. When I asked him if I could see Panova he rang her up, told her who I was and that it was all right my speaking Russian, and arranged for me to meet her at her publishers at 2.15 pm. By now the restaurant was open. I went in. There were two rooms, one with a 'buffet' where you were served over the counter. The people seemed to be students or intellectuals. I sat down at a table with two men. The window in front of us looked out on to the Neva. After the usual explanations about where I came from and why I spoke Russian, I said how pretty it was, how much I liked Leningrad, adding that I had travelled a lot and did not know a city I liked better. The older one asked: 'But have you been to Budapest?' He had lived there before the war. He talked about the new buildings around Leningrad, then the younger man, an architect, asked if the bombed houses had been rebuilt in London. I said most but not all. London was too big and needed decentralising; new towns were being built. The two men looked at each other and the architect said meaningfully: 'Every country has its policy.' I asked him what he meant. 'You are afraid of London getting bigger but our city is growing and growing.' I felt that there was something I ought to say in answer to his triumphant, challenging remark, perhaps explain that it was not the danger of revolution that made it better for London to be smaller, but it seemed too difficult to pick up. I fetched a dish of eggs and herring from the buffet and when the waitress came, ordered some cheese cakes. The herring cost 3r 50k and the cheese cakes 1r 50k; so I lunched for the astonishingly small sum of five roubles, perhaps a quarter of the cost of a meal at the hotel. The men discussed helpfully how I was to get to the Dom Knigi by bus. But I was late and tried to find a taxi, walking, and finally running, from one street crossing to another in search of a rank that everybody knew existed but nobody knew where. I tried another policeman in a cage, but he took me for a moron and, too late, I read the notice which said that he was not to be spoken to. Finally I found the rank and the taxi took me along the Nevsky, past the Kazan Cathedral where, from the office windows opposite, we had, in 1912, watched the Romanov tercentenary (the great procession of clergy with banners, then the Tsar riding past and the banners bowing to the ground). The Dom Knigi is huge, and there was a milling crowd at the lift. The brass plate outside gave the various names of the firms but not their floors and nobody I asked could tell me where the Creative Art publishers were.

I climbed huge stairs; half way up an attendant was sitting. I asked him; he looked blank; 'You don't know? – How odd that you should not know.' He put on his glasses and read slowly down a list. I got there in the end, almost half an hour late, but the Chairman was in conference and Panova did not arrive until a few minutes after me, then she took me into the Chairman's room. After Prokofiev had spoken with him, he had rung back while I was still there and judging by the cautious and embarrassed reassurance given by Prokofiev it must have been to make doubly sure I was 'all right'.

Here again I found a committee of six, but quite different from those in Moscow. They were lively, almost cosy, interested, knowledgeable, and Panova was like an old Petersburgian, though less elegant and more energetic. At the end of half an hour we got on to Soviet literary trends. 'We have several schools of writing,' she said. 'I belong to the same one as Ehrenburg. But he is chiefly interested in politics and I don't care about them. I'm concerned with personal relations.' This sounded revolutionary. We talked of war books, I said they were now more popular with us than they had been just after the war. Panova's face brightened: 'Do you think it is because of the relaxation of international tension?' I said I did. They spoke about the growing demand for books, how they had increased their production. They said they were allocated 20,000 tons of paper but could use twice as much. They published a monthly 'novel newspaper'. Panova's *Span of the Year* had come out in this. She, amiably showing off, went to fetch a copy and pointed out the size of the edition – half a million and yet you could no longer buy it in any shop. Books sold out on the day of publication. A dear little, thin man in charge of English books asked if Donne were worth translating? They were thinking of an anthology of seventeenth-century English poetry and another of Elizabethan dramatists (excluding Shakespeare). They gave me copies of Swift in Russian and their address to send books to. The 'English' director saw me out and showed me the way to Izogiz where I was going next. I could hardly bear to part from them.

Izogiz was quite a different story, though only at the other end of the same floor. The Chairman looked cowed and the woman assistant

Manya in Gloucestershire with
Simon, Sheba and Nicolette

he called in was the hard-faced, grim-jawed kind. They published books on art, as well as postcards and posters. But they were only the Leningrad branch. Authority lay in Moscow. If I got it from Nazarov (it was only now that I found out that besides being a Deputy Minister his special department was books), and if I saw the Moscow head of Izogiz, then they would do whatever they were told to do. When I mentioned the book on the Impressionists they looked very cagey. They did not think they had a file copy, the plates were most unlikely to exist. But if Nazarov were to instruct the Moscow office, well then, perhaps something could be done . . . I asked if I could buy it from their shop. But the Chairman seemed to think this was going a bit too far and made an assistant fetch it; all the same, I had to pay for it. I could almost hear their minds work: 'Is it safer to be civil or uncivil?'

I went away feeling suddenly tired. It was snowing again, the parcels of books I was carrying were heavy. The Nevsky was dark, crowded, with queues at the bus stops. There was no sign of a taxi, so I queued up for a bus. When I got out near the St Isaac I could not remember the way to the hotel and asked a well-dressed man. He offered to take me there, saying he was not from Leningrad himself, had just come from abroad. 'So have I,' I said, 'from London.' It did not occur to him I could be English – perhaps my battered clothes helped though they were probably still good enough to look as if I were an official. 'I was in Poland.' 'Oh! That must have been interesting.' 'Not at all.' He was emphatic. 'You were in Warsaw?' 'No. In X . . .' (I did not catch the name of the town.) 'You know, where our troops are stationed.' This interesting conversation refreshed me. So did a hot bath. But to go to Redkino was still unthinkable. I bullied Leontina to get me a ticket for a theatre (she said it would be difficult at the last moment). Then, during dinner, all at once, my decision seemed absurd to me. How could I miss such an opportunity. After all, I could turn back at any point if it seemed too discouraging – I could return from Gatchina, or Moloskovitsy; by then, at least, I would have travelled in a Russian train, or found out if the little man did turn up at one's elbow to prevent one from going. I apologised to Leontina. I had forgotten that I had arranged to meet a friend, I said; would she cancel the ticket; we might go to a cinema. She asked nervously whether the friend was coming to the hotel or I was going out. I said

I was going out. Indeed, I thought, I must go out soon for 10.30 pm would seem too improbable to Leontina. I might even really go to a cinema, Prokofiev had suggested I should see *Footsteps in the Snow* as an example of the present taste for thrillers – I might see a part of it, or the whole if again I changed my mind.

It was cold but not actually snowing. I turned left down the big street in the direction of the Nevsky where the cinema was. At the corner a subaltern and a civilian stood arguing. 'The Astoria is just here,' said the civilian. '*Is* it?' said the soldier with a broad, tipsy gesture, '*Valyay tuda* – let's roll there' – so the Astoria still had glamour, was still the place where it was tempting to break the mirrors.

Even in the dark the street looked dignified. Foodshops were open; I walked into two of them; they were crowded. I felt thirsty and asked if I could drink some *narzan*, the good Caucasian soda water, at what looked like a soda fountain, but they sold only bottles. I came out into the Nevsky. The Palace Square was deserted, vast, snowy, dark. Farther along I looked into the lit-up windows of a bookshop and noted travel books which seemed better than those we had seen in Moscow. But I said to myself I mustn't walk too much, or I will get too tired. It was close on 9.30 pm. I asked the way to the Baltic station and took a bus.

Once again I went to the inquiry office to check the timetable and to ask the number of the platform. The woman clerk on night duty was more stony faced than the one I had seen earlier. She confirmed 23.00 as the time of departure; I would get to Gatchina at ten minutes past midnight and to Moloskovitsy at 3.30 am. I asked where I should get my ticket? My question was evidently unexpected so I explained: 'I am sorry to bother you, but I am a foreigner.' 'You are a foreigner? Then you shouldn't be travelling to such a place at night. What will you do arriving at Moloskovitsy at such an hour?' 'My friends are meeting me,' I said quickly. 'Are you sure? Do they know that you are taking the night train?' At any rate there was no little man. I felt elated. I wandered up the big central hall. It was crowded and there were a lot of soldiers around. I wondered if Gatchina were a camp (it had been a *dacha*[18] resort in my day). A bookstall and two sandwich bars were open. I was still thirsty and asked for narzan. Soldiers and workmen were eating rolls with sliced sausage or herring and drinking beer. There was no narzan but I could have *moskovskaya*. Then, as I opened my bag to pay, I realised that I had left my money in my other bag at the hotel. It was 10.15. I ran out, fortunately straight into a taxi, and explained my hurry to the chauffeur. Entering into the spirit of the emergency, he speeded splendidly; at the hotel I took not only my money but my two brooches and my necklace – I did not think any- one was likely to steal from a foreigner but perhaps it was a pity to tempt them. I also collected the key of my room – surprise at my absence would come less early if it were not in the hall. I was back at the station by 10.35. If I were to be followed – I had certainly left many clues, my snatching my key from the inquiry desk, the taxi, my hurrying in and out all of which must have been noticed.

REDKINO

At the ticket office nobody seemed to ask for hard or soft class, so I just murmured 'One to Moloskovitsy' received my ticket and went into a waiting-room. It was warm, crowded with soldiers, sailors, work- men and women all sitting on the wooden benches. People glanced at me curiously but nobody said anything. One man strummed a balalaika; another got up and danced. Some people laughed. But it was not the spontaneous outburst of gaiety I associated with such scenes. Perhaps the dingy sleepy atmosphere was against it. A woman in uniform who was sweeping the floor looked with smiling com- passion at a pregnant idiot girl sitting hunched up in the corner and said: 'Every evening she is here. And a woman like that brings a child into the world.'

At last it was time to start. I showed my ticket at the platform gate and got into the little electric train, it had long carriages and sets of wooden benches facing one another in two rows with a passage in between. I sat opposite a pretty, neat girl who was doing petit point. Across the passage was a crowd of young boys in workmen's clothes talking loudly. Two were smoking. I lit a cigarette but the girl looked up with a severe expression. I asked her if smoking were allowed. 'Well, not as a rule.' So I put out my cigarette. She looked shy, puzzled, self- possessed. Judging by her small, fresh face, she could not have been more than seventeen. 'How is it you didn't know?' she asked. I ex- plained. She was uncurious, either through shyness or on principle? I continued talking to her and politely she put away her petit point to give me her attention. I admired the embroidery. 'As I have nothing to do . . I was just occupying myself,' she said; she was a *Komsomolka*[19] ('of course'!). She had finished her seven year school and was now, in the evenings, following the three additional classes. The first seven classes were free, the other three had to be paid for. She said, shyly, she was an orphan and had no one to pay the extra schooling for her, so she was working in a shop in Leningrad (eight hours' work, five hours' studying). She earned 400 roubles a month and had to buy her meals, but her lodging cost only five roubles a month as she lived in a hostel (the figures came hesitantly, as though they were true but needed some further explanation). Later, she would like to get a scholarship and become a teacher. Her hostel was in a factory settlement not far from Gatchina where she had relations. She started at eight in the mornings and came back by this train; most of the passengers were students. I thought, and said, she looked well in spite of her long days, adding that I supposed besides the shop and the classes she must have duties connected with the Komsomol. 'Of course' these days they were preparing for the Anniversary parade. She was modestly proud. People in the Komsomol had to show an example. I told her a little about England, though she didn't ask any questions. I was carrying Panova's book and said I had met her today. That was a little better, she had heard of Panova. But I did not think she was a bookish child; she tried hard, and failed, to think of any books she liked, though I believe she mentioned Shakespeare. I was evidently providing a difficult encounter; soon I left her in peace. Then she took out a text book with diagrams from her satchel and started doing her homework. She was a charming, pedantic Victorian miss, pretty and round-cheeked and very much the Girl Guide, anxious to combine helpfulness and civility to a foreigner, while giving an example of her country's dignity. She got out a little before midnight and told me the number of stations before Gatchina.

At Gatchina everything changed. For one thing, there was no platform. The little train puffed warmly behind me but all around was darkness, snow, emptiness. An old woman hobbled down after me muttering, 'Where can the station be?' I walked along the slope, caught up with another passenger, inquired and told the old woman. It seemed that the station was a dark hut some hundred yards farther along. We walked through the blizzard past an outhouse labelled

'Buffet': it was closed. Then a covered porch led to a narrow lighted passage where a few bored soldiers stood smoking and reading the posters. I read them too, hoping to find a timetable, for the inquiry clerk in Leningrad had not told me when the train left Gatchina. But there was only information as to how to get a season ticket, with sample forms etc. Another poster listed a large number of offences such as spitting, smoking – where forbidden, riding on the buffers; a third gave lively illustrated warnings against starting fires. I asked the soldiers when the train left. They said gloomily: 'One-thirty.' That meant an hour and a quarter still to wait.

I pushed open the door of the waiting-room and the ancient fug of Russia hit me in the face. Before me was a square, dimly lit room, heated by an iron stove, and filled with corpses lying, sitting or crouched on the benches round the walls. The thick sweetish stink made me reel outside, but it was cold there and I thought I'd better get used to the fug, so I came back and shut the door. The corpses were men, women, girls and boys resting with their chins on their knees or across each other's laps or shoulders. Everything was dark grey – grey faces and grey, threadbare, wadded coats and woollen shawls. Most of them were asleep except one old woman who was talking animatedly with two young men about a holiday and an excursion by steamer she had made while in Yalta, and three women who were chattering in a corner in some Baltic language. There was not an inch left on any bench. When I counted the bodies I found there were only about forty of them, but they looked like the whole grey population of the endless interior. I leaned against a corner of the wall; next to me, at the end of the bench, a boy in top boots lay curled up and grunted in his sleep. Later, tired of standing, I squatted on the floor. The little old lady who had limped out of the train with me came in and began a conversation with one of the women and was soon squeezed on to a seat. Then she called across to me: 'Come darling, come citizeness.' I went over and she offered me an inch or two she had managed to push free beside her. 'Your coat is too bright to sit on the floor,' she said. We talked a little. I thought she took me not for a foreigner but for an official on a service journey, so I explained. Across the room a packet of papers had slipped out of the pocket of a sleeping sailor and fallen on to the floor. Every now and then somebody woke up and said: 'He *will* get into trouble, we ought to wake him,' but then another voice would reply: 'Sleep is the most precious thing of all, let him rest.' After a time the little old woman could not stand it any longer, she walked over to him and shook him. He woke up, stretched himself, muttered thank you, and picked up his papers. A sergeant tottered in, lifted a couple of soldiers who were sleeping on the floor and propped them up against the wall. 'Smoking!' he addressed one who had lit a cigarette. 'I smoked for twenty-nine years and then I gave it up and I advise you to do the same.' 'He's drunk,' giggled the old lady. Reminded of smoking I went out into the porch to light a cigarette. It was very cold and dark, the blizzard was still blowing. I found a woman standing there, she said she was waiting to be called for by car. The drunken sergeant came out and repeated his saying about smoking, adding that it was disgraceful for a woman to smoke. I laughed. The other woman said reprovingly: 'Who's teaching others? You'll end up by losing your stars.' The man waved his hands. 'It isn't drink that has been the ruin of me, it's your kind of woman.' For a bit he stood mumbling, then broke out: 'Lutherans! Catholics! I know them all. I've seen through all the religions. And so have they too. They ought to be ashamed.' Then, turning towards me, concluded impressively: 'Anyway, if you're a Lutheran or a Catholic and you smoke you'll certainly go straight to Hell.' I could think of no suitable comment!

People were beginning to wander out of the station. I followed them towards the line, the snow smacking wetly at my face. Then I saw a little tall train standing high up on the bank, no light came from it. The soldiers were talking and laughing. I asked if this were the train to Moloskovitsy, they said: 'Yes, climb in, citizeness.' So high were the steps that to do this one needed to be an acrobat.

I wondered if it could be the identical train we used to take in 1913? As I pushed a door open the same hot fug as in the station waiting-room hit me and there was the same round black iron stove with logs burning in it inside the carriage. The wooden seats were the same as in the 'electric train' but the carriage was narrower and the people looked more countryfied – the men with trousers tucked into their boots, a family with children and a basket of provisions.

Two girls sitting next to me were whispering, their faces pressed to the dark window. But in no time everybody fell asleep. The journey was long. A few people came in or got out at the intervening stops, a man in a uniform, vaguely like a policeman's, came in at the station before Moloskovitsy, and another propped a gun up against his seat. The light was dim and the train shook too much to read comfortably, also, even though I had asked the girl ticket collector when she came through how many stations there were before Moloskovitsy, and had tried to count carefully, I was afraid of falling asleep and travelling beyond it. All the stations were in total darkness so one could easily miss one's stop.

Then, suddenly, we were there. I hurried out, though there was no need to hurry. Only after a long wait did the train move off, puffing its leisurely way along as though it had all Russia to wander in. Here again was nothing but darkness, cold, slush and falling snow turning into rain.

I had a curiously distinct memory of the last time I had seen Moloskovitsy. It was a grey day in early September. Father, Rikarna and I had driven the thirty versts from Redkino in the carriage, behind the brown horses with their yellow flowing manes and tails. In those days the station had been a neat house with a steep roof bordered with carvings and had a garden in front – a round formal flower bed circled by a drive. The station master had met us and given us tea while we waited for the train.

Now I wandered from the line in the blinding sleet, wondering what to do next. Suddenly, as I wiped my glasses and looked up, there was the steep outline of the station, with a little light shining through its windows. I had blundered to the back of it, and there, under my feet, all deep in slush, were the remains of the ring of pebbles that used to surround the flower bed.

I decided to go in and wait for daylight. There was the usual square room lined with benches, smaller than those in Gatchina, fuggy but cold. Three grey men lay asleep, face downwards on three benches. I sat on the fourth. A countrywoman, wearing the usual bootee-galoshes, tattered wadded jacket and grey shawl, sat down next to me. Her hands were scarlet with cold. I looked with horror at her knees covered only with a patterned cotton skirt, and put out my hand to feel how cold and wet she was. She smiled at me cosily. 'I'll just rest awhile. Then I'll walk to the village. It's about three kilometres. Perhaps it's warmer in the other room.' I followed her to the next room and there it was warmer, but smellier; such warmth as there was came only from the crowded benches on which the same corpses as in Gatchina lay about. I sat on the floor but again an old woman bustled over to me, pushed somebody aside and made me sit on the bench. She stood looking at me curiously. 'You're on a service journey?' 'I'm going to a little place called Redkino,' I said. 'Perhaps you know it?'

'Redkino? No. But I seem to have heard the name. Are you waiting to be fetched by car?' I mumbled. Somebody else said: 'Redkino? Isn't that near Slepino?'

Suddenly I remembered the three villages Slepino, Mishkino and Sapsk that stood on the River Luga. Two men came in. One of them asked a woman whether she could light the stove if they fetched logs. She said yes and went out after them. I followed them back to the first room, hoping they would light the stove there. The two men had pleasant faces and a wide awake expression. Perhaps, later, they might be the ones to ask how I was to go on? For a moment there was nobody around except the three corpses.

I sat down and tried to sleep. A few moments later, the old woman shook me. 'They're inviting you in to get warm,' and she pointed to a door I hadn't noticed, it had now been opened on to warmth and soft wavering light. I went through into a tiny cluttered-up room where the two were sitting on a bench in front of a stove; the only light came from the fire. They gestured hospitably and made room for me.

'Come in. Come and get warm.'

The warmth, the sudden intimacy, were heavenly. They shut the door.

'You're going to Redkino? On a service journey?' Before I had thought what answer to give one man said:

'I was on the train with you.' Then, as though to the room at large: 'I said to myself, that's not someone from our parts. Sitting there so quiet, so reserved.'

Here goes, I thought, and if he's a policeman who has been following me, so much the worse.

'I'm a foreigner,' I said, and told them my whole story. There was a moment's silence. The atmosphere grew warmer. One of the men remarked:

'I always say, everybody should do that – go and see their birth-place.' The other man nodded approvingly, and they settled down to discuss where Redkino might be; they decided it was between the river and the three villages. There was a bus, they said, it met the train from Leningrad at two o'clock. That was nine hours off, but now it didn't seem to matter in the least.

The old woman came back and the men told her my story. She said:

'We've had strangers before, but never from abroad. It must be that times have changed.'

'You're right,' I replied. 'It wouldn't have been possible a year ago.'

But between us there was the unspoken question: was it really possible now? Had I any right to be here by myself, or had I taken the bit between my teeth at my own peril and perhaps at theirs? None of us knew the answer, and, strangely, I realised, it made a bond between us and put me under their protection. They began to discuss my journey on. The post van might leave earlier than the bus; someone said I could hitch-hike but the general opinion was that this was not a good idea. 'It's all right for us, but for her, a stranger and going to such a remote place. Who knows what people she might happen on?' 'You must be careful,' they said, 'there are many *zhuliki*[20] about. In an out of the way place like this anything might happen, so, when you get to Redkino go straight to the *sovkhoz*[21] and introduce yourself, then they'll be responsible for you.'

I felt utterly at home with these people, tied to them by close bonds, convinced that I should see them all again.

Long before the bus was due, I went to meet it, which was lucky as it came and left before its scheduled time. I thought it impossible that I should remember the road and yet I knew which way we would go because that was how we had driven from the station. I was sure the road was no wider than it had been in our day and it was certainly much muddier, sticky, yellow, churned-up mud, but then I had never been in these parts so late in the year. When it arrived the bus was nearly full. Opposite me sat three men in good dark coats and fur caps. From their conversation it seemed they were going to various villages on some inspection job.

I was fascinated by the landscape, so utterly familiar it was, sad, grey, flat under the enormous sky. Here were the forests; this part had been 'State property', our estate started farther on, and I remembered Rikarna saying that the State forests were better kept than ours and drawing my attention to how upstanding the trees were. Now all the woods looked neglected and unkempt and the tree trunks were thin, like strands of grey dishevelled hair; many trees had fallen. Behind the telegraph poles and wires (they existed in our time but didn't go all the way to Redkino) other trees had been felled to prevent damage to the wires. We stopped at a small village with some houses built not of logs, but of boards. Farther on there was a roadside chapel and still farther, a couple of hundred yards from an old village, a few graves with crosses but no church. After that the landscape was just as I remembered it, except that the log huts now mostly had roofs of wooden slates, and there was hardly any thatch left. The woods and fields did not appear to be better cultivated than in our day, and there were no new houses until we reached Slepino.

The road followed the same curling river, made the same bend, with the low hillside on the right, and climbed where the horses used to be sent up at a gallop. When we reached the turning to the left over the stream there was Slepino, settled in its curve. The houses looked the same, except that there were certainly more of them. We made a longish stop and some people got out. Here were the log barns I remembered, now they were buckling at the knees, and in some places a new one had been built alongside the old one. We went on, past Mishkino. A woman asked the girl ticket collector to let her down at Redkino 'on the hill'. I said, 'I'll get off there too.' We stopped and the woman climbed out with a parcel and a heavy suitcase. I said I'd help her carry them, but she replied 'No': for if I were going on a service journey to the school I'd not be going her way she was going up the hill to the settlement. 'Have you been here before? Would you like me to show you the way?'

'No,' I said.

'Well they're sure to be expecting you. It's only a little way, down-hill to the right.'

The weather had cleared. It had grown cold but was still. The sky was grey with clouds and light watery patches. There was nothing to be seen except the snowy fields, the muddy road and a few huts up on the hill. Here the road had changed its direction. It used to swing down, over the wooden bridge and round the church, then past the houses, along the valley to Sapsk. Now it by-passed Redkino. I walked down, slowly.

Suddenly, only just over the crest of the hill, there came a burst of red and rose, domes, roofs; closer together than I thought they would be, but more splendid and tremendous. Everything was there, the great low houses and the old chapel with the steeple and the 'new' octagonal church with its two domes. All of it glowed an unbelievably warm pink, against the grey sky, the dull earth, and the brownish wisps of bare trees, looking like smoke, which veiled it a little. It was real, solid, huge, exuberant, gay, like a great ripe fruit, alone in all this endless grey space.

Here was the road to the church where we had talked with the man with the scythe. I saw that the church was now only an empty shell with broken windows, and that those curious double crosses in the graveyard in front of it, were falling sideways, and that there were no railings between them and the road. No garden ran up to the house which had lost its wooden verandah where we used to have tea. Only the steps leading to the balustrade remained, and the pebbles which traced out the formal flower beds. Here father had planted a fir tree for Fira and another for me, I could see the place where one had been pulled up. But the river was still there, with its same shallows, its same ford, its same bend where the women used to bathe, and its same sweet, light, rapid tinkle, which made me thirsty as though today were a hot, green, summer's day. And there was the place above the river where the rowan tree grew and you could stand and look at water and not be scolded. I walked round and looked at the house and the old chapel at an angle to it – a design I had never seen before, perhaps because I was small and probably children never look at the whole of a house, or because there had been more trees, or because when we stayed there the trees were in leaf. Seen as a whole the house was much bigger than I remembered it, though I remembered all its different parts. Now there were no stone urns, no oleander trees, no lilacs. Shorn of all its prettiness it looked great and battered, but more beautiful, I thought, than ever. Certainly, whoever painted it a red which had faded to these many rich pinks did it a service. The park had become open country; of the long avenue only a few silver birches and the poplars were left, the crab apple tree had gone and so had the lawn with its daisies, its tobacco flowers, its pinks and its sunshades. All I saw was a muddy playing-field with a seesaw and a swing and many stumps of trees. The 'dangerous' old chapel stood firm, but the 'Agent's office' was gutted, as was the dairy; the stables were standing but empty. Prokofievna's pond was lost in the slush but the ducks and geese were still padding around.

I walked on, past the ruined laundry and the 'old kitchen', where the wreaths of dried apples and mushrooms used to hang. The road was getting deeper and deeper in mud. An old woman with a cart and horse was walking towards me – an immemorial cart, straight out of Nekrasov,[22] with a high 'collar' on the horse's neck. The woman and a couple of men passed me with no more than a curious glance. But as I went towards the house, children stalked me, turning up from every side, following me from tree to tree.

Sooner or later I should have to declare myself, and I did so when I saw a tall teacher, dressed in some sort of uniform and a blazer, cross the garden calling to the children. At first her face was closed, but she warmed at once when I told her a part of my story: I said I was English, I had a Russian mother and we had often stayed in Redkino. Now, I have been invited to Russia on business and had taken this opportunity . . . She welcomed me, saying she would call some old inhabitants to talk with me. The house had been damaged during the war, it was occupied by the Germans and the Russians shelled it. That was why the verandah and the cherry trees were gone. 'But come in, you must be tired,' she said, 'you can't have eaten, let me get you some borsch.' The ground floor was not used in our time, except for a few rooms at one end which were the servants' quarters. She and a girl took me upstairs to see some rooms that had been partly restored. We went through the back door and from the landing peered down into the hall. The teacher said, 'You can see it was a beautiful house, a pity it was so damaged, some parts are unsafe and they can only be restored little by little.' The room she first showed me used to be the drawing-room, a great square room; they had patched it up and whitewashed it, and the moulded ceiling had survived. I remembered where the piano stood; next to this room was the sitting-room – it had kept a little of its moulding and blue paint.

Next Yurik, a boy of twelve in a good warm coat and cap with flapping ear pieces, took me to the farm to see an old inhabitant – Aunt Liza. We walked some way through the wood, past men working a mechanical saw. Then we came to a clearing, in it stood a log cottage and a barn in front of which a woman was working. Yurik left me with her. She put down her chopper and stood talking shyly.

Her husband was out at work. She had lived at Redkino since 1921, she came from Mishkino, but her husband had been born in Redkino.

All at once we are back in 1913. 'I remember the *Barin*, a fine up-standing man he was. I remember him driving up to the house, the troika drawing up, the horses arching their necks; fine horses, chest-nuts with yellow manes. I used to walk from Mishkino with my Granny, when we passed the house and I wanted to pick the flowers, lovely they were, Granny always said I mustn't.' Aunt Liza talked of the people of those days. Stepan Dorofeich (the sly agent with a beard, who was so disliked by the peasants and was always trying to get another piece of land to add to his own) had survived wars and revolu-tions and died peacefully only two years ago, owning a lot of land. He had married all his daughters to important people, they still lived in the neighbourhood, so did his widow.

During the Revolution, Aunt Liza told me, the house stood empty and peasants came from all sides and carried away mirrors and furni-ture and broke and looted. Then there was the civil war, some General arrived, Yudenich,[23] she thought. Then came peace and the school was opened, at first for adults. Aunt Liza and her husband had only just got their own house when collectivisation began. She did not mean the one in which she now lived. This, she told me, stood 'where the kennels used to be for the dogs with the gold medals.' (That was before our time, Bogdanov the former owner had taken his dogs with him except for one borzoi who ran away to follow him.) The 'manager' had come with carts and men to shift their first home together with four others. Aunt Liza's husband didn't want it moved but it couldn't be prevented. The *kolkhoz* had to get rid of it. There was great poverty then, nobody lived decently. Last year they turned the kolkhoz into a sovkhoz, and this was better; Aunt Liza owned forty-five *sotniks*,[24] bad land, but they get paid piece work for what they do for the *sovkhoz*. At present she was helping the men on the wood cutting. During the war the Germans overran the whole neighbourhood in no time. 'We hid in the woods. We got bread from the Partisans. They were shooting at the house from over there. It went on for weeks.'

Our teeth were chattering with cold, and at last she asked me in. It was a small but solid looking two room log hut, with electricity (a bare bulb in each room) and as everywhere a wireless. The front room was clean, with, on the table in the centre, a white cloth, and there were *ficus*[25] in pots, and good pieces of furniture – obviously from the house – perhaps that is why she took so long to let me in, though who could have expected peasants not to take what was going, and because they had good furniture it did not mean that they hadn't been hungry. Perhaps seeing that I understood all this, she became cosier for a time, then suddenly her voice took on a note of lamentation. She showed me photos of her children: a boy died of starvation during the siege of Leningrad, twin boys now in the army – 'they took them, now they're in the Far East, there's no knowing if we'll ever see them again' – a small boy was still at school, and a daughter had married and was living in Leningrad. Aunt Liza was unhappy about her.

'Why?'

'What's the good of having a family these days? Look what happens to them, how they change.'

The daughter is a biologist (that at least is a change unthinkable in our day, and for the better). She married a teacher at the institute where she worked. Aunt Liza showed me two photos, one of the daughter before her marriage, a soft, lyrical-looking country girl, the other after, with her square-faced husband, a hideous baby, and the girl herself now seemed to have a hard, sly face. The change was so terrible that I could hardly find words to comfort Aunt Liza.

I noticed an ikon half hidden by the ficus. 'You are a believer?'

'Of course.'

She took me into the inner room where there was a bigger ikon and two small ones on either side of it, one was of Our Lady of Spassky. The lamp was not lit – 'it's difficult to get oil' – but a white embroidered towel hung round the centre ikon.

'How should one not believe? Perhaps clever people like you don't, but to us faith and prayer are all that make life liveable.'

These were the very same words I had heard before. She told me a long strange story about a dream she had before they moved, in it she saw a brightly lit chandelier, with the Spassky ikon in the middle of it, rising into the air, circling around and then settling over the spot where their present house is. When the place was occupied by the Germans, there was a priest at the church, and one day she went in and asked him for the little Spassky Madonna and he said she could take it. The children, she said, don't pray, but perhaps they remember what she taught them when they were small. They don't laugh at her ikons.

Redkino

Little Venice

'That's how it is with young people. We do what we can before they are seven, and perhaps they will remember and come back in later life. Party members don't pray, but who knows what is in their hearts.'

I took leave of her. I had been crying with her. Of course I was very tired, but it wasn't only that.

I walked up the rise through sparse woods and clearings. Overhead the sky was a pale, cold, clear-washed green above soft clouds. The path turned left and then the house blazed at me with a warm, intense radiance and the gold and silver of the birches were caught in the sunset which itself was invisible so the house seemed to be the only source of light. It shone strongly, peacefully, unchangingly, never, I thought, so beautiful as now, and it was telling me something which I must wait to understand.

The light was bound to change soon and, with resignation to something that had not been communicated, I got out my note book and sketched so that at least I'd have something visible to be remembered. Dark roofs with strong, fine shadows below, the white line under the eaves, the rose walls, the out-houses and the chapel on the right and the domed church on the left, splendid, outflung, stripped to its bare bones, all softness gone from it, yet softer than ever with its rose flames; all these demanded recalling.

As soon as I began to draw small children appeared from nowhere and surrounded me. They talked, they were friendly, and little Tanya turned somersaults. When I had finished they followed me up to the house and led me to the front to show me the windows of their classrooms. We walked round to where the pleasant teacher had met me, now another one was there in a tattered uniform and with a stony face. We were standing outside the back door, she questioned me: how was it I had been able to come? Why was I alone and not part of a delegation? I gave my explanation. But the meeting had turned into a 'Meeting' and the children, no longer individuals, stood grouped behind the teacher as a class. 'When you knew this house,' she said, 'it belonged to landowners?'

'Yes, but it seems very suitable for a school.'

'Like all landowners' houses.'

'In England also many large houses have been turned into schools and institutions of various kinds.'

'Well, since you are here, you can tell us: do the children of English workers and peasants go to school?'

I felt crossly surprised at this first meeting with old style propaganda taken seriously and indeed I was little prepared for it after the intimate encounters of the day. I gave answers, about English education, about the taxation which has obliged many landowners to give up their houses, about present social conditions.

'And what are the wages of an English worker, assuming the exchange to be three roubles to the shilling?'

I pointed out that she must have got the exchange wrong, but I told her in sterling.

'How are we to know what a pound is?'

'Twenty shillings,' and I gave her the approximate wages of various workers.

She calculated mentally and asked indignantly: 'An agricultural labourer gets that much *a week*?'

'Yes.'

Angry, and disbelieving, she turned the conversation: 'And may I ask, how it is that when whole delegations come . . .' I think she meant to say 'and tell us one thing, while you tell us another,' but she changed it to 'and you come by yourself.' I repeated my explanation. Very angry now, and anxious to keep her face before the children, she almost hissed:

'Well, there's one thing. When you come to the USSR you see what you see.'

'What do you mean?'

'Well, you see what you are allowed to see, and if you were to ask me questions I would, of course, answer what it is laid down to answer and not what isn't laid down.'

Afterwards I thought I should have taken this up, but at the moment I was only anxious to end this unpleasant conversation. I felt oddly embarrassed for her in front of the children.

'Well, you'll be late for your bus,' she cut me off. The bus was not going until six-thirty and it was not six yet, but she insisted with frank rudeness. I tried to hold my ground a little longer, asking her what she taught.

'Russian literature.'

'Well, then you can advise me about Soviet books to publish in England.'

'Certainly. If you want books that it would be good for English children to read, I can give you a list.'

I asked her to lend me a pencil and she sent a child into the house for it, but stood in the doorway not letting me pass. Then she dictated the names of half a dozen 'patriotic' titles and repeated that I would be late. So I was not to see the other teacher again, and by now I was afraid of asking for her in case I should get her into trouble, so I told the monster to say goodbye to her for me and set off.

Two little girls followed me and soon other children caught up with us. By the time I got to the crossroads on the hill and sat down on a stone, I was surrounded. I asked them about their school and where they came from. Some were from Redkino and came to school daily, others were boarders from outlying villages. They got up at eight, and started lessons at nine, those who lived in did prep in the evening. All of them were Pioneers[26] or in the Komsomol. They asked if holidays were longer in England (they have a week now, a fortnight at the New Year, a week in the spring and three months in summer). Did English children become Pioneers earlier than they did (at nine)? They were learning German.

'It's mostly English in town, but German in the country,' they explained. They started Russian history in the fourth form, mediæval history in the fifth, foreign in the sixth. Now they were doing Wyatt's Rebellion, but they had begun with William the Conqueror and they knew his dates. Yurik, who was better dressed than the others, said he was going on to the 'ten-year school' at a little town some way off. The other boys didn't know if they too would go there. All would like to be mechanics. The girls laughed, they didn't want to go on to anything. Is there electricity in England? Metro? Cinema? Theatre? Puppet Theatre? Circus? Servants? – 'Yes,' I say, 'much as in the USSR.'

'And you have temples, and one temple for burying rich people.'

'I don't know of one,' I laughed. They said shyly: 'That's what we are taught.' 'Perhaps you mean a church where the kings are buried?' They thought that was probably what they meant, then asked, 'Do the kings come from rich families?' I said they got big wages as they had big expenses.

'Who is your king now?'

'We have a Queen – Elizabeth.'

A little girl asked, 'Does she wear a golden dress?'

'Well, not usually, but she wore very lovely things at the Coronation.' I talked about the Coronation. The girls said:

'It must have been very pretty.'

There was a warm smell of bread as a cart with freshly baked loaves passed us on its road to the school. The children followed it a little way, then came back. They told me, 'It's bread for our supper, baked in the village on the hill' and added that they need not go back yet. A young woman from the village who was waiting for the bus joined us.

The children asked what countries I had been to and which was the best. I laughed: 'Yours, of course!' Then I said I thought everyone loved his own country best and they agreed. Suddenly Yurik became portentous: 'Do the Americans have more bases outside their country than inside?' he asked. The young woman sitting by me laughed, but looked a little shocked and remarked, 'What a political question, Yurik.'

'What do you mean?' I said, 'Aren't the bases inside a country just part of that country's army?'

Then all at once I felt cross, not with poor Yurik, but with the head teacher, and went on:

'What would it mean if I asked you whether the Soviet Union had more bases inside the country or outside?'

Yurik drew himself up with a mixture of shyness and good faith:

'The Soviet Union has no bases anywhere.' I was reduced to speechlessness. However, the young woman wasn't:

'These are secret things they don't tell you about, Yurik.' Recovering my wits I said that this was a senseless conversation as nobody wanted war. The young woman agreed to this eagerly. She was very friendly and interested. I asked the children once or twice if they should not go back, for it was getting dark and very cold, but they stayed until the young woman shooed them off. She was going to the cinema in Slepino. At last the bus arrived. Just before it came to a stop a drylooking, upstanding old man, walked up to the road. He had heard about me and had come to have a look. We talked about Redkino in the days of the Benensons and of the Bogdanovs. Then, just as the bus was drawing up and several people were coming to meet it, he said in everybody's hearing:

'It must be a lot better in your country than in ours.'

I didn't know what to answer.

'Don't try to pull the wool over our eyes,' he went on. 'Tfu' he spat, 'that's what it's like here.'

As we crossed the dark countryside I was grateful for the two hours' rest in the bus. I dozed off, woke up to churning worries and then dozed off again. I was angry at the lies the children were being taught. All the time I was speaking to them I was torn between a passionate wish that they should hear something true and an unwillingness to shake their trust in what they were being taught, to destroy whatever faith they had. At least I had tried to be scrupulous in answering their factual questions.

We reached Moloskovitsy about nine, it was dark, cold sleet was falling and there was slush on the ground. The train was not due till one o'clock, but at least when it came it would be an express direct from Tallin. The station waiting-rooms were cold and dimly lit. In the front room, the usual corpses lay face downwards on the benches (two seemed to lie on top of one another with their coats bundled over them), but this time most of them were singing and the people in the back room were laughing at the songs. I walked across the yard to the hut marked 'Buffet'. It looked inviting for a bright light streamed from its door. Outside two drunks were quarrelling in front of a watching, sympathetic crowd, inside there was a little counter with a waitress behind it, and an older woman who was keeping her company. At four or five small tables sat some men and boys who were talking about the drunks and worrying about whether one of them wasn't going to the dogs. Earlier in the day he had very nearly hit the policeman.

I felt too tired to join in the conversation and opened a book. A pity to have done this as it marked me out. At once there were comments about people who were 'reserved', who read instead of talking. But I was too tired to talk. Some young boys at the corner table were discussing their courses in biology. They had been doing jobs in the country and were now going back to town. The smallest and best dressed among them pulled a wad of money from his pocket and treated the others to portions of fish. A woman remarked that boys earned too much. I ate a slice of black bread with ten grams of cheese which cost a rouble and bought five sweets for thirty-five kopecks, but they were nasty. A tall young man showed off his gloves, he had bought them a year ago, the waitress examined them with interest and he offered to sell them to her for 150 roubles. He was also proud of his coat; 'they' had given it to him for the holiday. Another man holding a suitcase and with a parcel hung by string over his shoulder came in, a little tipsy. He asked the way to a village, and bought a drink remarking: 'Funny how drink draws me.'

I began to feel more and more isolated by my 'reserve' so I went back to the station waiting-room. The boys from the buffet came in and crowded round the ticket office worrying about the chances of getting on to the train. Tickets were not sold until an hour before it arrived. The clerk told them that the Tallin express was more expensive than the ordinary trains; nineteen roubles the fare would be. There were nine boys and they hadn't enough money, so some would have to wait for the slow train which wouldn't come in till four.

When I asked for my ticket the clerk said she didn't yet know if there would be room on the train. However I 'insisted', saying I must be in Leningrad because of my job and that I had a reservation on a plane for Moscow which I would miss if I did not get on the Tallin express. Within a few minutes I was given the ticket: 'But it's for the "general" carriage,' the clerk said. I did not ask for explanations and hoped that someone would show me which the 'general' carriage was.

The train arrived late, but it was an altogether bigger, newer, smarter train than the one from Gatchina. Above where the luggage racks usually are were shelves on which people were sleeping.

I sat down hoping to sleep, but a man with a vaguely familiar face took the seat opposite me and after a few moments said: 'So you got the bus back.' I realised then that he was the man who had sat opposite me in the bus going to Redkino and was suddenly convinced I'd been mistaken all the time: I had been followed, after all, and now perhaps something was going to happen to me. But what? I risked nothing except an interesting detention. I said, 'Yes.' He told me he had been to a village farther on; I wondered if he had been driven back by car or if he had been on my return bus without my having noticed him.

He said he was an engineer and that he had to travel 'all over the region'. He had spent fifteen years in the army – been in the siege of

Leningrad and all the way to Berlin. 'In Leningrad I commanded . . .'
But I meant to show him that, at any rate, I was not collecting information and interrupted: 'You know I am a foreigner.' 'I wondered if you
were.' I explained why I was in Russia. He thought a little, then said:
'And you visited your birthplace?' 'Yes.' Perhaps because I was tired,
or because he looked so pleased at having guessed right, I felt happy;
either I was wrong in thinking he was a 'tail' or there was nothing
to do except wait and be as simple as possible. I also realised, that when
one is inside the country, everything seems different. From outside
one thinks with horror of 'disappearing'. But 'inside' people have this
or that happen to them and that's that.

The man was in his late thirties, big, sturdy, well-dressed but with
an unshaven face, probably well off but certainly unpolished.

I said I had not realised how much people around here had suffered
during the war and he talked about the siege of Leningrad: 'You
walked along the street and it was quite empty, only one or two
people perhaps.' Then he talked about Berlin and the Germans, but
not venomously. He goes to Poland and to Finland, where he used to
have a dacha; now, if he had time he would build one outside Leningrad; credit is available, but he has no free time. His daughter aged
twelve is at a school of music; it sounded rather like the ballet school:
they start at ten and go on for eight years, doing general lessons and at
the same time beginning to specialise. There is a lot of competition, he
paid 400 roubles for a single lesson to make sure the child would get in.
Now she already makes some money giving performances at 150
roubles a time. He told me proudly that she was booked up all through
the holidays. In the end he asked me to get him a concert accordion
for her: they were very expensive in the USSR he said, about 6,000
roubles. 'You can send things from abroad now,' he told me, 'the
money goes through the general trade agreements.' I took down his
name and his address. By then I was quite reassured but the conversation was uninteresting – too public anyhow, and with the
better dressed sort of people all round, and this man was happily part
of the machine, moving smoothly and making machine sounds.

There were some flirting couples with an old-fashioned look
behind me; the men paying compliments and the girls putting them in
their place; a storyteller was keeping the people in fits of laughter, but
I was too far to hear his tales.

I offered the engineer some remarks about England but he was incurious.

LENINGRAD

Having started at 1.45 am and done 100 kilometres, we got in at 4.20 am. The engineer said he would see me to the Astoria; I replied I would take a taxi, but we couldn't find one.

We stood in the street which was growing lighter, watching the occasional Zim or Pobeda swishing past. Then the first bus trundled over the bridge and we decided to take it. It was crowded. The engineer got off when I did near St Isaac's and walked with me to the turning to the hotel. I thought that, after all, he was a kind man. My clothes were sodden, I was chattering with cold and I had run out of powder long ago – so I was no ornament to him.

St Isaac's Square was deserted and the front door of the Astoria locked. I tried a side door where two women were sitting in a lobby, they said I must knock on the front door, then the night porter would have to open it. He opened, apologetically and incuriously, and I went up to bed and warmth, but I couldn't sleep.

I was booked for the afternoon plane to Moscow but asked for a car for 10.30 so that I could see more of the town before I left. When it arrived, I gave the chauffeur a list of places I wanted to look at. Leontina approved, and when she saw me, merely said: 'So you're back.'

Up Rossi Street we went to the old Alexandrovsky Theatre, the street and the exquisitely proportioned theatre smart in its yellow stucco. The Alexandrovsky Garden was snowy, stark, bare, with the Bronze Horseman silhouetted on one side and the dark mass of the St Isaac on the other. I got out and followed the paths where I played as a child and Rikarna had taught me to read by writing with her umbrella in the sand. I recognised the garden, but I realised that what was moving was not to recover the little scenes I remembered from my childhood, but to discover all this grave beauty – to see what I saw when very small without being aware of it.

The taxi took us over the river to the old Stock Exchange, now a naval museum, stockily handsome, then past the Peter and Paul Fortress and over another bridge. Colour is intrinsic to the beauty of Leningrad, the grey of the sky and the stone, the black and white of the stone and the snow, the gold and the bronze and the green of the sky and of the water, the hardly perceptible colours that are both muted and intense, give life to all of it. I stopped at the Cathedral which is 'in use' and went in past the beggars. The main church is on the first floor, it was packed to bursting point for a Solemn Mass. Most of the congregation were old or middle-aged women in grey shawls, but some were younger and some well dressed and there was a sprinkling of both very old and very young. I asked a smart looking woman in her forties if it is a feast day. She was shocked that I didn't know it was the feast of Our Lady of Kazan. I explained I was not an Orthodox. She went on more warmly:

'Well, it is a great popular feast day.'

I edged forward through the almost solid crowd. All the faces seemed on the point of tears. The Mass was ending. I walked along with the crowd, past old women sitting impassively on the stairs and people stopping to cross themselves or kiss the ikons (none of the ikons any longer had precious stones or gold, but in some you could see where the stones had been). Though there was no Mass being said, the crypt was almost as crowded as the church. Here, some priests were leading prayers to which the people chanted the responses. A tall young priest with an open, spiritual face looked like a sixteenth-century Russian. I bought two candles (they were the thinnest of brown wax tapers and of differing sizes and cost three to ten roubles each). I put them up on a big holder – there are many candles around the ikons. Outside the church women were selling wax flower garlands to hang around the ikons and I bought one for forty roubles.

We went on to the Smolny, now a seat of government, it can only be visited by appointment. The low classical house adjoins the fairy disarray of the domed monastery, which is part empty, part occupied by offices and not completely restored.

I asked the chauffeur about religion but he was unforthcoming and only said there was religious freedom. I stopped in front of another church, almost as big, and almost as crowded as the Cathedral; the service was finishing. There were more men here, some in uniform. At the back, where it was less crowded, women – mothers and grannies – were showing small children the ikons and explaining them. Since from seven onwards each of these attentive children will be taught to hate everything to do with religion, what could these women be feeling? No wonder they looked as if they were taking great trouble. It occurred to me that the grannies have borne Russia on their shoulders, tearful, tough, unbeatable old things.

On our way back we stopped at the Gostiny Dvor, this was a disappointment. I remembered it on a snowy evening going there with mother in her sables, the light and the luxury. But now the same shops inside the gallery looked as if they could never have sold anything but these few, shoddy, hideous goods.

I returned to the taxi and found the chauffeur reading a book which he tucked away when he saw me. I asked what it was, he showed it to me – *The Conspirators*, a huge, grey-paged spy story about 'German plots against the USSR'.

At lunch at the Astoria I heard two men talking at a table behind me and glanced back. Both were in their forties, one, who seemed to have come up from the provinces, looked like a neat businessman, the other was in a uniform of some kind. 'All the same,' said the businessman, 'they did manage to have a hotel like this in the days of private ownership.' The other replied. 'But now it's up to first class standards.' I felt furiously indignant as I chewed the horrid food. 'What *was* good in the old days,' went on the one in uniform, 'was their banking system. You put your money in the bank and it was safe, and nobody interfered with it.' Then they discussed the relative advantages of socialism and capitalism but after a while lowered their voices: I had not turned round again but perhaps my ears looked attentive?

As I went up in the lift, alone with another woman, she looked with interest at the wax garland hanging over my arm and asked where I got it and how much I had paid. She said it was pretty and that the price was right, then, lowering her voice, added: 'I make them myself.' She asked what I would do with it; I said I'd take it home to England. 'You'll keep it in your house?' I think she wanted to know if I had an ikon.

The young Intourist chauffeur who drove me to the airport was the first really convincing enthusiast I had met. He too had lost relations who died of hunger in the siege, but what was foremost in his mind was the rebuilding. 'Look at the new houses, good and well planned all through, with proper yards, not slummy wells. Whole new quarters are going up and there is a new law, that Leningrad should have a belt of fruit trees round it. Groups of young people and schoolchildren go out on Sundays and plant trees' (as in Israel, I thought). He pointed out the Victory Park planted in honour of those who are twice Heroes. I asked him if he were a Party man, he said no, it would mean too much work. I then inquired about the churches I had seen this morning – were they 'working'? 'Yes,' he said, 'there are many believers.' He himself went to church. 'It makes no difference in work – between believers and unbelievers.' A touching boy. He almost had tears in his eyes when he was talking about the trees.

At the airport a smooth handsome Intourist character took me to an empty suite which was very smart indeed. Two smallish rooms all in pale blue velvet with gold and cut glass. Suddenly I became extremely nervous – had they caught up with my visit to Redkino? He put on the wireless and twiddled the knobs (perhaps to drown my cries?) but, in fact, he was only showing me that he could get London. He told me there was some trouble about my luggage, another jolt, but it proved to be only that, now that it was not being weighed together with Billy's discreet baggage, it was overweight. In an excess of courtesy, he asked an attendant to bring in both the luggage and the weighing machine. The fee for overweight was very small but, even so, he wangled that I shouldn't pay it, saying he knew foreigners had a hard time with their exchange, which made everything seem very expensive to them. For Russians he argued prices were not high. He is paid 1,600 roubles a month and on that he can afford 'things foreigners can't have.' Food is cheap in 'dining-rooms' – five roubles for lunch – the dining-rooms belong to institutions but are open to the public. Food is twice as expensive in restaurants and three times in first class hotels.

At the airfield, where the passengers were showing their tickets to the woman official, he led me through and I wandered off to the plane in advance of the rest. By now I was so tired that I slept during the whole journey.

MOSCOW

At Moscow airport the local Intourist man and the Zim chauffeur went into consultation: rehearsals of the parades were going on and the centre of the town might well be roped off. '*Nichevo*,' I said, 'You can drop me off anywhere and bring my luggage when you can.' I felt carefree, Russian and sleepy. But the chauffeur replied: 'Perhaps we'll manage,' and he did. The cordon began some blocks from the hotel, he got out of the car and had a 'talk with the lieutenant'. We were stopped again twice but each time he went off and came back saying he had 'talked it over with the lieutenant' and he ended by swishing round into the square, scattering soldiers who broke their ranks to run out of our way, finally he drew up like a troika at the front entrance of the hotel.

I woke up too late to go to church and settled down to what turned out to be a morning of telephoning. As usual, Intourist wouldn't give numbers and took a long time getting calls, most of which had to be repeated later when the heads of the institutions had arrived. All this, and ordering lunch upstairs in advance so that it should not take too long to arrive, and booking my plane for the following Friday took me till 1.30. It now seemed that I wouldn't be able to see any of the people I was supposed to see: Surkov, the Secretary of the Union of Writers is on holiday (but I am to see Apletin); Chakovsky, the editor of Foreign Literature is on holiday (but I can see Dangulov); Riurikov (who works on the Literary Gazette) has been replaced by Kochetov who is not there on Saturday; Professor Belza (musicologist) does not exist at the Moscow University and is unknown to them; Chernyshev, an architect, is puzzled though amiable, inquires into my Russian and will see me.

'Foreign Literature' has small offices in a wing of The Writers' House. Dangulov, the editor, is thirtyish and bright. He called in two women editors. The atmosphere was almost as cosy as at the Creative Art publishers in Leningrad. The magazine is a monthly and reviews theatre and art as well as books. It is going to publish translations of Mauriac, Caldwell, Hemingway, Sartre. They asked my advice about Dylan Thomas, Graham Greene (his stories), plays by Sean O'Casey, John Lehmann's memoirs, they would like other literary memoirs, and unpublished letters by Shaw and Galsworthy and an article on the new production of Shakespeare. Are Balchin's later books (after *Small Back Room*) too psychological, they ask? They have looked at T. S. Eliot and found him 'really too decadent'. They suggested Russian books for us.

I left late for my appointment with Chernyshev and, having refused the car they offered, waited anxiously for the Intourist one which arrived late and the driver couldn't find the House of Architects.

It is a vast, tomb-like monstrosity. A long perch of a woman met me in the hall, where I left my coat and was surprised that I was alone (Comrade Chernyshev was expecting English *visitors*), but she was not at all surprised that I was three-quarters of an hour late!, Chernyshev, an avuncular *homme sérieux*, occupied a huge, lofty, sombre office with velvet curtains drawn. I was impressed at his seeing me alone, 'You would like to know about our architectural trends? We did Constructionism in the twenties, but the materials were bad and the colours ugly, so people got fed up with it. Then we went in for neo-classicism, now people don't like that either. It is a difficult problem to find a style which combines simplicity and economy with dignity and tradition.' He looked depressed. Architectural books, he told me, were published by the Academy of Architects and the Architecture and Building Press. He rang up the head of the Press and arranged an appointment for me 'after the holiday'; like the others, he explained on the telephone to his colleagues that it is 'all right' my speaking Russian.

By now I was again late and rushed back to the Writers' Union. Apletin, the head of the Foreign Commission, received me accompanied by a young, clever-looking, Jewish girl who is his English reader and knows a fair amount about English literature. It was near closing time and the eve of the three-day holiday, but I was tempted to hurry in any case, as when I asked Apletin about 'new trends' in Soviet literature, he lost his temper: 'There are no new trends,' he said. 'It's all an invention of certain people.' I apologised for troubling him at an inconvenient time and said I would ring up on Wednesday if I were still in Moscow. He said they might try to arrange for me to meet a writer. My tentative suggestion that I should talk over suitable English books with the girl on Wednesday morning went over badly.

I dined hastily, not bothering to change, and, not having Billy's technique, arrived at the Bolshoi after the last bell. The attendant showed me into a box where people who come late can see the remaining part of the first act. In front of me were two women whom I took for foreigners, as they had long diamond earrings and were wearing not only elegant dresses but wearing them in a manner that went with them. They proved, however, to be Russians. The ballet was a new production of *Swan Lake* with Plisetskaya and I found it lovely. Spacious sets, uncrowded, well-organised colours and Plisetskaya beautiful and perfect – tender as the white swan and excellently wicked as the black one. The court scene was Renaissance and a little heavy, the lake water more real than ever and the swans again applauded. All the same, the enchantment was there.

I took a car to go to the Yelokhovsky Cathedral. It was a long way off and I talked about religion to the driver who was delighted to know that I went to church. He too is a believer, and so is his wife. This morning he had been to a requiem for his sister-in-law. Their son is in the Komsomol, but they don't interfere with each other's ideas. He said there had been indignation at the revival of anti-religious propaganda and that Khrushchev had mitigated it. People always went to church, he said, not just since the war. Perhaps there was a revival during the war but religious freedom came gradually. At one time things were very bad, there was persecution, provocation, mockery, but 'today people aren't allowed to mock'. No new churches were being built, but of those that had been restored some have been put back into use. He thought there were thirty in Moscow, but the people wanted, and asked for, many more. 'Even Party members go to church, though it isn't good for their career. They marry in church. It's more difficult about funerals for the Party gives them a Party funeral, but their relations say prayers and hold services for them and some Party members even ask for Masses in their wills. Officers too go to church, but usually not to the Solemn Mass.' During the Revolution, he went on, many churches were destroyed, some of great beauty and historical value – 'They were blown up deliberately. But when Lenin heard of it he was angry; it was that that made him move the Government to Moscow – so that he could be on the spot and stop it.'(!)

When we got to the Cathedral the Mass was nearly over, but there were still a lot of people praying. The chauffeur took me across the road drowned in melting snow, he was sorry I had started so late and suggested that perhaps I could come to the afternoon service, then the nuns would show me around. The crowd was much the same sort as in Leningrad: some men and among them some soldiers and many small children. On the way from the Cathedral to lunch the driver pointed out some disused churches and places where no trace of a church that had been blown up remained. He said he too was once in the Komsomol and an unbeliever, but 'a man has to have faith'. He remembered what he had been taught as a child. I asked him if it was a disadvantage to him in his work. 'Not at all,' he replied, 'believers are even more trusted because they are known to have a conscience.'

In the afternoon I went to Ostankino. It is an incredible place, looking from outside like a Regency villa, but built entirely of wood, as a theatre and for parties, by a Prince Sheremetyev. He married a serf, who was an actress. Next to it is a church, painted and domed. As I had arrived after the ticket office had closed it looked as if I should not be able to get in. But two women who had just been round told me I must *insist*. I did just this and was successful. There are beautiful parquets and crystal chandeliers, also wooden chandeliers, faked to look like bronze which are at least curious, but all in all the proportions are crushing and there is a hideous excess of richness. No wonder it is difficult for the Russians to find a style! Nevertheless, the theatre itself has an enchantment, with its movable pillars and intimate auditorium. But by the time we came to Prince Sheremetyev's colossal den, I hardly needed the propaganda posters and the map of the Meshchersky estates spread over half Russia to feel, they must have needed a special needle's eye.

It was the 'eve of the holiday' and everyone told me 'our people are having a gay time.' So I went into the streets to observe them. They did not look gay, nor even very leisurely, more like a Saturday afternoon crowd in a London shopping district, though there was an occasional family out for a walk with a child, and occasional drunks. I went into GUM, the big universal store in Red Square; it was crowded, obviously a centre of attraction. A banner read 'Buy presents for the holiday' and the present shop was packed with a solid row of people window-shopping in front of the painted boxes.

After dinner I went out again. The shops were closed, the same uninspired crowds were about but thicker now, and there were more drunks. One group of young people was following a boy with a harmonica – perhaps they at least had been dancing. The general effect was neither grave nor gay nor even animated, somehow neutral. A workman of about thirty asked: 'You are out for a walk?' and fell in step with me. 'Yes,' I said, 'and you?' – 'I too, it's nice to get a breath of fresh air.' We talked a little. I tried to think of a way of spending an instructive evening with him, but it was definitely a 'pick-up' and Rikarna's upbringing was too strong. In the dark and snow, muffled in my good fur coat and black shawl, I looked relatively smart and probably of an indistinguishable age. As I left him, regretfully, two women were saying: 'All that fuss about the holiday, it's only an expense.' In front of the hotel, a van directed a sizzling searchlight at the portraits of the leaders across the square.

The Intourist bureau, after saying it was too late to get a place for me to see the parade and that I could very well watch it from the balcony on the first floor of the hotel, ended by presenting me with a ticket for a Red Square 'tribune'. I started off at 9.15, wandering across the Manège Square with some straggling groups. The Square itself was cordoned off and there were double cordons at the entrance to the Red Square. The guards misdirected me and I walked all round the GUM side, lined with 'tribunes' and rows of MVD, past the Execution Place, beautifully decorated with bunting and red gauze fluttering up representing a flame (last night it was lit up and looked very realistic) till I came to the front of St Basil's and to a 'tribune' next but one to the Mausoleum. There were no seats anywhere, but the crowd was so thick that it held us up. The weather was fine, almost warm, with sunny patches. Around me there were French, Chinese and some Soviet citizens. A tall Russian next to me said good-humouredly: 'Why don't you push through to the front?' A woman came from behind and joined me; he encouraged both of us: 'Go on, push on, like women.' We did so with general approval. Children were shoved through or handed over and put in the front of the tribune; only a solemn Pioneer girl and boy behind me refused to budge. Some yards in front of us I saw a row of MVD and farther on detachments of troops. I asked who got tickets for the tribunes, a woman replied that it depended on your service and your rank.

By now the members of the Government had inconspicuously assembled on the Mausoleum. Zhukov[27] drove out of the Spassky Gate, standing up in his jeep and I wondered how he managed not to fall. There was some faint but friendly-sounding clapping. A General in another jeep drove towards him from the Manège side, and followed him as he inspected the troops, they went from regiment to regiment in both squares. Zhukov stopped in front of each battalion and shouted something ('He's saying good morning' my neighbour told me), and the troops shouted '*Zdravia zhelayem*'[28] in the good old style, followed by something not understandable and hurrah. Then Zhukov went up to the Mausoleum and made a brief speech in a clear, deliberate style. His voice carried by the loudspeakers echoed so that each word was sounded twice – it might almost have been deliberate as the effect was curiously emphatic. He talked about industry, the relaxation of international tension – though some people still resist peace – and ended on a hurrah, echoed by the troops and followed immediately by the band playing, by salvoes, and by the march past.

It was a pretty sight, the decorations were plentiful and bright, the perfect timing of Zhukov's entry as the Kremlin bell tolled ten, the echoing shouts, the guns, the crescendo rumble of the parade deepening to artillery fire, the clatter of tanks and the roar of flights of planes in formation – all this should have been stirring, and must have been in wartime, but now the crowd wedged round me was like pastry that wouldn't rise. Some regiments were clapped, so were the cadets of the Zhukovsky Academy, but the sound was faint, possibly the space was too vast to give it its proper value.

The military parade didn't last long. Then there was a march past of various clubs of athletes, looking charming with flags representing different sports, borne aloft by some of the athletes on bicycles, others in ski suits, with snowballs. All this ended a little before eleven and then the 'demonstrations' started. The whole city seemed to pour past between the MVD cordons: districts, industries, all with banners, slogans, bright bouquets of paper flowers and people on the outer edge of the stream looking round smiling and waving. But by now the tribunes were emptying fast and some women behind me remarked: 'It's a shame, it happens every time, as soon as the demonstrations start, the tribunes empty.' I too walked off past St Basil's towards the river, along the raised footpath above the demonstrators who were streaming away, a little more loosely now. Many people were strolling slowly in the mild sunshine. Two middle-aged men wearing good coats and fur hats were, it seemed, worried journalists. One said: 'They force the pace. It's all very well for Ehrenburg to push us along. But all this is just a little NEP[29] to butter up the foreigners.'

At each street crossing I argued amiably with the police and the

MVD until finally, after showing my pass, I was let through and reached the hotel. On the balcony of the first floor, a dozen foreign delegations were shouting slogans and waving with frenzied enthusiasm – this was the first spontaneous jollity I had seen. The demonstrators filed past with their everyday faces, but turned to wave when they heard the roars of the delegations. I stood for a little while on the balcony, in wonder and disgust. In disgust at these frivolous foreigners, in wonder that the splendid picture did not move me. From my balcony, the demonstrations were a scarlet river of banners moving in the sunlight towards the Red Square with St Basil's in the distance.

At lunch, in the dining-room with the net curtains decorously drawn so that the demonstrators were invisible, I was joined by a Belgian businessman and a drunken Syrian who was travelling de luxe for pleasure. Our meal took a long time.

The Belgian was sadly frustrated by the slowness of Soviet business methods. 'How are you to know whether they are in earnest or not? Nobody will see you except in solemn groups, and everything has to be explained all over again to the next committee. All the same contracts, if they come off, are so big that it is worth trying.' The Syrian didn't like his food and brawled with the patient waitress. We finished about 3.30 and I had a short rest before going to tea with Ehrenburg.

He received me in his cosy study. He looked old, experienced, clever and worn. I asked him if I could meet Obraztsov[30] or would it be a nuisance for him; thus challenged, he gave me Obrazstov's telephone number and said he would mention me to him. We talked about Dostoevsky. 'The young people don't like him much,' said Ehrenburg, 'they read the early works, but *The Possessed* is really too remote and will not be included in the reprint; they read the *Karamazovs* but skip some chapters, for instance, those on Zosima.' I asked if they lacked an inner life. He replied, 'No, if they did they wouldn't read Tolstoy, but Dostoevsky's philosophy of suffering seems forced to them. It's different for our generation.' Talking of rising Soviet authors, Ehrenburg regretted that they left all their other occupations for the sake of art too early – in fact as soon as they have brought off a moderately successful first novel – say 45,000 copies. The temptation to security divorced them from life. He, Ehrenburg, was kept busy with public works. 'Unsuccessful authors eke out their living with work for the cinema and the radio. A moderately successful first novel brings

in, say 60,000 roubles – and on that the author can live modestly for
eighteen months and write his next book. An unknown author gets
2,000 a sheet, an established one as much as 4,000.' I was startled at
Ehrenburg's unawareness of, or deliberate ignoring of, the more usual
standards of life.

On the way home I had another look at the crowds. This time they
seemed gayer and more relaxed. When I reached the hotel I went to
bed, for a cold that had been hanging over me was now beginning to
make me feel ill. It had been a frustrating day.

After breakfast I took the electric train to Zagorsk and walked up the
hill to the monastery;[31] inside the gates are lovely houses and churches.
I went into the first church. A weekday service was going on, there
were a lot of candles and a great crowd. I saw many men and young
people and many young monks. A little server shooed me away with
horror from the sacristy door saying women were not allowed in
there; he called a priest. I explained I was a foreigner and asked to talk
to someone. The priest went off to consult 'authority' and when he
came back told me if I wished to talk to someone I would have to have
a letter from the Patriarchate in Moscow: they were very glad to talk
to delegations but . . . I said I wasn't a delegation but I saw their point!
I went into another smaller church with golden domes; this too was
crowded and a young priest was leading the prayers. I put up a candle
and as it is difficult to reach the holder, because of the crowd, people at
the back asked me to put theirs up for them. I stayed a long time in
that church. More than the others, in Moscow and Leningrad, it had
an atmosphere of devotion and suffering. Afterwards I wandered round
the enclosure but I didn't go to the museum; with its policeman outside and its notices it didn't attract me.

Back in Moscow I went to the Tretyakov Gallery[32] and raced,
under the shocked eyes of the attendants of whom I asked the way, to
the two end rooms to see the ikons: some beautiful huge Rublevs, including the three angels and other, earlier and later primitives. Notices
on the walls informed visitors that these pictures are displayed to show
the vitality of the beginnings of Russian painting, which has a historical interest, and expresses human sentiments such as pity and the
love of mothers and children. Also it already shows the beginnings of
that realism which came to its triumphant climax in the nineteenth

century! There were not many people in these rooms, a few students, a couple of girls talking about the pictures with curiosity, an oldish couple on an educational outing. It struck me that the tone of the notices was exactly that of Rikarna who saw the history of painting as just like the progress of pupils at a gymnasium – from pathetic scribbles to the capacity, attained in the eighth class, to draw things just as they really are. I glanced through the other rooms. Probably some of the pictures would look well in a different sort of historical gallery. Some are painted realistically but with a little freedom. The latest prize pictures are as 'Millais' as ever though more dramatic and include the one of Stalin dreamily surveying fields and tractors, a print of which we had seen at the airport when we arrived. But there were other recent prize-winning objects, rococo china figures and groups; they were of the utmost exuberance and were entirely after my heart.

I changed for the theatre but as my cold was bad and I shivered as soon as I took off my Arctic clothes, I ordered dinner in my room. The play was Mayakovsky's *Bed Bug* at the 'Satirical' Theatre which is the only one that attracts an intellectual audience, and when I got there I found them alive, excited, and almost like an audience at an art theatre anywhere else in the world. The play and its production, though the farce is overdone, fascinated me. It starts during the NEP period. A young man, Prisypkin, incorrigibly Russian in his weakness, abandons his working-class girl friend to marry into a *nouveau riche* family. He learns manners from an elegant Diaghilev type who is his best man. At the wedding breakfast there is a sudden panic when two policemen come in, but they are only offering congratulations and join the feast by the end of which everyone is dead drunk. Then there is a brilliant cinema transition which shows that the house was burnt down. The next act is in the 1960s when the brave new world has been achieved, with no love making, no germs, and everybody wearing plastic dresses. The Russian's body is found and resuscitated out of scientific curiosity. It is now that his tragedy begins: he cannot bear the existing aseptic society, he wants something to cheer his soul – vodka, love, cosiness. His only friend is a bed bug which has accidentally been resuscitated with him. He carries within him a virus dangerous to the new society, the plastic students are infected and begin to sing romances and dream of love. He and the bed bug end happily as exhibits at the Zoo, Prisypkin in bed and swigging vodka. For all its savagery against the bed bug, the meaning of the play, emphasised by the production, is at least ambiguous. My sympathy was with the bed bug and Prisypkin.

Even my cold was improved by this intellectual stimulus and I went to bed with happy thoughts about the revival of the twenties. Blok's[33] work reprinted in editions of 100,000 and gone in a day, and this brilliant, anything but socialist-realist, production of the *Bed Bug*.

I spent the morning at the Architectural Press in a pleasantly stuffy, almost Dickensian office, where I was seen by the usual committee of four. The firm publishes 600 titles a year and ten monthly magazines. The books are depressingly grey and the publishers agreed that printing standards had gone down. The Chairman remarked, when I asked if they do much colour reproduction, 'You [in the West] have to compete for the reader's attention.' The implication being that they have a captive, famished readership.

Obraztsov, whom I had rung up the day before had offered me a choice of either coming to his theatre or to his flat at seven. I chose the theatre.

He is pleasant in an untidy, bohemian way, likes England and has written an essay about his journey there which has been a great success here and which he would like to have published in England. We talked about Russian books for England and English books for Russia. I joked about Galsworthy. He found it hard to believe Galsworthy is not completely contemporary and asked me for a list of really up to date books. I said it was not easy to compile a list off the cuff but I would send him one. Some current books would not be suitable. 'What for instance?'

'A lot of Graham Greene.'

'Why?'

'He is a religious writer.'

'Well, that is certainly decadent.'

'We do not hold the same opinion on that subject,' but I agreed that certain of his books wouldn't do for the USSR.

'Do you mean he is something like Maeterlinck?' asked Obraztsov. What he doesn't like about Western Europe is its traditionalism.

'You can't go forward if you're looking back. America is different.' I said I had the impression that Russians didn't much like the Americans though they were impressed by them. He exclaimed at once:

'No, we like the English much better. But traditionalism means imperialism.' I pointed out that no other country has given up their colonies with England's good grace. He looked sheepish.

He gave me his book and we parted on the best of terms and I am to get in touch with Mezhkniga about his other books, *My Profession* and *The Traditional Theatre of China*.

After lunch I went to the Patriarchate. I had called there the day before but the only official visible told me I should go to Zagorsk first, or else to the Novodevichi Monastery where the Patriarchate had its publishing office. He was obviously principally concerned to get me off his hands. Finally he told me to come back the next day when there would be someone else there.

The Patriarchate seems to consist of two gloomy houses on either side of a yard, behind a church. I found the same official there, he called another who asked me to wait and went off and had a long conversation with an unattractively smart young priest. This official returned, he was a layman and repeated all the usual line about freedom of religion. I asked if this applied to teaching children and he said yes: parents teach them and school teachers no longer interfere, even a priest can teach children when he visits his parishioners. I began to feel impatient, sure he wasn't going to tell me anything I could be certain was true. He seemed to sense this and suddenly I felt sorry for him, after all what was the poor man to do, how could he be sure I was not a *provocateur*.

I was to have a final meeting with Mezhkniga at eleven and before that I checked with the Intourist office to make sure that they had my reservation for the plane to London for the next day. They had not the least idea and wouldn't know till the evening.

At the Department of Foreign Trade Korovina met me at the door with the same polite and patient smile, and took me to Zmeul's office, the talk was rather more businesslike, now that I knew more about Russian books. And they ended up by showing me a mountain of books that they are going to send me. So friendly were they that our leave-taking was almost human.

By now I had glanced through Obraztsov's book and had asked to see him again to discuss it with him, so I went back to his theatre. Most of what he writes is true and fair, I told him this, but asked how

In Corfu

Still Life

he could write about the East End slums without mentioning the new
buildings that were going up, and told him that he put wages so low
that, according to him, a workman's wife can only afford one dress a
year. He said that was what English people had shown and told him.
I believed him and said I wished he had seen more and different
people and more things. He laughed and told me that the people he
saw were English and they must have been patriots, so it was impossible that they should have deceived him about such things. I said
all the same he hadn't seen enough and told him that most English
workers live well and certainly better than the Russians. He said
seriously: 'Yes, but we had to start farther back.' There we could
agree. I explained that the reason why I was arguing about his book
was that it is much fairer than most, so it was a pity it should be spoilt
by inaccuracies. He asked me what I thought of some other passages
e.g. about street walkers, Americans in Grosvenor Square, and a piece
he would have liked to put in about the Queen being a simple woman
in private life and only a fairytale princess on State occasions. When I
said that all that was true, he seemed to accept my good faith about the
rest. I said, 'It's a pity so little is known about England in Russia.' He
replied, 'It is nothing to the ignorance of foreigners about Russia: I've
been asked if it were possible that I had only one wife and had lived
with her twenty years.' We agreed that a competition in ignorance
might well be held.

On the way out Obraztsov pulled me by the arm into the theatre.
They were rehearsing *Konyok Gorbunok*[34] and had reached the trans-
formation scene – when the little horse and the rider fly off into the
clouds. The set was lovely and Obraztsov talking about his theatre was
enchanting.

But, back at the hotel, I realised that my cold was worse than any
cold I have ever had and that my hot room felt like a catafalque.

All the same later I went shopping for souvenirs off the Petrovka –
but here I saw only the same Palekh boxes and painted spoons as at
GUM. The embroideries were not worth looking at, and the little
secondhand shops had nothing but white elephants. When I got back
the Intourist bureau announced that I had a reservation, but they would
neither reserve a room for me in Helsinki nor send a cable to Ralph at
my expense.

That evening I ended up at a Galsworthy play, *The Skin Game*.

The butler had side whiskers and wore a brown suit, and called the lady of the house 'Missis', the *ingénue* was out of Turgenev, and the *femme fatale* was splendid in rivers of satin and lace. The costumes, however, did not claim to be contemporary – though whether the audience realised this was another matter, anyway they loved it, particularly the *femme fatale*.

The journey, until I reached the comfort of Sweden, was blotted from my mind by cold, darkness, sleet, fatigue and my cold, all I recall is that the polite Intourist man at Leningrad airport was more polite than ever and had to go on entertaining me for a very long time, because the plane was waiting for news of the fog in Finland.

Helsinki was unbelievably neat and cosy. A 'boy-scouting' young man, who liked to be helpful to foreigners, showed me the way to Stockman's store and then gave me tea. But, because of a congress, there was no room to be had in the town. However, the clerk at the airport, unbelievably, telephoned Stockholm without any fuss and that night I slept in the luxury of a room that was neither too large nor too small.

Second Journey to Russia
Spring 1956

MOSCOW, RYAZAN, LENINGRAD,
VLADIMIR, SUZDAL

Since her first visit in 1955 the political situation and the mood of the country had been transformed. Early in 1956, at the Twentieth Party Congress, Khrushchev had come out with his Secret Speech exposing Stalin's crimes, which had at once been widely and quietly publicised (though never formally published) throughout the land. He had also done a great deal to remove the ever-present fear of war, deliberately fostered by Stalin, and to start bringing the Soviet Union into uneasy communion with the West, under the general heading of co-existence. In May 1956 the country was still in a state of shock after the traumatic experience of the de-Stalinisation. But some of the dams were down, and already the more intelligent and articulate, particularly among the young, were in a state of ferment, often behaving recklessly, especially in conversation with foreigners, for all the world as though the Terror, so recently past, had never existed. It was a mood which, spreading, was to lead to the Polish defiance and the Hungarian uprising later that year. But, with all this, the Soviet bureaucracy, as Manya was to find, clung stubbornly to its old habits of evasiveness, procrastination and suspicion.

This time Manya went to Russia for a specific purpose, to negotiate for a book on the Russian ballet; it was to be heavily illustrated with photographs by Baron. The texts were to be written by Russian experts and translated, the book would be manufactured in England and the Russians would buy sheets for their market. Baron meanwhile waited in London to receive his visa should the project be approved by the Soviet authorities. The initial correspondence had suggested that they liked the plan.

We flew up into clouds then, through a rift, we saw the frozen sea, its ice thinning, bluish, pockmarked with thaw, rough as though the waves had frozen instantly, farther on dark islands and the brownish ice of lakes was sometimes surrounded by black water. Clouds again, then an expanse of empty white land ending in mist and as we were coming down to Helsinki I saw the trim cottages and the lace of the birch trees, the well-kept woods of red birches and dark firs.

The aerodrome at Helsinki is very unlike a Western one, so much more country all round and the woods starting immediately outside the airfield; the snow was still lying under the trees, and above us was my childhood-familiar sun most mild, pink, mist-wrapped in a milky sky.

On the plane to Moscow I was surrounded by Arabic-speaking delegates; they had a neat, mouse-faced leader and among them was a raw, hot-eyed peasant boy. I remembered enough Arabic to ask them where they came from. 'From Syria,' they said. At 7.30 pm the sky was a tender, greenish-blue with clouds that were only just pink, but by eight o'clock it became dark and only the dim, widely scattered lights of villages showed up.

MOSCOW

A prosperous-looking American helped me with my hand luggage. He was met by Russians, including one with a lean sophisticated face. I found out later the American was Michael Todd, the Hollywood super-producer, and the Russian, Alexandrov, in charge of films at the Ministry of Culture. The Syrians stood in a bunch in the waiting-room round a Russian girl with a Mongolian face who spoke Arabic with a Russian accent. A microphone was brought in and they all spoke into it, each saying (in Arabic) that he was a Moslem and how delighted he was to be in the Soviet Union. Another Intourist welcomer greeted an Australian delegation – mainly iron-haired women. At the Customs I was taken correctly in my turn, though Todd was obviously the guest of honour. The official licked his pencil and wrote down endlessly the numbers of my travellers' cheques. By now we had all been dealt with except for a Mongol guest who was still waiting. He spoke no European language and could not say how much money he had. 'Send him back to the Far East,' joked the customs man.

The driver of a cruising limousine which I took told me the winter had been hard. I asked about Stalin. He laughed. 'Now he's dead they beat him. But, after all, it was we who set him up, *all* of us.' He believed that Beria had got hold of Stalin by denouncing a murder plot, and that after that, Stalin wouldn't let anyone else near him, and bumped off those who approached him. Stalin, he said, knew nothing of the country except what he'd seen in films! This driver came from a kolkhoz where things had got a little better under Malenkov – quotas had been lowered, prices raised on produce sold, and the *kolkhozniks* were sometimes paid as much as three kilos of bread and twenty roubles per work day, of which they had to do 200-300. (A work day is not a day but a task, e.g. so much land to be ploughed by horse plough, and this may take less or more than the target.) The technicians who had been leaving the kolkhozes were now beginning to come back.

As we came into the town the driver pointed out that there were no Stalin portraits put up for the 1st of May. 'But,' he went on, 'the trouble wasn't only Stalin. The cult of personality had affected all of us. For instance, just fancy naming a kolkhoz "Molotov" – as though he owned it!' Then he turned on the foreign radio to demonstrate the noise of the jamming, in spite of which he had heard an English broadcast at 6 am. 'Does the jamming come from somewhere in Europe?' he asked. 'Perhaps from West Germany?' That it was being operated in the USSR had never occurred to him.

I slept late. Mezhkniga rang up to ask if I had been 'met' and hoped the room they had got me at the Metropole was all right. (The Metropole is more dilapidated but cosier than the National and I had a vast room with a bed alcove and a bath.)

By the time I had finished my telephoning, unpacked and come down it was nearly one o'clock.

A nice, sunny day and there were women selling little bunches of flowers. The fashions were less extreme than last year – shoulders less padded and hats less high. There were no portraits of Stalin in the streets, only of Lenin and Marx and some of the Praesidium with either Khrushchev or Khrushchev and Bulganin. There seemed overall to be fewer portraits and more bunting than last year. There were the usual slogans in honour of The People's Friendship and many about the Soviet people marching towards Communism. Over a cinema I saw Yugoslav posters and there were Chinese posters over the hotel.

I took a taxi to Mezhkniga. Here I was told that Zmeul (President) was away. His huge office was occupied by Ivanova, his *zamestitel* (second-in-command); with her was Belchenko, a handsome boy; the atmosphere very sunny and more relaxed than last time. Baron's photos which I showed them were much admired and our project liked, but I was told that whether or not it came off would depend on the Ministry of Culture, with whom they would get in touch. They would like to find a basis for contracts which would suit both sides. Then they spoke of other things. Could we publish children's books, fairytales, for instance? Could we pass to other publishers the books we didn't want, would we like an agency? All this while we had tea with lemon, waffles and chocolates.

Afterwards I asked about Stalin. A frozen moment followed. Then Ivanova shrugged and with a schoolgirlish smile said the principle of collective leadership had always been essential to the Party; there had only been a temporary deviation. Belchenko, looking hawklike, said the same and that the principle applied not only to central authority but all committees. They said opinion had been prepared gradually. Children and young people had had things explained to them by the Party agitators, who went on explaining until they were sure the children understood. Ivanova then remarked: 'You think our story a little thin?' I protested that I admired their leaders' courageous revelations . . . 'But you wonder where they were when all this was happening?' We laughed and agreed that mistakes could happen anywhere.

Sunday, and I went to church where I found the usual crowd, some men, some children and a number of diplomats.

At twelve o'clock I had an appointment with Bocharnikova at the Ballet School. There was great enthusiasm over the photos in the book I showed them. I was asked if I were seeing someone at the Ministry of Culture. I said that Mezhkniga was to arrange an appointment. Bocharnikova tried to speed things up by herself telephoning the Ministry but with no result so she gave me various numbers and advised me to go to the Ministry direct.

I rang Gradov who said that the Head of the Theatre Department would see me on Thursday. Then I asked whether he'd mind my trying to contact the Ministry of Culture; he said 'No.' I called Stepanov from the Bureau of Passes. He said why hadn't I rung earlier? It was three o'clock now, they were closing at four o'clock but all the same he would see me. He liked the idea of the project and the photos but did not see why they should buy sheets from us. They would want copies as gifts to show to the Institutes, though in a year's time, he added, they would be able to do as well themselves. He also did not see why Baron should be their guest.

Went to see Ehrenburg. He spoke of the change in the position of artists. Nowadays when Gerasimov painted a Munnings everyone protested. The difficulty, he said, was not Party control, but the bureaucratic barrier between the artist and society. It was being broken down but there was still much to do. The Russian public were more alive and more serious than the public in the West, and they were becoming more and more educated. Everyone felt deeply connected with the Party and with the people. 'If a man grows roses he feels it is for the country, whether or not he calls the rose "Socialist Construction" or "Beauty".' There had been a time when every rose had to be called 'Socialist Construction' or something of the sort, but this was no longer so. I should look at the new exhibitions and read Martynov's verses which had been recently published. This poet had been writing for eleven years, but had been unpublished, during this time he had circulated his poems in typescript. He ran a study circle at a factory and read his verses to its members. Finally a demand had been created. Here was a great difference between the Soviet Union and the West: their public was alive, co-operative and being educated.

As to political change – nobody here wanted capitalism or Tsarism; the conditions for such régimes didn't exist. The people criticised this thing or that but within the Party framework.

I asked if a writer could defend religious themes. 'There are no such writers,' he said. 'If a young man wanted to write that sort of thing he'd go into a monastery.' The coming change, would, he believed, be the development of initiative which had been strangled under Stalin. The middle generation, he felt, were having the hardest time; those who grew up before the Revolution had stamina and the young people were tough.

I went to the Yelokhovsky Cathedral: it was crowded and there were many men in the congregation as well as some nuns with absorbed, civilised faces. I asked to see a priest and made an appointment for Good Friday. After this, I lunched with a Russian friend who has maids. They work an eight-hour day, conscientiously, and have fixed holidays. Children, she says, are taught honesty, democracy and truth at school and have secret elections to their committees. She believes her son is more careful to speak the truth and to confess his faults than most children in the West. We talked of the Russian ballet and said it emphasised the expression of emotion and had saved classical dancing by mixing it with modern. The dancers were well educated, took the usual school examinations and were taught the characteristics of the different periods they represented in ballets. She suggested that by the end of the nineteenth century the Russian ballet had exhausted the benefit it had derived from foreign influences. Petipa[1] did much for it, but after him the ballet froze. Then came Isadora Duncan, Diaghilev, Fokine – they were opposed but they had an influence which is recognised today (e.g. it is admitted that *The Fountain* is influenced by *Prince Igor*). A new era opened in the thirties with *The Red Poppy* and this culminated in *Romeo*, then it declined, partly owing to heavier scenery, etc.

As I waited for Mass on a bench in a yard, an old woman came up and began to talk. When I told her I was a foreigner she said: 'You don't know how they oppress us.' I asked: 'In what way?' She glanced at the wall behind me: 'I daren't tell you, but we are much oppressed.' Since there was nothing comforting I could say, I held her hand.

I went on to the Red Square. When I arrived the tribune was crowded, but, like last year, I was pushed to the front with other women. On the stroke of ten Zhukov drove out; this time he was clapped as much as but (I thought) not more than Khrushchev. There was the usual inspection and the same greetings and speech as last time, then the anthem (the men took off their hats); when it ended a gun salute followed, which was much appreciated by the spectators. There was a march past of academies, military schools, airmen, sailors; all, particularly the members of the academies, were admired by the crowd for the way they marched. Then came armoured cars (no tanks), guns, a few planes (no jets). The long intervals were filled in with music. Then there were the gymnasts, rather dull except for some girls in peasant dresses with hoops. All the same this athletic generation have better figures than their forebears. Finally there were the demonstrations and, as usual, people at once began to leave the tribunes. Most of them were foreigners, Mongols predominating. I had a long walk back to the hotel through cordons.

After dinner I set out on a 'pub crawl' with a friend. The streets were crowded and the traffic constantly diverted. Our driver argued frenziedly with the militiamen, protesting that he had foreigners in his cab; usually he got his way. The beer-hall in Pushkin Square was closed 'for repairs' so we went to a snack and beer bar – an extraordinary sight: over all the floor, growing like flowers, were double-tiered tables for people to lean on. The party at the next table to ours were arguing loudly. One shouted: 'You can't live all your life and not ask questions.' I turned and inquired, 'What questions?' The man looked at me and said calmly: 'Would you like me to crush your spectacles into your eyes?' An elderly waitress gave a shocked giggle. We drank our beer. A slightly tipsy ex-airman joined us. He said he had left the Air Force three months ago after thirteen years' service, of which he had spent the last years in Port Arthur where life wasn't much fun for a bachelor. Then he had made the mistake of going first to Gorky and now he couldn't get registered in Moscow though he had been born there. He was living with his parents and was looking for work, but work was hard to find in Moscow and life expensive, especially when you got fined every week for living there illegally. A nice boy, friendly – though slightly glazed. As we drove away our taxi driver asked if at home we had holidays like the 1st of May. I said ours were not so organised and we had Christmas and Easter. Was our Easter at the same time as theirs, he inquired. His parents were believers but he wasn't. He knew there were plenty of believers but not amongst his friends.

At the Metropole the waiter placed us with two Greeks, one of whom spoke English. He was a businessman who was going to Odessa because some dispute had arisen over the quality of his deliveries. He sold bauxite. Negotiations were, he said, very slow, especially at first, when the Russians didn't know their needs or the quality of the goods or the customs of foreigners. Now they were easier, not because of the relaxation but because the Russians were more used to trading with foreigners.

The lights were going on and off, the music blared and people were dancing. Some men had no collars but, on the whole, most were not too badly dressed, yet the general impression was of poor figures and drab clothes and my escort said he had never seen so many un-attractive women. I went to bed tired and depressed.

I travelled to Zagorsk. There was a large holiday crowd at the station. In the train a girl sat next to me with her head in her hands, sleeping. Beside her was a peasant woman sitting on two sacks; farther on an old woman with a handsome face, in a brown shawl, was eating apples. Beyond her were two children and finally a hatted, gold-toothed lady with a boy. She shooed him off to make room for a man to whom she was, it seemed, keen to talk about the boy. She told him her son was sixteen and now doing well at school, but he had missed a lot in the sixth and seventh forms because the teachers had been bad. Now he thought he might join the army and catch up while there but she didn't want this. Standing next to them was a flirting couple – a pretty, slender, very young girl with grey-blue eyes and dark lashes, munching apples, while the young man said over and over: 'And I waited for you. I thought it isn't possible that she won't come – what can I have done to offend her?' Neither were quite looking at each other. Flirting here is very formalised, the men making all the going. Finally the girl said she wasn't going to get married for a very long time – not till she was twenty-one or twenty-two; the boy's face fell.

I gave my seat to the old woman with the sacks and went to smoke in the corridor. Looking out of the window I asked two men if we were passing kolkhozes; they replied 'No – dachas and a military camp.' The boy's mother joined us. I said her boy was nice. She told me he was keen on natural science and wanted to get into an Institute but she doubted if he would. She had seen the May Day celebrations on TV. I said we had not so many TV sets as in the USSR, whereupon she suggested that perhaps wages were higher in Russia. She was a war widow and received 350 roubles a month for her son as well as getting his ten-year schooling free. The best pupils went on to Institutes where they studied for five years on a grant. (I thought she seemed possessed of a middle-class anxiety to show off to a foreigner.)

At Zagorsk station in the crowded buffet, I bought a stale cheese sandwich and two sweets costing sixty kopecks each. A gipsy woman followed me about after I had given her some kopecks, saying: 'Daughter, I have two things to say to you; cross my palm.' I found myself calling her 'thou' and feeling annoyed by her wheedling though not by her obvious rascality. I refused to be told the two things and got away.

From half way down the winding road Zagorsk looked like an old print. A pale blue sky, grass, budding trees, the village climbing uphill and the monastery domes ahead. In the square, outside the monastery gates the radio was blaring music and, surrounded by a ring of lookers-on, young people were dancing – many girls with girls and some boys with boys. Inside the gates people were waiting in the garden between services. I asked a rather greasy young Brother where I could hand over my letter to one of the Fathers; he said at the Academy on the right. A few students in semi-mufti were sitting on the doorstep or walking in the garden. One took me through the house to the yard and brought out the priest – a handsome, young man with soft fair hair. We walked up and down the path, he saying there was complete freedom of religion; children didn't have to join the Komsomol – true, if they did, they ceased being believers since religion couldn't logically be reconciled with their materialistic faith, but some came back. It was difficult to say if there were a revival or not as no statistics were kept. I could see for myself how many people came to church. Those who married in church were genuine believers. I quoted Ehrenburg on there being no religious writers. He said it was true that if an author wanted to write a spiritually inspired work he could publish it through the church press. This priest was saying as much as I had any right to expect, but I felt no contact and his smooth voice and smile appalled me.

I joined the old men and women sitting on benches on the church steps in the central square of the monastery and later visited the museum (the churches were closed till six o'clock). Only one gallery was open – it showed tapestries, china, glass stuffs.

When I came out some of the young people were still dancing in the square while others were walking up the station road singing and playing concertinas; there were many drunks. Going back in the electric train I found myself sitting opposite an old woman with a fine face, and a younger, cosy one. A girl sat down next to me and tried to hang up her bag above my head. I offered to help and nearly dropped it on a well-dressed lady behind me. Her companion protested crossly; the bag contained potatoes. I apologised. The old woman looked at me with a smile: 'That's what happens, and all on account of helping other people's business.' She had a lovely face, dignified and reflective. She said she was living in one room with her niece and her niece's husband; they had fourteen square metres, a bed and a divan; the divan wasn't bad. The younger woman, a dumpy energetic type, was saying she had thirty-five roubles left and would take them to her daughter, with whom she was spending Easter. The old one asked how she would get to church from her daughter's; she said they had a church nearby.

A woman sitting by the window called out: 'Look, they're bringing in a corpse!' A drunk was carried in and dropped on the floor at the end of the carriage. His relations stood around him, smiling. I couldn't see him but people were saying: 'Fancy putting him down like that, with his hands sticking up; now they're turning him over on his side; that's better; there's a draught though, he'll catch cold.' A good-tempered looking militiaman joined the group – children ran up to see the sight. At a small station two militiamen and some Komsomol girls with first-aid armbands carried the drunk out and laid him on the platform where his family crowded round him again.

I liked the old woman more and more; so on the way out of the station when she got separated from her friend I followed her. From behind, bundled in her colourless coat and brown shawl, hobbling with a stick, she looked a tiny thing. I asked her if I could take her home. Her face lit up. 'Why darling, I wish I could ask you in, but I live with my niece and nephew – the way we live I couldn't ask anyone in. If you knew the way we live. I've wandered from pillar to post for years.' I asked if she would have tea with me but she didn't think there was anywhere one could get tea.

I had supper at the Metropole. There was much gaiety all round and the young people at the next table stared at me in a friendly way; I went up to them and said I was a foreigner and interested to know if they were students or artists. The worried waiter followed me, saying hadn't I forgotten something at my own table and shouldn't I go back to it, but the friendly boys said: 'Sit down – have some Caucasian wine, vodka, chocolates, dinner.' I sat down and we drank to peace and friendship. 'What does anybody want but peace and good conditions? We're all tired of the threat of war.' They said they were three brothers and their two wives. The table was covered with drinks, sweets and the remains of a good supper. When the waiter brought the bill they clubbed together but wouldn't let me contribute. They kept asking me to dance; I said I was much too old, they must ask their ladies; finally they did so. Meanwhile the waiter had become increasingly worried and kept on saying he must clear the table, but they paid no attention to him. However, while they were dancing he came back and told me he really *must* clear up and would I please leave. I said 'Yes' but didn't. When the boys returned I told them what the waiter had said, they pooh-poohed it. But the next time after they had danced they returned with changed faces saying: 'We are expecting so-and-so, I am afraid we need your place.' I got up at once; they looked very sad and embarrassed.

Went to Mass, then at 10.30 am Belchenko came in a smart car to take me to see Kabanov, the Head of the Theatre Department of the Ministry of Culture. We entered an immense office with a self-conscious-making runner to the desk at the end where Kabanov and Moskhateli (his deputy) were sitting. Belchenko introduced me and supported me, briefly but competently. I explained our project. They liked the photos and the book and said everything would be all right as far as the theatre side went, but the question of paying for the photographer's stay was Stepanov's business. There was no precedent for that. I said his stay would be expensive for us, cheap for them (in roubles) and that in the reverse situation we would certainly have asked the Russian photographers to stay. They seemed moved by this and Moskhateli said to Kabanov: 'After all, there are people whose board is paid for.' They ended by agreeing that they would get together with the Ministry and let me know the result next day.

I went on to an exhibition of Saryan's pictures about which everybody was talking. He is an old painter, said by officials to have been previously known in Moscow but never before shown in this big way. I thought he had been influenced by Matisse, Gauguin, Van Gogh, etc. – bright colours, abundance, fruit and flower pictures, portraits, landscapes. Two people looking at the pictures said the colour was artificial. But an older man showing round a younger one remarked: 'People who don't understand might ask why has he used muddy colour on that face, but look at the expression.' The young man commented that this was unlike most Russian painting. The older man went on: 'Yes, he's a sort of Frenchman, but that's all right. The West has produced much that's good.' They stopped before a portrait with a streak of green, bringing out the whiteness of the hair saying: 'All the same, one must be bold to paint green hair.' The 'Comments Book' at the entrance was surrounded by an amused crowd. It had remarks such as – 'Picasso says one man turns the sun into a yellow blot, another turns a yellow blot into the sun. Saryan does the latter. The struggle for Saryan is also the struggle of the younger artists. Pity he wasn't known till now.'

I went on to a mixed exhibition. There was a big crowd in front of Goncharov's pictures which broke up into arguing groups. In one, a well-dressed bourgeois couple were saying to an intellectual-looking older man: 'That nude will drop off her sofa, the man can't draw; and the colours are all wrong and very dull.' He answered: 'Art is not photography; Goncharov's pictures are more real than the old realism. They're not just a slice of life but his view of it, his mood. His colours would be warm if the mood were gay; after all, the West has produced Matisse, Van Gogh, Cezanne – not so bad, so why shouldn't we learn?' In another group a tall girl student was cornered but holding her own against what looked like a kolkhoz manager, he was saying that Goncharov was 'not helping our socialist construction.' She replied: 'We should think about socialist construction and do it, but not talk so much about it – talk has turned it into clichés.' She liked Goncharov and felt he conveyed more of reality, painting the way he did. The man said this was going back to what we had left behind, to French art. She said: 'Why not? We don't mind copying Rembrandt, why stop there?' He replied: 'This is copying from our enemies.' She turned on him: 'Who are our enemies? In art we have none.' At this he became threatening: 'You must be under somebody's influence and we'll find out whose.' Evidently alarmed, another student drew the girl away, saying: 'Better look at the pictures.'

I asked a student who was looking at the Comments Book if she liked Goncharov's work. She said: 'Yes, I do' as though answering a vital challenge.

After Mass I went at ten o'clock to see Obraztsov. Goncharov is a friend as well as a pupil of Favorsky; he is about fifty. Obraztsov himself greatly admires Turner. He asserted that photography was documentation and that Cartier Bresson had shown how good it could be, but that art (painting) was image (*obraz*) and it presented the artist's opinion of the world. 'Because of this there is a quarrel between those who see art as documentation and those who see it as opinions.'

I went on to the National to see an American lawyer about a form of contract to be worked out with Mezhkniga for the Ballet book. He said he had come out mainly as a tourist but also to pursue the question of royalties, but so far he had failed to see anyone though he had good introductions.

I went on to the Yelokhovsky Cathedral; it was jammed tight for Good Friday. I was taken in by a dvornik through the foreigners' gate into a space outside the sacristy door where people were waiting. A priest came out in his vestments; we talked by a lectern; the crowd was four yards away. I said Christians abroad felt and prayed with the Russian church; I didn't want to press him on the religious situation. He said much the same as the priest at Zagorsk. Children needn't join the Komsomol. It was difficult to know if there was a revival, but certainly those who came to church came for no worldly advantage. The Church was entirely supported by voluntary contributions – the sale of candles helped a lot. There were no disputes now between Orthodox, Catholics and other Christians. I felt he was telling the truth so far as he went but it was like talking through a glass screen. As I left, I looked up and saw an intensely human, warm expression, perhaps trying to convey a genuine message.

Later at the Bolshoi I saw *Romeo and Juliet*, an immense tableau presented on an immense scale and the dancers looked tiny under the great architectural décor. It was beautiful in terms of a Renaissance picture, though there was too much detail.

I spent most of the morning at Mezhkniga working over the contract for the Ballet book, but as yet no answer had come from the Ministry of Culture. Finally I went there to see Moskhateli who told me that so

Near Siena

North Uist

far as the ballet was concerned everything was agreed. It now only remained for the Ministry of Culture to agree the financial terms. By about five o'clock I went to see Boni who said that since I wanted to spend a few days in Leningrad why didn't I go there at once and they would have the answer for me by the time I got back. (He must have known that it is impossible to get a ticket on the day itself.) I said I'd go as soon as I could get a ticket.

At 11 pm I went to the Cathedral. The traffic was stopped several streets away as the roads were blocked by crowds. I walked to the foreigners' door, then I edged towards the Russians who were separated from us by a grille; they were jammed tight together, men, women, young, old; their eyes closed, their faces recollected; some were crying. I went out on to the steps and found a huge crowd chanting the litany then I walked about in the still, dark yard. Later I went back into the church where, at midnight, the procession started from the altar to the ringing of bells. The Russians holding lighted candles embraced each other, saying 'Christ has risen'. The service was to go on till three o'clock but at about one I came out. I thought I'd never get through the crowd, but it parted obediently when the militiaman sent someone to guide me and said that I was to be let through.

RYAZAN

I went to the Kazan station, took a ticket to Ryazan, climbed into a hard carriage and sat down at a 'Pullman' seat under a window. Opposite me sat a girl in a shawl, Zoya was her name. She had been travelling for a month and five days; the trip would cost close on 5,000 roubles (return?). Her employers had paid one way. She showed her tickets all round the compartment. She had started out on a sleigh pulled by dogs from a place in Siberia, then she had taken planes and trains and had had to sit on her luggage most of the time. She had spent a week at one station waiting to get away. She told me about the splendid hunting and fishing in Siberia and how people adopt little bears as pets. The climate, she said, was good. She had gone out three years ago with her husband, when there was a call-up for the virgin lands. The pay was excellent – 2,300 roubles and 1,800 expenses and long leave every three years.

Now she was going home to her sovkhoz, half way to the Black Sea, to bury her mother, sell their house and pick up her little girl whom she had left with Granny. She had an Easter egg for her. I asked what her job was. She said: 'With prisoners.' I suppose I looked startled. 'Prisoners, you know,' she repeated. 'But you can't know. You don't know the truth – the thousands of innocents sitting there. There are several hundreds in my camp, all with sentences of twenty-five years and over – some forty-five, some more; that means for life, of course, but theoretically they might survive. Thousands there are in Siberia. They say Vlasov is out there: he wasn't killed[2]. And Trotsky's wife and a son of Stalin's whom he had by that actress. In another camp I'm told there was a lovely woman; all she had ever done was to refuse to be Beria's mistress. The numbers he put away! That one had her little daughter with her. She was there for many years. Then the Commission came to sort out those who were to be freed. This woman came to one of the guards and said: "If they let me out I'll go mad." They called her up to the Commission and told her she could leave. But she had a heart attack and died on the way out of camp. The little girl asked the other prisoners: "Why have mother and I had such a hard time?" Many went mad or had heart attacks or strokes when they were amnestied; many died on the way home. It's terrible when you know the truth.'

'Surely many more will now be let out,' I said, 'and aren't conditions better today?' 'Yes, they're better,' she answered. 'Now the prisoners are paid for their work, but some managers are dishonest and profiteer on their food and pay. I have banged on the table defending their rights; they have rights, the same as anybody else, I said "we're a democracy".' And indeed, she looked as if she might have banged. 'Things are bad,' she went on. 'People have become heartless.' 'That there are such as you,' I said, 'shows that they haven't altogether succeeded.' 'I've been through a lot,' she continued. 'It's changed me; I've aged. Look, that's what I was like when I went out.' She showed me a photo of herself – just a little Komsomol girl, with painted lips. Now she was handsome in a weather-beaten way. I said so. She had always been tough, she said. At fourteen she was a Partisan. The Germans had occupied her village. She and her brothers carried messages to the Partisans. Then she and her mother, and many more, had been rounded up and some were shot, others escaped. She hid in a ditch. Her mother had been holding the baby; he was killed, she was wounded. 'Are you alive?' her mother had called out. They had got away.

This was a sad time for her – sad that she hadn't seen her mother again. Her mother who had always been afraid of losing her daughter as well as her boys (they had been killed in the war), afraid of Zoya dying before her. 'Are you a believer?' I asked. She said defensively, 'Yes, even though I was in the Komsomol. So is my husband, even though he has been a Party member for eight years. Of course, they taught me not to have any religion, but I never believed them. My parents were religious.' She said that many things were wrong in Russia. There was a lot of graft. And then things like 'the way we despise the Jews. Why should anybody be despised?'

We arrived in Ryazan at about one o'clock. Zoya came out on the platform with me and we embraced, hoping to meet again. I walked down the street: it looked a village street with little wooden houses with carved window frames, some painted blue. There was a whole quarter of such houses, though from the train Ryazan looked an ordinary town, with a new quarter built in plain, grey, utilitarian blocks. I asked a man sitting in a doorway if there was a hotel. He said: 'Yes, go on till you come to the asphalt; it's a couple of hundred yards on the right, next to the gastronom.' The asphalt was a big, wide street which still had some wooden houses on either side, but these merged into stone buildings, some imitating the pattern of logs and wooden window frames. Farther on there were urban buildings, some nineteenth-century, some probably new but built in the same style.

The hotel couldn't have changed in seventy-five years. The restaurant consisted of four rooms, three facing the street but shaded from it by Venetian blinds; all were joined by archways, hung with blue crushed velvet. The tables and chairs were shrouded in white cloths and there were white slip covers on the tall wooden chairs, and white vases on the tables with a bunch of bright artificial flowers in each; on the walls, brown Victorian scenes of picnics. I saw no portraits of leaders.

At breakfast an officer joined me at my table. He had been at Ryazan ever since the war. He was an engineer who had stayed on in the army – what difference was there, he asked, whether you did your job as a civilian or as a soldier? He said the town was growing and so were a lot of towns because the peasants were leaving the country for industry. The best quarter, he told me, was farther up near the river which was now in flood but nice in summer when you could bathe in it. I should see the town museum.

I took the trolleybus up the long street and came to a square with a monument to Lenin, then I turned up another wide street which ended in a garden and a church. I got out and walked through the garden – it was an old town garden with a new-looking monumental archway leading into it; holiday crowds were walking about. What seemed to be a church proved not to be one but a monument put up, in the 1950s, to a local chief who, in the sixteenth century, drove back a Tartar Khan and made him renounce the tribute paid to him by the Prince of Moscow. Beyond it is the kremlin which stands on the bank of the river.

The town is curiously open to the sky with sounds coming from the country and the river, the 'noisy spring' rushing along and the hooting of river boats. The whole gives a feeling of width – wide main streets and wide flat country stretching around it.

From where I stood I could see how the town culminated in the kremlin, with churches massed around it – the kremlin itself overhung the harbour and looked out on the dark river and beyond it to the flat country stretching away endlessly. The river is the Oka, one of the sources of the Volga.

I asked a little old woman the way to the museum. She showed me, then asked for alms and for my name so that she could pray for me; when I looked back I saw her still standing in the street crossing herself.

The museum is a small, square building in a yard between two churches; beside it is a house – perhaps belonging to the clergy or a government office. It is a plain building but decorated magnificently in barbaric colours. The little museum must once have been a private house; it has shallow stairs, small, well-proportioned rooms and beeswaxed floors, shaded by Venetian blinds. I saw a Guardi, a Guido Reni and some eighteenth-century French pictures. A little of what must have been the original furniture remained and some chandeliers. People were admiring the place which was well kept.

The churches next to it were closed and dead so I asked a woman where there was a 'working' church. She looked startled, then pleased and told me how to get there. The church of Saints Boris and Gleb is on the outskirts of the town. Again, I asked my way of a woman. She inquired: 'It's the first time you come to church?' and took me under her wing. We passed beggars in the church garden and a chapel where people stopped and crossed themselves, then we went through a wide doorway where priests in pink vestments were standing around, finally we entered the church. It was packed with what seemed a fair cross-section of the population – men, boys, children, many young girls and families. They passed candles up to the front of the church where, after a time, strip lights were switched on and the initials XP in electric lights shone out disconcertingly. Down the nave a space was kept free and after a long time a procession moved down it from the altar with the pink priests chanting. But of course this was only one church and on an Easter Sunday afternoon, and there were plenty of the townspeople outside.

After tea I went to the station. There were two ticket offices, one civilian, one military. I stood at the end of the civilian queue and asked the two men in front of me why I hadn't been able to buy a return ticket at Moscow. They said return tickets were only issued for journeys between Leningrad and Moscow, adding that certainly the availability of return tickets was a desirable system but it had not yet been applied to other stations. Tickets were sold only an hour before the train's departure and then only if there were free seats on it, if not, you waited for the next. I got a ticket and then went to wait in the buffet. The two men came in and joined me at my table. We all ordered caviar sandwiches (at five roubles) and they ordered vodka and beer, but the beer pump had gone wrong. They had a quarter of vodka each, which makes a small tumblerful and only turned a little pink. I asked how many put one out cold? One said he was not in practice, but he used to be able to drink eight or nine. He lived in Ryazan and was seeing off his brother-in-law who was on a service journey from Siberia where he had lived for a number of years. The Siberian spoke happily of his Far East town; he had seen it grow up; everything was changing; it was really exciting. When he came to Ryazan or to his home town nearby, he felt this was the old world and that in it nothing changed. Life was out East. He had a wife who came from Ryazan and a child. Today he had spent seeing his wife's family.

We got into a carriage with an odd number, as he thought we could smoke there, but the other people objected so we stood on the platform at the end.

The man told me he was preparing his examination for 'Candidate of Sciences', as well as general papers. There were two special subjects – German and Diamat:[3] he felt quite sure of passing all except Diamat: for what with the changes he didn't know the right answers, neither did the examiners. I asked if the cult of personality had really gone so deep into philosophy. He said the revelations had been very upsetting. Evidently it had to be done, but why do it in this way? He and his friends, Party and non-Party, had discussed the question; most of them were unhappy about the method. Things had to change but they were already changing gradually – opinion was being prepared so a sudden push was hardly necessary. Had *he* known? I asked. 'Yes,' he said. As a young man in the thirties, he had taken part in the fight against the *kulaki*[4] and in searches. It had seemed right to him at the time, as it would have to any romantic young man – it was a fight against the enemies of the country. Later he saw that things were going too far, had, in fact, gone much too far.

It was difficult to know what to think now. It was not only the cult of personality that had been wrong. The Russians had boasted too much – they had claimed inventions before they had been checked, for instance a way of creating organic life, then they had found that the experiments couldn't be repeated under controlled conditions and the whole claim dropped into oblivion. Many products which had borne foreign inventors' names had been re-named, so that if you asked for them the chemists said they didn't exist, but now the foreign inventor's name had been brought back, though joined with those of Russians'. The period of isolation had been very hard for all scientists, among whom he had many friends. They needed foreign books and journals and wanted to exchange ideas. He was very interested in his work and owing to conditions in the Far East, had had opportunities of specialising. He added: 'We have to face the possibility of a new war, though we hope it has receded now; all the same we have to be prepared at least to defend ourselves against every form of warfare.'

I mentioned a book on Pavlov[5] which claimed he was an atheist and said I had since heard he wasn't. 'That's right,' he replied; he had known people close to him. Pavlov was a believer and had supported the church in Ryazan which had remained open, thanks to him. Some people said he did this to please his wife.

He went on: Stalin had been bad about the peasants, he seemed to think they lived on roast chicken. Today people realised that the peasants had to have an interest in the products of their work so now they were paid, though the new conditions had not as yet reached all farms. You could still find some where nothing had changed.

People had had many shocks – after the stability of Lenin and Stalin's régimes, there had been Beria's fall, then Malenkov's, now this. Perhaps Malenkov had been too near to Stalin – a clever man – said to be related to Lenin, perhaps a nephew? Collective leadership was all very well but somebody had to be on top and it was natural that it should be the head of the Party. Khrushchev was now clearly on top.

We talked about books. He knew Azhayev, the author of *Far from Moscow*, and didn't think very much of him, his second book was, he considered, very bad. The pipeline described in it as finished in 1948 had only just been completed. He asked me why publishers printed books that just lie around and didn't reprint those that are wanted. I said there was a difference between the Soviet system and ours; we tried out demand, the Russian publishers printed to a plan.

We kept being jostled by people coming in from other carriages or going to the WC or drinking from water taps, so we went to the other end of the carriage and were joined by a soldier, a sailor and a woman. I asked the Siberian about the health service. Medical care, he said, was free in the clinics and the hospitals, but medicines were paid for. Sick leave, if the worker had kept his job for a given time, was paid by the employer; it was in proportion to the wage. If the sick person had not been long enough in a job to qualify, then he must show he had changed his post not through his own fault. Old-age pensions were scaled according to years of work. There was no sick or old-age pension for people who did not work for the State. However, a domestic worker who belonged to the Union and proved his employment by letters from his employers could claim. Under a recent law employers had to give a fortnight's notice of dismissal (if due to a reduction of staff). During that time the worker should find another job. Jobs were easy to find, so unemployment pay was not necessary. He asked me what happened with us. The sailor inquired: 'What is this "with us" and "with you"? What are you talking about?' He was obviously puzzled and very curious. The woman wanted to know about pensions for cloakroom attendants. The Siberian said that if they worked for the State they got one. As we reached the end of the journey the Siberian said he wished we could meet in Moscow but he couldn't invite me to his place as he lived in a hostel. I asked if he would come out with me and my friends. He said he'd love to and gave me an address, suggesting that I send him a post card. But he refused to be given a lift in my taxi when we arrived – possibly genuine embarrassment at my going out of my way. In saying goodbye he made a point of stressing how nice it was to talk with foreigners – adding that of course in Moscow people were more stiff, not unfrozen yet, but outside it was different.

MOSCOW

In Moscow there was still no news from the Ministry about our book, so I asked to see a market. I was told there were thirty in the city and was bear-led to the biggest. About 1,200 people usually come here to sell their goods but there were fewer today because of the holiday (Easter Monday). On a normal day there were up to 24,000 shoppers but not all came to buy, some came mainly to look. The market is open from 7 am to 6 pm (4 pm on Sundays).

Outside the stalls were shops for the kolkhozniks where suits could be bought from between 1,087 and 1,623 roubles.

Later that morning I and some friends were taken to see a trial in the lowest court (the People's Court). There was a woman judge and two lay assessors, a man and a woman. First we had a talk with the judge in her small study off the court-room. She explained that each sub-district of Moscow had a People's Court. The Appeals are heard by the Moscow Court of Appeal and the Regional Court. Murders (for which people are now shot) and some political crimes go straight to a higher court. The judge and the assessors are elected by the District (by secret vote); there are seventy-five assessors who act in turn for short spells. If they are working, their wage is paid to them; if not, they get ten roubles a day from the Ministry of Justice. They have no special training but the judge has. Each Republic has its own procedural code, but several follow those of the RSFSR (Russia). There are separate codes, for civil and criminal law. Decisions are by majority but a minority report can be put in to the Appeal Court, and an appeal is possible even where the decision has been unanimous but it must be lodged within five days. The accused can have his own lawyer to represent him and in that case pays full fees; if the lawyer is appointed by the Court, then he pays according to his means. The accused can ask for witnesses – if he does so before the trial the judge allows them to be called, according to his discretion; if the accused asks for more witnesses during the trial, the judge and the assessors decide together whether they should be called.

At this point the judge told us we must go into the Court as the trial was already twenty minutes late in starting. The accused, she said, was Victor Shatskov, born 1938, finishing technical school where he was studying to be a watchmaker. He was arrested in the District on the 3rd of April, accused of stealing a foreign-made watch from an invalid. He was allowed out on signature (no bail), i.e. on his promise not to disappear. People under eighteen were not usually kept in prison before trial; after that it depended on the gravity of the crime and the character of the accused. The file contained the report of the militiaman and the Minutes of the proceedings at the Police Station signed by the magistrate and the accused. The value of the watch was 340 roubles.

We went in. The judge and the assessors sat on three tall chairs on a dais, with a table in front of them. Below were places for the Prosecutor, the Counsel for the Defence and the clerks. On benches at the back sat militiamen and five men and three women.

Shatskov was called and given a chair facing the court. He was asked for his documents and gave his TU card. Then he was asked if he had received the charge less than a week ago. The injured party (Polivanov) and witnesses were called and stood in a row, and they were warned to tell the truth on pain of two years' imprisonment. It was ascertained that the mother and father of the accused were present. The accused was told his rights – to question witnesses, call new ones, put in documents; also he was given the names of the judge and the assessors.

The Prosecutor asked if Shatskov had anything to add at this stage and told him he would want to question his father and his teacher.

The judge then read the charge: stealing a watch from Polivanov who was drunk at the time and also suffering from a fit. The accused had tried to escape but was arrested. Shatskov admitted he took the watch – two other watches had been found on him. He had no past record.

The Prosecutor and the Counsel for the Defence agreed on the order of the questioning. Shatskov was asked his name, age, where he was born: near Voronezh in a village called Makhrovka, he was Russian, not in the Komsomol, he had finished his seven-year schooling and was now in a technical school. He lived with his parents and younger brother and sister. School work 'not bad', likes games (a little doubtfully). Asked what social work he did he said he read newspapers 'with a circle'; he liked reading but had no favourite authors. After replying to these questions he was told to give an account of the crime. He went to a *stolovaya* (beer-hall) with a friend, Salatin, from the technical school. Salatin bought vodka and drank it, standing next to Polivanov.

Polivanov, who had been drinking, twice gave the boys twenty-five roubles to buy vodka. Then he had a fit. Several people, including the boys, helped him. Salatin held his hand, then Shatskov took his watch. He didn't mean to; he was drunk. He had no need of a watch – he had one of his own and another one which a friend had given him to mend. He had never drunk vodka before. 'What do you think of your action?' 'It wasn't right. I know I committed a crime.' 'Will this be a lesson to you?' 'Yes.' A long scolding followed, ending up by the judge asking again if Shatskov was sure he hadn't meant to take the watch.

The man assessor asked: 'Did you know there is a law against taking vodka in a beer-hall?' 'Yes.' 'If you had observed it the rest mightn't have happened.'

The Prosecutor: 'Why didn't you confess at once?' 'I was drunk and frightened.' More questions about sport and social duties followed, and Shatskov was asked why he was not in Komsomol. Then: 'Have you read *The Young Guard* and *How Steel was Tempered?*' 'Yes.' 'How, after reading such books, could you get drunk? Does your father drink?' 'No.' 'It doesn't look as though you were so very drunk since you thought of hiding the watch (it had been found in his sleeve). Are you sure you hadn't intended stealing it?' 'I don't remember how it happened.' 'When did you come to?' 'At midnight.' 'When were you questioned?' 'Next morning.' 'Who are your friends? Name them.

Where do they work? Have they a record?' 'No.' 'How do they behave?' 'Well.' 'So you were not under bad influences. How much did you drink?' 'First a quarter on our own – then a litre between the three of us.' 'Was your crime discussed at your school?' 'Yes, the Second-in-Command on the political side called me up.' 'Does the Komsomol know about it?' 'Yes.' 'Has it been discussed by them?' 'I don't know.'

Judge: 'I see you have had bad conduct marks. Why?' 'Absenteeism, but only once.' The Defence began to question the boy and drew attention to his repentance, drunken state and fright.

Polivanov was called. He is a war invalid on a full pension and unemployed. Asked to give an account of what happened, he said he was going to buy fish, wandered into the beer-hall and was tempted to drink. He had an epileptic fit – doesn't remember a thing. He had bought the watch some years ago for 175 roubles, or perhaps 280. His pension is 400 roubles of which he has at the moment 50 left. He had been an officer and has a son.

Defence: 'How is it that you gave money to boys who are the age of your son, to buy vodka?'

Witness Bolshakov (the policeman) is called. He had been there. He says Shatskov was drunk. (His report was most unlike an English police statement. He was uncertain about the time and couldn't remember names.)

'Couldn't you get the boys out of the beer-hall?' asked the Counsel for the Defence. The militiaman said he had no right to go in.

In the end the boy was sentenced to five years, but the sentence was suspended. The proceeding was curiously paternalistic – it seemed to me well adapted to dealing with young offenders, but you could see how the same procedure (who are your friends, etc.) could be used for tyranny.

LENINGRAD

At eight o'clock I went to the station and caught the train for Leningrad. I was very tired and took a sleeping pill. I woke to find a woman in her thirties, rather pretty in a dark-eyed, soft-complexioned way, in the next bunk. She smiled at me, said how well I managed to sleep and was delighted to hear I was English. We talked cosmetics. She said the best thing to clean the skin was to chop cucumbers and soak them in rain water with a little lemon peel. Her skin was a good advertisement for this treatment. Her husband was working in an institution and so was she. They had no children. They had a maid. She was going on a business journey with a man from her office, he was in another bunk. When he woke up, she explained her excitement about being with a foreigner. We talked about Stalin. 'Some people think it wasn't such a good thing to tell.' 'We knew about most of it, but all the same it was a shock.' She had been to an Easter service and afterwards had eaten the traditional dishes, *paskha*, *kulich* and eggs, but she wasn't a believer – how could one be when it was now known that God didn't cause thunder? She said her grandmother was religious, but neither she nor her mother were. She appealed to the man. He said he couldn't be so sure that there was no God. An attendant brought us tea and the woman pressed me to share her home-made cake. As we arrived at the station I invited them to lunch at the hotel; they said they'd love to come and would in any case ring me up, but didn't.

The Europa Hotel is less smart than the Astoria and equally old-fashioned. I went to the Dom Knigi and asked for Panova's address which the secretary gave pleasantly, without any fuss. I rang her up and said could I come and see her? She answered that she was washing her hair, then the manicurist was coming and she had a meeting at the Union at two but she could come out at four and meet me at the publisher's office. I went to buy galoshes – got some rubber bootees for sixty roubles. A man of whom I asked the way walked with me and inquired whether the English were pleased with Bulganin and Khrushchev's visit. It was nice that things were going well internationally but he couldn't understand why B and K hadn't been allowed to meet the common people?

Panova came with freshly dyed pinkish hair. We talked about her books, personal relationships and collective life in the Soviet Union. 'Don't you believe that people's feelings have changed?' she said. 'I have been married three times and have grown-up children. We love and have dramas just as we always did. Our Russian temperament has not changed.' Her *Span of the Year*, she pointed out, is about human relationships. It is not primarily social criticism, though it also describes everyday reality. After leaving Panova I went to the Hermitage, where I saw a heavenly French exhibition, from twelfth-century enamels to contemporary paintings – a room for Matisse, another for Picasso (early) and so on. Some people were puzzled, some admiring. A professor was showing three young men round. This group talked as a coterie which knew more than the philistines. Other people were saying that the painters must be laughing at the public.

Afterwards I walked about and had another look at the Moika and at our flat. Leningrad is different in the spring light, pretty but less poignant, or perhaps I was less moved the second time I saw it.

Having now seen the city pretty thoroughly and having gaps between my next appointments and no need to return as yet to Moscow I thought it would be fun to take the late night train to some country station and then get out and walk around and perhaps talk to a few peasants if I met any who looked chatty. So I went to the station and took the electric train and, as out of a lucky dip, took a ticket to a station whose name I didn't know. Next to me two young men were talking. 'I'll tell her straight out she must make up her mind – she must say one way or the other,' said one. 'That's right, you tell her straight out.' 'And if not, I'll try Irina.' 'Ah, don't you do that; she'll need to get a divorce.' 'Well, we'll get it. We've got money.' The train was dark; only one man had a glowing cigarette. I had a feeling of the remote country.

At each station the conductor came in and announced its name. He was careful that nobody should oversleep and pass their destination. '*Khozyaika*,[6] isn't this yours?'

At the station where I got out I ate sour cream and a little sugar and black bread in the small restaurant, with some peasants. I asked an old woman: 'Are things better now in the country?' 'They got better under Malenkov but haven't improved since. He was a good man.' A peasant said to me: 'One must hand it to your Churchill. It turns out he did warn Stalin but he didn't listen. Who knows? Perhaps the war could have been avoided if it hadn't been for him. Or at least it needn't have been the way it was. Stalin destroyed the top ranks of the army and he didn't arm us properly. But for this we mightn't have been overrun. Khrushchev is on top now, but perhaps Malenkov will come back. He is much loved. Stalin was an *izverg* (monster). He killed and massacred. Some of the revelations we only learned of recently; for instance, that he killed Kirov[7] and others too, allegedly for murder.'

All the same, he personally had been less surprised than some, for 'Stalin was never my Grandpapa. I couldn't bear to look at the papers, even though I was in the Komsomol. But you couldn't say anything or the "black ravens"[8] would come. When we had the letter read to us we were delighted.' I asked if he thought Stalin or Beria were most to blame. He said Stalin. I then inquired whether Stalin's portraits had been removed – I hadn't seen any. He said there had been one at this station but people kept turning it upside down at night, so finally it was taken away, and replaced by pictures of Mikoyan and Khrushchev. Everybody in the neighbourhood who had been sent to camp had come back. Most of them had been arrested after the war. They were now working and not being molested. I asked an old woman if there were much feeling against those who had collaborated during the war. She said it depended on the person. One man (now back) had prevented people from escaping, saying if they didn't stay on everybody would go to camp. That was bad but another (also back) had been good to refugees and was only sent away as the result of intrigue. A man called Seryozha came in; he said he had been tying up logs for freight but would finish quickly and come back to talk, or would I like to go to his house? I went.

He lives with his wife, daughter and old mother. They have two little rooms, the front one with two beds covered with white sheets with insertions; the pillows also have insertions and the table has a linen cloth. The wallpaper is blue; there are paper flowers (such as are made and sold at some stations) and a picture made of cut-outs, also a charming Victorian one, a small ebony clock made in 1870 and some home-made mats. The mother explained that she had worked for many years, in fact her hands had never been idle. She showed me the crochet bed covers she had made; her daughter-in-law had made the insertions (beautiful work) and the cut-out picture. The old lady is philosophical and tough. She said things are hard but if you work hard you can live. When her other son comes back from the army they will build him a house and he will marry and she hopes the sisters-in-law will get on. Seryozha told me he earns 500 roubles and his wife earns about the same. They have a cow and chickens. Conditions in kolkhozes depend on whether or not the manager steals. He suggested I should go to the village soviet and ask to be shown kolkhozes. I agreed, because not to go might be worse.

A tight-bunned secretary received me and became polite on hearing that I was in the Soviet Union on an official invitation. The President was not there but would I come back in an hour. I returned and found a lean, surly type in khaki. He didn't know how to handle the interview. He couldn't read my English correspondence with Mezhkniga but saw the address. He suggested that my Intourist coupons were out of date; I pointed out they were not. I couldn't however produce my passport as it was at the Bureau in Leningrad. He said I'd better get my visit laid on there; if I did then he'd be glad to show me round. I said: 'All right' and I went back to the peasants and met Seryozha's daughter – a neat child with china blue eyes; he adores her. Then back to the station.

The following morning I took another trip. I left Leningrad by train and got out at a wayside station which looked nice. Here I got into conversation with a peasant woman who invited me to her home to tea. To reach it we had a long walk through muddy fields where there were a few patches of snow still left and many holes full of water. I was glad of my galoshes. It was drizzling. On the verges of the roads pussy willow was flowering. Some had been cut; people use it for decorating their homes. The village we reached after going through endless fields was a poor one. It was part of a kolkhoz. At the cottage was a girl who was a neighbour and the woman's husband, Gleb. The atmosphere was very friendly and we had bread and eggs for tea. They told me how their kolkhoz worked, what they had to give to the State and what they got in return. They were allowed to keep a small private plot for themselves. It might be thirty to sixty sotniks according to the size of the kolkhoz but now they were worried because the Twentieth Congress had decided that if all members of the family were not working on the kolkhoz the size of the private plot might be reduced, or even taken away. The women have to do 250 work days, the men 300. Young people get through the work in a short time but the older ones have a job to finish it. Their pay used to be fifty-two kopecks a day but now they do better as they have a new Manager, a local man, honest and a trained agronomist; in fact, all round things are better. There are five villages in this kolkhoz; before they were amalgamated the peasants were paid piece-work, which they liked. The old lady had been injured by a bull and cannot work. She does not get any pension because she has a house and a cow and a husband. Gleb, however, is not well but hopes to get into a high invalid bracket in which case he may be paid as much as 270 roubles. All the same they worry a bit about security in their old age. They could sell a bullock, and their cow they could sell alive, but not for meat.

The houses of the kolkhoz were built by a Leningrad factory. It charged the kolkhoz with the cost and a peasant when he arrives can get a house on the instalment plan for 21,000 roubles but when he leaves he loses what he has paid unless he can sell the house to a new-comer. (Of course, they can only sell to someone who is acceptable to the kolkhoz.) But, alternatively, they can actually shift the house to another village within the kolkhoz if they can find a buyer there. All this tends to make them feel tied to the soil, more so since the Twentieth Congress, because since then the authorities are stricter about keeping identity cards, without which no one can move.

This couple are religious people. The man told me how, on return-ing from the war, he found his mother's grave but it had no cross on it, so he made one and planted it. They have an ikon and a proper towel. The old lady wishes her grandchildren to be baptised.

We talked a lot about the horrors of the war and also about what a good thing it was that there was less tension now; people from the West could come to the Soviet Union and some Russians could visit us.

We were drinking tea when a man in a leather jerkin appeared out-side the door. Seeing him through the window I thought he looked almost like the caricature of what I should have expected – square, tough, smiling with gold teeth and accompanied by a lean assistant. They were let in by the old lady who at once offered them tea. The man gave his name and they sat down politely; the assistant was silent. The couple treated them as officials who might have dropped in to discuss some village matter. 'Jerkin' asked how they were and who *I* was. Then he looked at my papers and commented on the absence of my passport. He also asked what we had been talking about. We said we were having tea and chatting about this and that, the hardships of the last war, and so on. But again he asked what we had been talking about. I said we were saying that things were better now – Russians came to England, English people to Russia. If he wanted to know more about me he could ring up the Ministry of Culture or Mezhkniga (mentioning high officials). The old lady stood up and said she wasn't used to being asked what she talked about with friends. She was a veteran collective farm worker; she spoke at meetings; everybody knew her. Jerkin smiled, sipped tea and said he meant no harm. Perhaps we would like to finish our conversation and then he would give me a lift to the station. I said, 'Good – better than walking.' The old man talked about his pension. Jerkin said that under the new law his position would improve. I asked Jerkin his rank. He said he was the Secretary of the Regional Committee. I said 'goodbye' and then went out and walked up the street to where Jerkin had his jeep. He remarked that I shouldn't move about without my passport – 'Surely your Embassy must want to know where you are every hour of the day?' I exclaimed: 'Why should they?' 'Suppose something happened to you?' 'Why should it?' 'Nothing will, of course; all the same, it's awkward.' He suggested the best thing would be for me to go to Leningrad with them.

We dropped the assistant, but kept the driver. Jerkin sat in front with him, leaving me in the back. I made polite conversation. He was a little on the defensive. 'What's that big church?' 'Don't you know that religion is free in the Soviet Union?' etc.

Jerkin came from Leningrad; he had done five years in the army, had a degree in history and was studying, by correspondence, to be a candidate for Party membership. Eventually he would like to become a teacher.

It is funny how self-conscious this sort of incident makes one. I tried to be relaxed but it was difficult not to do too much or too little explaining.

The first part of our long drive was over indescribably bad roads which required great skill on the part of the driver. When we arrived we went to the Astoria, though I had told them I was staying at the Europa, but Jerkin insisted that as the Head Intourist Office was at the Astoria my passport was probably there. He went in and left me with the driver for about twenty minutes. The man said, 'You mustn't take offence. All along the Soviet Union has had the whole world against them.' He had only just left school when the Finns attacked them (!), and then the USSR had suffered so much from spies. But things would gradually improve; there would be more understanding between nations and more people would travel. No one wanted war. Everyone had suffered too much.

When Jerkin returned they drove me to the Europa. I asked them if they would have dinner with me. They were going to have a long drive back, and though I thought their driving me to Leningrad unnecessary, I supposed they had done what they thought was their duty. Jerkin refused politely.

Later I rang up Panova and asked to see her. She said would I come to the Writers' Union restaurant where we could talk undisturbed. We sat at a table in the middle of the restaurant, talked a little about my *Listener* article which she had read. She said we put things more directly than they could. Then she asked me what I wanted to talk about. I told her the whole story of my expedition to the country. She looked sad but said I mustn't think anything would happen to the peasants I'd been having tea with. Times had changed and we couldn't judge from abroad. She was only sorry I had been treated discourteously. But I must understand.

Gabovich and Slonimsky came in. Panova introduced me to them, stayed a little, then said she had to go, telling me before she left: 'Let your heart be at rest.'

Gabovich had come to Leningrad to talk with Slonimsky about the text of our ballet book. They were glad we had met and were anxious to discuss the criticism of the Soviet ballet that had already appeared in the British press and might be expected again, e.g. that it was concerned with propaganda. I said that occasionally it gave this impression; e.g. in *The Seven Beauties* the peasant riot scenes seemed rather like propaganda, since they only cluttered up the plot. They said that *The Seven Beauties* was taken from an epic poem. If we wanted to make a film about Cromwell, wouldn't we put in both his love life and his political activities? I said we were unlikely to make a ballet on that theme. They agreed that *The Seven Beauties* was a bit complicated and that this was possibly a weakness in some of the others. But their aim was to express great stories through ballet. The weakness of our ballets was not attempting enough – short ballets didn't give dancers sufficient scope. I asked if they knew Diaghilev's last ballet – *The Prodigal Son*. They said they had seen photos of it and had studied them carefully. I then recalled the supper scene. They said that kind of thing was clever but not moving – or was it? We talked a lot about the difference im-

posed by scale. At the Bolshoi you had to have huge tableaux, otherwise the dancers would be crushed. This and big crowds influenced the
whole style. They asked me if it would be a good idea to bring *The
Fountain* to London. I said 'Yes'. They remarked that Margot Fonteyn
too was keen on it. I ate with them and went home.

I had rung up Gradov in Moscow to know if he had had a reply yet.
He said 'No'.

Since I had more time to put in, I again took the electric train and went
for a walk in the country, just looking at the land and feeling how
much it was in my bones.

The train back was full. In the carriage next to mine men were
singing. After a few stops an elderly woman and a man came in and
sat opposite me. He said he was a widower. Asked by the woman why
he didn't remarry: 'Well, what about it?' he replied. They looked up
at me laughing. 'What do you think of that?' she asked. 'You've just
had a proposal,' I answered, and we talked all the way back, or rather
Klava talked nearly all the time. She used to be a librarian in Moscow
but she left in '51. The first time she said this she only implied something disagreeable, but the next time she explained. 'I found myself in
the dock. There had been a mistake.' She got ten years but served only
two as after the amnesty of 1953, she was released. She had been ill and
they put her in a Home for Invalids. She recovered but didn't like the
Home because it was full of chronic invalids and mad people. In the end
the officials in charge helped her to get a job as a housekeeper to an
engineer whose wife was a nurse. They lived in a place where there
were some smart and learned people. The couple have two daughters,
a dog, a cat, a cow, chickens and a vegetable garden. Klava works in
the house, looks after the cow, but not the garden – the family work
that themselves. She earns 200 roubles and is content. Her mistress says:
'Make this or that for dinner' and she does it gladly. Why shouldn't
she?

The other day the daughter went to do some shopping in Leningrad
and lost 1,000 roubles. The money was in her despatch case but it
didn't shut properly. All the people round us nodded in sympathy and
indignation at the zhuliki who must have stolen the money. But
Klava said: 'Well, her mother told her when she came back that it was
God's punishment.' 'Why was she punished?' 'That very day she had

told me not to believe in God, and that there was no Heaven or Hell.'
Everyone agreed that the girl deserved something.

A beggar woman walked down the carriage singing the Litany of
Our Lady. People gave her money and somebody remarked: 'On one
side the Litany, on the other side the songs.' (The workmen were
singing.) The old man who had 'proposed' to Klava lost some of his
children in the war. But he has one son left who works in building.
'In my day,' he says, 'there was not so much education – I only did
four classes. Now they do seven or even ten, but they aren't much
better off. What happens? They come to Leningrad, and having no
connections and no strings to pull – what do they do? . . .' 'I know,'
said Klava, 'go into building at 400 roubles.' 'That's right.'

As we were getting near Leningrad I told them I was a foreigner.
'Well, what do you think of the way we live in the Soviet Union?'
asked Klava. '*Khorosho* (Fine).' As we parted she invited me to visit her
'family'. They were, she said, very hospitable, and would enjoy seeing
a foreigner. Better come in the evening, then they would be sure to be
in. 'You will see how a cultured Soviet family lives.'

The prospect was attractive and so next evening I took the electric
train. Klava had said it was a tiny place and everybody would know
the house. But when I arrived there was no one about except one
woman sitting on a bench in the station. I asked her where the engineer's house was – she didn't know. I inquired at the ticket office.
The clerk said she didn't know but that they were sure to tell me at a
house nearby. I was about to go there when two very young policemen popped out of the ticket office. They had heard my inquiry and
wanted to know who I was and why I was going to see the engineer.
I had no time to ask myself what I should say, but my impulse was not
to tell the whole truth. They looked to me very unlikely to believe
that I was going at the invitation of the housekeeper. So I told them
about having been invited to Russia by Mezhkniga and said I wanted to
meet some cultured people to talk about books. 'How is it then,' one
of them said, 'that you haven't got the exact address?' He was obviously a conscientious worrier. The other tried to calm him down but
he insisted. 'How is it that you are alone if you are a foreigner?' I said
he was behind the times and showed him my passport. He looked at it
and complained: 'How are we to read that?' I pointed to the Russian

visa, but this still didn't satisfy him. The other boy argued, but it came out that what was really worrying the worrier was that he believed I was a Russian official sent to 'test' them. 'What could the test be?' To pass it, should they know the engineer's address and show me the way – or not help me? I teased him. He began all over again, asking the same questions. 'I've already told you.' 'Will you repeat it again?' I obliged. 'But how is it that you know the name of the engineer but not his exact address?' I said: 'For God's sake, dear man,' an expression that was still quite normal, but he says – 'Why God' – surely I was not a believer. I said we mostly are in my country. Which country? And that started it all up again. I wished now I could see someone responsible; I asked the boys to take me to their chief. But since I'd asked to see him, they felt it must be the wrong thing to do. The argument became good-tempered, when after one had called me 'Mum' I told him he ought to call me 'Granny'. 'I'm fifty and you must surely be of an age to be my grandson?' But, he complained that I didn't look like a Russian Granny. We argued about this too. Now another idea entered his head. If really I was a foreigner but not a delegate I must have come through 'contacts', i.e. the engineer is my 'contact' – he had been in touch with me when I was in England. This was not at all so good and I only just managed to go on joking. Finally the return train to Leningrad arrived and the other boy begged me to take it and to come back some other time, the implication being when these two were not on duty. I took the train and spent the journey in the deepest worry.

MOSCOW

Now I felt it really was time to get back to Moscow, so I took the late train and found myself in a sleeping compartment with a Finn. We laughed at this sort of thing being taken for granted in the Soviet Union, talked and went to sleep. Soon after we arrived I went with Gradov to see Boni who said they had come to a decision. They liked the project but would not pay for the photographer's stay. I said I'd see what Collins said to that. I mentioned I'd met Slonimsky and Gabovich in Leningrad. Boni said they had been commissioned to write the text for our book. I asked, if London agreed, whether it would be possible to get a visa in time for the photographer to come out before the ballet season ended? He said this would normally be difficult but they'd do their utmost and were fairly sure it would be all right.

Went to Mass, then got a cable from Mark Bonham Carter, agreeing that Collins would pay Baron's expenses. I telephoned Boni. He said he'd ring the Soviet Embassy in London at once about the visa. I cabled Baron to apply for it.

Then I went to the Artists' Union Committee. Here I met Goncharov, dark and bright-eyed and looking like a painter anywhere. The rest of the Committee were more stuffy. They plunged at once into the theory of painting. A man who was, I think, Secretary of the Union said that art must be useful. I asked what he meant by that. He said the Soviet Union had left abstract art behind in 1910. Giorgione's 'Sleeping Venus' was wonderful, so were Picasso's plates but not his distorted oils. I said the distortions in some cases were caricatures expressing his opinion of the world. He said personal opinion was only valid if it expressed that of a group. Rouault and Braque were interesting but there was something lacking in their work. At this Goncharov broke in saying he liked them. The Secretary said art must be influenced by social aims. This started an argument but all agreed that art must be ennobling. I asked whether the social aim of art had to be conscious (Goncharov said, of course not) and whether, if an artist had had a real experience and expressed it he would not reach to a universal level. Goncharov agreed that art was ennobling by being human, real. I inquired how democracy in art was to be gauged. Goncharov, without saying very much, seemed to convey that no external tests of 'usefulness' were possible, but he too rejected abstract art. At one end the Secretary was repeating clichés, Goncharov at the other could have been on common ground with David Jones,[9] but they managed a *modus vivendi*. I suppose the test will be whether they go on showing better pictures.

As I was leaving they invited me to the Tretyakov anniversary celebration that was taking place that evening at the Bolshoi. I accepted. The girl secretary at the Artists' Union had told me I must wear evening dress, but I found everybody else in afternoon dresses or suits. It was very cold as the heating had been turned off. Photographers and TV men were flashing all the time. There was a huge portrait of Lenin over the dais and a large number of officials standing under it.

Speeches followed – including one by Grabar who said the Tretyakov Gallery was the best in the world. A worker from the Red Banner factory also congratulated the gallery and spoke of the boundless talent of the Russian people, saying that new artists would show even more widely the heroism of the Russian people and the struggle for Communism, as outlined by the Twentieth Congress. Later I spent an hour and a half getting details of the voltage at the Ballet School and trying to arrange a meeting with the Bolshoi Art Director to discuss Baron's timetable.

SUZDAL AND VLADIMIR

Since I could do no more for the moment I left at 1 am for Kursk station; it was rather sinister – full of rough-looking types and drunks. I got a ticket for a 'couch' in a general coach. The fact that a bunch of soldiers were also getting into the coach worried me a little as, if stopped, I would look as if I were trying to get into conversation with them. However, about a third of the passengers were civilians. The conductor said I had the right to a couch and tried to dislodge a boy who was lying on it, but he was sleeping so soundly I said to leave him in peace. The other passengers sympathised – 'Nothing sweeter than sleep'. The conductor agreed.

Near me two jolly girls told me they were going to relations in Vladimir: one of them had a ticket for a bunk and climbed up, the bunks were in two layers over the seats; two soldiers climbed on to a top one and flirted sedately with the girl until she said she was sleepy. The motherly young conductress called out to them: 'Don't fall off, children.' The soldiers then came down and sat with the conductress, huddled in friendship, asking her: 'Who knocked out your teeth? Makes you look old!' (She had a mouthful of steel teeth.) She let everybody smoke and every now and then came and swept up the ash.

My neighbour was a woman who had been travelling for six days from beyond Frunze on the Chinese border. She dozed at first, then in the early hours sat shivering in her cotton dress and short jacket, her legs under her. I wrapped her in my coat and she relaxed and talked. She lives near Gorky with her husband, a factory worker, and their sons. Last year her daughter married a soldier and went, nervously, to live with him in his native village in Asia. Now she likes it except that it's so far away. Her mother had just had three weeks' holiday and visited her. She described the scenery – 'All mountains all round, you look up – it's frightening. Snow; tall, thin trees stretching to the sun, poplars, birches. Hot springs leap out of the mountain. They catch them in pipes. The pipes go all round the houses and to the fields. You can bathe in natural hot water. All the irrigation is artificial – there's hardly any rain.' Her daughter is a teacher, a typist and a pay-master in a Children's Home. She was lucky to get this job at once as there are hardly any schools yet in that area. Her son-in-law is a driver. 'Wages are low there but they can grow what they like and have thirty sotniks of their own, so live well. They grow everything, only buy Lent oil,[10] sugar and salt.' Her daughter has two cows, a bullock, a heifer and poultry. 'It's green there now – tall grass, they had tulips for the 1st of May.'

The night was noisy; a baby cried fitfully and snatches of song came from the next carriage when the door opened. Dawn broke at three o'clock. By four o'clock I could read. There was a wet light out-side and I saw soft spring woods, birch mostly, grassy clearings and little houses with three windows in honour of the Trinity.

Soon the girl climbed down from her bunk. She had wonderful chestnut-gold hair that went well with the Russian landscape. We col-lected our things and stood by the door, for we were approaching Vladimir. A young soldier pointing at the churches said there are always many churches in merchant towns.

I breakfasted in the old station dining-room and admired its painted ceiling. People were eating extraordinary meals – herrings with cucum-ber, red cabbage and red berries. I ordered the same with black bread – there was no butter except on sandwiches. Having eaten, I went out and saw a little street climbing up to the town with its kremlin on an escarpment and churches higher up. I walked on and at the top there was a view over the vast, dark plain, a winding river and the harbour. Cocks were crowing and I had the same feeling of width, air and of noises coming from a far distance, as in Ryazan.

I decided to go first to see Suzdal and walked along a big street with pale green and pink stucco houses, to the bus station where there was a long queue waiting for tickets. The office was closed until the Suzdal bus arrived; the queue waited patiently. A fairly well-dressed man wearing a floppy hat said: 'One can go by taxi at fifteen roubles a head

if there are four passengers.' He was evidently ready to pay, so I said
I'd keep his place in the queue if he'd go and look for a taxi. He went
and found one and another passenger – a boy going to a kolkhoz near
Suzdal. As we were walking to the taxi we picked up a *babushka*
('Granny') who came with us.

We had the usual talented driver who ably negotiated the fearful
road. The land was dark and flat, so flat that when we climbed an
almost invisible hillock we saw miles and miles of tumble-down huts
with pretty painted carvings, villages with big white churches and one
far off on the right that was wrapped in mist. The mud was appalling.
The driver said the road had been built for the Tsar to go on a pil-
grimage. I saw many churches in the distance and I asked if this were
Suzdal. 'Yes,' said the well-dressed man, 'only Suzdal can look like
that.' But as we arrived, the driver remarked: 'It's a drab sort of town,
really.' The well-dressed man, drinking it in, turned to me saying:
'Don't worry, you'll have nothing to complain of.' At this the driver,
looking apologetic, said that he was used to it so perhaps that was why
he didn't see its beauty. The babushka and the boy got out. We went
on and I had a little conversation with the well-dressed man. As we
had both come to see things I expected he would be hard to get rid of.
But when I told him I was English he looked very startled and when I
gave him a chance to duck out he took it.

Almost at once, I came upon the market-place – looking just like a
scene out of *Petrouchka* – the crowds, the stalls, the carts with vendors
standing up in them, selling little pigs, goats, sheep. Blue-painted
booths in the background and the white churches. Beyond the live-
stock market people were selling sacks of new potatoes to the accom-
paniment of much bargaining. In the middle of the market-place I saw
a 'working' church, its doors open; people were going in; there were
candles in the dark interior and an old man reading prayers to which
the crowd was responding. Mass had not yet started.

Later I went to the 'hotel' which had astonishingly a board with the
timetable of the buses and a list of monuments. On the first floor, there
was a row of little rooms, neat and painted blue; most were empty. At
the end of a corridor I found the usual primitive WCs behind a common door – one for men, the other for women – no running water
and no paper. The hotel didn't serve food and the 'Tea Room' was
farther along the street, so I walked downhill, through deep mud, past

a church used as a store-house. In front of me was the town (village)
spreading out on the right with a still stream mirroring two white
churches. I crossed a narrow plank bridge with railings on one side of it
and went up to a church – I found it locked, but its defaced frescoes
were visible through a broken window. Then I went across the valley
past another church to where the town peters out into another village
which has a pink nineteenth-century church. The whole place is really
a collection of sprawling villages centred round the kremlin which
stands on a green hill surrounded by other hills which once were
fortified. All around are many churches and monasteries. The view
was indescribable; the limitless flat, green and greyish-brown land, no
trees, and all these white churches and golden domes, widely scattered
on low hills, standing out against the sky.

On the plank bridge which I crossed, two women were talking.
'I've done my work, now I'll get no pay till the end of the year.' 'I've
managed to get some.' 'Well then, you intercede for me!' (They were
presumably referring to the fact that kolkhozniks had until recently
been paid only once a year after the harvest, but were now supposed
to be paid every month as an 'advance'.)

I went into the museum, formerly the patriarch's house, where a
nice-looking man, possibly a teacher, was taking round a group of
young people. He started with the Stone Age and palaeolithic man –
showing them the remains found in 'digs' round Suzdal, then went on
to 'the mystery' of where the Slav tribes came from. 'They brought
higher culture with them' he said and talked a lot about 'our ancestors'
who traded with the Arabs (Arab coins had been found here). Finally
he came to the conversion of Russia. 'At that time feudal lords were
tightening their hold on the peasants; part of this process was their conversion.'

Suzdal is a very old town, the cradle of Rus, its first capital. Later
the capital was moved to Vladimir and then to Kiev. The earliest
churches were destroyed by the Tartars.

In the middle of the room was a stone coffin with a skeleton inside
it. The guide said it was a Christian prince, buried in pagan fashion,
with one arm crossed over his chest, the other straight down. A
mother called to her eight-year-old son to come and look at the grisly
sight. The next room contained plaster casts of heads and some carved
stones of the eleventh-century church which was pretty well destroyed

by the Tartars. The guide described the sack of Suzdal, the nobles and the clergy being burned in the church where they were hiding. After this we saw prints of tortures inflicted in the monks' prison. The monastery had been used by the Tsars to put away their unwanted wives, said the guide. He went on to explain that part of the break-up of feudalism was due to Stenka Razin's[11] rebellion and part to the reformation of the Church which resulted in a new church subservient to the State. It was bitterly cold and the children complained that their teeth chattered. The guide took us out into the courtyard between the patriarch's house – a pretty sixteenth-century building – and the Cathedral, the first story of which looked very Norman, with its round arches and carvings, but much had been added between the fifteenth and seventeenth centuries. Inside it was rather ugly, much too narrow and tall, with most of its frescoes covered over by nineteenth-century paintings, though a few of the old ones were now being exposed. The guide said the later paintings were by what Khrushchev had called 'Vladimir daubers'. This did not refer to the earlier paintings which were good and were now being restored after being X-rayed – layer after layer of daubs had to be removed.

Then he lifted a coffin lid and said the dried-up body inside had belonged to someone the people had thought of as a saint – he did it very coarsely; some of his audience were a little horrified, others joked. A man asked if the churches were going to be restored. The guide replied, 'Yes', the structures were and the frescoes but they would not be given back for religious use.

An odd scene was created by a boy who looked the guide straight in the face and asked, 'Why only the structures and the frescoes?' A Komsomol girl cut in: 'Because it isn't necessary,' but the boy would not be silenced.

We came out into the courtyard under a grey sky but it was warmer than in the cold church. Someone asked how many churches there were in Suzdal. The guide said there had been forty, now there were twenty and one had been restored for the use of the clergy in 1948. He was asked if the destruction had been done before or during the Revolution. He said, 'Neither. In the thirties when we thought – wrongly – that our old culture must be destroyed and a new one built on its stones. Now we realise that old art has value.'

I went back to the 'working' church, then to the market, gay as ever; inside the enclosure onions were being sold and plates of cooked cabbage, and sunflower seeds.

I lunched at the 'Tea Room' canteen. Two lorry drivers joined my table and ordered rice with shreds of pork, *aladyi* (small pancakes with sour cream) and beer. I had milk soup, cutlets and jelly for 5r 25 k, tasteless and too much. The waitress refused a tip.

By this time it was two o'clock so I went to the bus station to discover ways of getting back to Vladimir. Several people were waiting hopefully without tickets and the clerk said that she must keep three tickets for people with children, invalids or other priorities. The queue grew quickly, but the only person who seemed agitated was a made-up girl with curls and glasses who was a newspaper correspondent and said it was disgraceful that tickets should be sold out in advance.

A young man came to the top of the queue and announced that he had priority. 'If you have, come along,' said the people in the queue. 'What is it?' – 'I'm joining my regiment.' – 'Why?' – 'I've served seven years; now they want me to go back for three months' retraining. I have to be at Petushki by eight – that's where all the contingents from the neighbourhood are gathering.' The clerk reserved not one but three seats, which meant there were none left. The people in the queue were laughingly disappointed and wondering if they should wait indefinitely or go home. I went into the office and told the clerk I needed to be in Moscow at least by tomorrow. She said probably I would be, adding that trucks passing by often offered lifts, but a man remarked: 'They'll drop you half way there or when they pass the militia post, because they haven't the right to take passengers.' By now there were some twenty of us waiting. At 2.40 a bus arrived; the clerk came up to me and said: 'This woman wants to sell her ticket; buy it.' I did, after asking the two people who had been ahead of me in the queue if they minded, they said 'No' and, anyway, it was my luck that the woman had offered it to me – my fate.

Next to me sat a woman with a baby and on the other side a man was carefully holding an infant; behind him was a sad-looking, half-blind Southerner with a concertina, and next to him his wife, also blind, at least in one eye.

Soon we came to the soldier's village where his family – about fifteen of them – were waiting to say goodbye to him. There were tears and kisses while the bus hooted and the driver shouted 'We'll be

late.' 'Don't be heartless' roared the soldier's family. He climbed back
with some friends. The bus was now full to cracking. The blind man,
with the sad face, suddenly began to play a gay song, the people took it
up, and we went hurtling over the atrocious road across the desolate
country, singing song after song. There were no trees and no tractors –
just fields and turned-up earth.

After a while we came to the town; here we were preceded by a
funeral. The coffin was carried in front of a crowd of mourners, its lid
was borne separately. It had red bunting on it. People discussed who
was being buried; they decided it must be a woman worker. One said:
'The Heavenly Kingdom be her lot.' The others joked; the bus hooted
and passed.

Outside Vladimir station a big crowd was waiting, sitting on the
pavement and on benches, eating and playing concertinas. There was
no direct train to Moscow till after midnight, but there was one at six
o'clock which meant changing at Petushki. I went to have another
look at the town. It has a lovely plain white church on a hill. The
public garden is pretty with the tracery of its birches showing up
against a background of pink, blue and green houses and a blue band-
stand. I visited a 'working' church.

Endless columns of soldiers were marching down the road; however, to my relief, there were no soldiers waiting at the station. I suppose they must have had their own train. A few women sitting on a
bench and a couple complaining of the upbringing of modern girls
and some young men were all I saw. Finally the Petushki train came in
and its passengers poured out in a disorderly fashion and those waiting
got on board.

A young man talked about the difficulty of travelling and what
hard work it was to be a speculator, travelling constantly in and out of
Moscow (carrying food out and selling it outside). 'Almost better to
be in a kolkhoz,' said one of the women. 'Well, no, not that.' I offered
English cigarettes. They were excited that I was a foreigner but less
interested in England than in personal things – How old was I? Was I
married? Had I children, etc.? A woman opposite me turned out to
be much older than I thought. 'I'm two years older than thou – buried
two husbands.' The train stopped continually at small stations. At one
of them a family got out and a boy from the next compartment
darted in, saw my Ehrenburg and borrowed it. Another boy sat down

next to me. He wanted to know about wages and prices in England. I said not all our wages were much higher than theirs but that our prices were much lower, e.g. you could get a good suit for £15 or less. He was overcome – at that rate a worker could get two suits with one month's pay! The boy was a casual labourer – he earned 300 roubles and said he could buy nothing but black bread on that. But he lived with his parents in a factory settlement.

He is a rolling stone and wants to move on. He thinks the present conditions awful and is sure they are better abroad, but is made cheerful by the fact that under the new five-year plan such engines as the one pulling our train will be replaced by electric or diesel ones; and also by seeing a cement road being laid – 'wonderful slabs joined by seams'. Finally we get to Petushki where the Ehrenburg reader brought back my book.

A fat woman and a high-school girl swept me into the station waiting-room. I bought sweets at the bar and offered them to the pair. The fat woman said: 'And you so old treating us young ones!' (I wonder what I must be looking like). The waiting-room was full of boys going off to their regiments; most were in mufti and a little drunk. They sat on the floor in front of us, talking cosily. They told me that the kolkhozniks mind being called-up, but that factory boys don't as army life for them is not so very different from their normal life.

We got into the train. A soldier sat down next to a girl and nudged her. She moved at once to sit between a fat lady and me. The fat lady scolded the boy – 'You can talk but you mustn't hurt a young girl's feelings.' A sergeant came in with two very young soldiers. He said they had been travelling since yesterday. They'd met a man who wanted to know if there were wizards; they told him 'Yes,' there were, and explained that the way to become one was to climb up a pine tree holding a glass of water at midnight on forty consecutive nights. This story was considered a tremendous joke.

'How do people live in England – in barracks?' a girl asked. The others laughed at her and said that English people liked privacy and having their own home, so did the Germans, who built good houses – POWs in their district had been building them up till last year. It was possible to get two-thirds of the money needed to build a house on credit from the State and when you paid this back you owned the house. They explained that employees get flats from their organisations, the rent being deducted from their wages. It wasn't a trouble-some system, but you never owned your flat.

The sergeant had been in the army for fourteen years, living in distant parts all that time, but he liked returning to his home town where he still had his mother and a brother. 'Everybody likes his native place. Those born in Moscow won't move out even though offered better housing elsewhere'; others – like himself, for instance, couldn't stand city life with its noise and bustle. Housekeeping in towns was troublesome and expensive. Some people even took their friends out to restaurants – 'less trouble and no more expense'. Women, he was told, were beginning to go to restaurants – but not alone, that would be shocking. He then remarked that he knew it was different in England: 'There a woman goes to a restaurant at midday, orders a whisky, perhaps with nothing to eat except a few sweets, opens her *Times* and sits reading the newspaper and sipping her drink for several hours!'

The sergeant grew gayer and gayer, then as we neared Moscow two policemen came in and asked him for his papers. His face fell. It turned out he was not only twenty-four hours late but had no travel order for one of the boys. Evidently he had got drinking with them, missed his train and picked up one extra. He and the boy were taken away and did not reappear. The women looked sad and bothered. 'Arrested him, poor fellow,' they lamented. One woman was worried about her own documents. I was too, but so tired and sleepy by now that I had no difficulty in relaxing. In the end, neither the woman's papers, nor mine, were asked for.

MOSCOW

Almost all my afternoon was taken up with inquiring about Baron's visa. I was still being told that it would be all right but felt anxious. I was also worried about his timetable. Eventually I was promised I'd be able to send a cable that night or at the latest the next morning, in time for Baron to take his plane.

I met Gusev and Kogan at the Bolshoi; both were amiable and sophisticated. They agreed that the plan for Baron's visit was work-able, especially as a timetable already existed for publicity photo-graphs wanted by Covent Garden. They thought the book a very good idea. But, right at the end, they told me I must get in touch with Stepanov for them to have the Ministry's final consent. I was horrified as I had been convinced, after Boni's assurance, that everything was settled and, besides this, I had had the assurance of the Ministry of Foreign Affairs and that of Kabanov, Moskhateli and Bocharnikova.

A nightmare day. I spent it telephoning to everyone I could think of to get the confirmation that all was in order for Baron's visit. First I rang Boni (back in half an hour), then Stepanov (away), then Kabanov (ill), then Moskhateli (ill), then Boni every half hour from nine till four. Finally he answered: the plan was easy to work out. I said I wasn't worrying about the plan but about the order from the Ministry. Boni asked if Baron was still in London. I said I didn't know. The Ministry of Foreign Affairs had promised his visa for that morning.

Boni: 'Well, I can tell you he hasn't had it yet. Ring me up to-morrow.' I said telephoning was no good. 'Then come at ten o'clock.' Gradov rang me up to ask for news. I asked if the Ministry had changed its mind. He thought not.

During the day I had two nice conversations with taxi drivers – first with a woman. 'You and I are thin because we smoke and we smoke because we're tired. If I had a husband to influence me I might stop but I only have two sons, eighteen and fifteen. The elder is at a Technicum; he gets a grant of 250 roubles. The other day he came in and said he had subscribed a hundred to a loan. I said: "How could you? You might have given less." He said: "No, we all had to." And it's called "voluntary". I earn 500 roubles; they came and asked me to subscribe 400. I said I wouldn't; finally I gave 200.' 'Could you have refused?' 'How could I? We're always frightened. The boys will earn all right when they are trained – 500–600 roubles from the start. But the elder still has one year at the tech. It's hard keeping a job in Moscow and easy to get a job in the provinces, but I have my family.'

My second driver was a gay young Southerner. He said: 'I make 800 roubles but I can't live on that so I steal another 400 roubles.' 'Don't you ever get caught?' 'A good thief doesn't get caught.' When I got out I offered him a tip which he refused, saying: 'That won't get me out of trouble and you might need it.'

Went to Mass and talked with a priest. He said things were getting better and priests were coming 'back' (from camps) and chapels in churchyards had been re-opened.

At 9.30 Boni rang me up cancelling my appointment and saying that the Ministry's final decision was that there should be no book. Appalled and almost incredulous, I asked: 'Why?' – 'The theatre is busy.' – 'But Kabanov, Moskhateli, Bocharnikova, and on Tuesday, Gusev and Kogan, all said the theatre and school were delighted with the prospect!' – 'They have a lot of rehearsals.' – 'How is it that you only know this now?' – 'The ballerinas have fallen ill.' I said I must insist on seeing Stepanov and 'bang on the table'. I rang again but Stepanov and Boni were 'out'. I'd been warned that this sort of thing does happen but that it is unusual. Anyway, it is quite intolerable and I won't give up yet.

Today I spent the morning telephoning Boni but couldn't get on to him till about 12.30. I repeated that I *must* see Stepanov before I left and I also asked what I was supposed to say in London – 'that all the ballerinas are ill?' He interrupted: 'I'm called on the telephone from Paris [this wasn't true as I could hear all that went on] and will ring back.' I waited but he never rang back. There seems to be nothing more that I can do so I may as well go home.

Third Journey to Russia
Winter 1961

Manya's third journey to Russia was made for pleasure. She, therefore, decided to visit the South which she did not know.

The Khrushchev era was now in full swing. Khrushchev had survived the upheavals which followed the de-Stalinisation, and which nearly cost him his position. In 1957 he had counter-attacked and soundly defeated the so-called anti-Party group which had sought to pull him down. He had put himself on the map as a world statesman, travelling widely and meeting the President of the United States as an equal. He had survived the fiasco of the Paris Summit Conference in the summer of 1960 and the initial impact of the great quarrel with Communist China. He had another three years to go before his fall. But although to the outside world he appeared to be undisputed master in his own house, this was far from being the case. Life was easier in the Soviet Union. There was more to buy in the shops. Fear of the secret police had dwindled. The prison population had been enormously reduced. The intellectual life of the country was transformed. But still nobody quite knew where he stood: what was permissible on Monday was heavily forbidden on Tuesday. And already the great promise of catching up with America had a hollow ring: the spasmodic, erratic, unco-ordinated industrial and agricultural reforms had not lived up to their promise. The Party was unsettled; the peasants seemed to be as poor as ever; the urban workers found it hard to make ends meet. Far from thanking Khrushchev for making life a little easier, people grumbled increasingly because the improvement was too slow. Khrushchev had brought the Soviet Union into a new era and freed it from Stalin's strait-jacket; but it was also an era of muddle. There were already nostalgic backward looks to the bleak and bloody certitudes of Stalin who, for all his harshness, was a strong, silent leader of unlimited strength of will. Khrushchev talked too much, boasted too much, clowned too much, changed his mind too often – and, with all this, he remained a prisoner of his own Stalinist past. The visionary dynamism which so impressed the West counted for all too little among his own people, who despised him and were later to allow his manifest inferiors to destroy him. Much of the prevailing mood is reflected in these pages.

This time, with no business to transact, after spending a few not very memorable days in Moscow, I went to Rostov. The charming hotel at which I stayed was straight out of Chekhov and there were no political portraits hanging on its walls. The town is famous for its pretty girls, and the maids were indeed dreams of beauty.

My room was large but it had very sinister-looking ventilators which I suspected of containing microphones. The restaurant was elegant but the food bad and the water heavily chlorinated.

No other foreigners were staying at the hotel and a Union Jack stood on my table as a warning to other visitors. Moreover, when I moved farther away from the noisy loudspeaker it followed me.

I went out for a walk early next day and was stopped by an old Jewish woman who wanted to buy my scarf. After I had warned her against such transactions, we went on together, talking. She told me that both her parents had been burnt alive by the Germans. As for Russia's present rulers, she thought of Khrushchev as 'a kind Papa who sees that children who lack clothes in which to go to school get them'.

After we parted I got into conversation with a middle-aged engineer who asked me how workers lived in England and obviously disbelieved every word I said on the subject.

That evening I proudly spotted my first *provocateur* – Polya was a friendly young woman who joined me in the snack-bar of the hotel. Soon she became excessively confiding and invited herself to my room for the following afternoon. I had no doubt of her intentions and looked forward to studying her technique.

Next day, with my mind at rest, having found the nigger in the wood-pile, I welcomed to my table at lunch two young men Peter and Fedya who introduced themselves as ardent Communists and passionately interested in Constructivist art. After a long discussion on its merits we agreed to meet again at dinner.

Polya came at six; she set a few traps which I avoided and I commented severely on incautious talk with foreigners. But she was still clinging to me when I went to meet Peter and Fedya. Thinking that she was safely outnumbered and curious to see what their reactions to each other would be, I dined with the three of them. They seemed to dislike each other at sight, but to bury their differences in the excitement of a further discussion on Constructivist art.

When we came out the street was crowded with Rostovians taking the air or going to the cinema. The young people wished me to see a theatre built in the Constructivist style; it had been damaged during the war but was now being repaired and would soon be functioning again.[1] We walked there, the door was invitingly open and the lights were on inside so we went in and up to the gallery from which there was a fine moonlit view.

I was feeling delighted with the eagerness of my artistic young friends when things began to go wrong. Polya and Peter vanished, then Fedya said he had lost his way and went to reconnoitre. While he was gone I heard distant voices and whistles. When Fedya returned we went down together and straight out into the arms of a posse of policemen headed by a man in mufti. A watchman, who had not been there when we arrived, stood by with a rifle. Within minutes Fedya and I were being whirled into the night and off to the police station for an identity check. There we were questioned together and separately by two men in uniform and by the man in mufti.

My bag was emptied on to the desk and an interpreter sent for from the hotel, to read my travel notes. After this my things were put back into my bag and we were driven to the theatre where flashlight photographs were taken of us separately and together; then we returned to the police station. Once more my things were taken out of my bag and this time my travel notes were carried into another room. Meanwhile, I was questioned without a pause. There were references to 'spies' and to 'undressing in empty theatres'. I said, 'But surely not in this temperature; the thermometer is well below zero.' After which that theme was dropped. By then it was 3.30 am; the policemen's faces were grey and Fedya sat in haggard silence. I said we had gone to the theatre with Peter and Polya but this was not followed up.

At 4.30 am the man-in-mufti drew up a statement for us to sign. It said that we had entered the building without authorisation and had recognised our error. 'Was entrance to the theatre forbidden?' I asked.

'No, it wasn't forbidden but it was a building with a watchman.'

'But the watchman wasn't there,' I protested. The man-in-mufti was unmoved. I pointed out that I could not have known that an authorisation was needed to enter the building and said I would not sign the statement unless this fact were included in it. It went in as 'Harari claims she did not know she was doing wrong.' By now I was very sleepy, so I let it go at that. A little later I was driven back to my hotel.

I woke up late and wondered, 'What next?' Had they arranged for me to stay another day, as I had asked, or would they send me at once to Krasnodar or perhaps to Moscow?

I went to the Intourist Office and told the guide, 'They have spoiled Rostov for me.' He looked as if he were genuinely puzzled by my remark. I wondered if he knew nothing about what had happened or if he just wanted my version? Anyway, I gave it to him, and expressed my surprise at the police making such a fuss. With an air of embarrassed sympathy he muttered something unintelligible and suggested I should have breakfast.

In the buffet a waitress suddenly became confiding. The day before she had motioned a woman away from my table but had not interfered with Polya, the *provocateur*, so I assumed that she was definitely 'one of them'. Now she told me that she was born in China of émigré parents and had returned to the Soviet Union in 1954. With this background she was still more likely to be 'one of them' and I decided that she was fishing for my reactions to last night's events, but, how could one be sure? Perhaps she was just feeling human, certainly she looked rather sad.

After breakfast the Manager summoned me and solemnly warned me to 'take my last night's experience seriously.' He added that, for the present, I could proceed with my journey but that a report had gone to Moscow and that further action might be taken. I repeated that I could not understand what the fuss was about? He said 'It looks bad. You had better take warning.' It then emerged that I was not to have my extra day in Rostov and as the plane for Krasnodar was leaving at one I would have to start in half an hour's time. While I was packing Polya rang up. She said she wanted to let me know that she was all right; 'in spite of spending so much time with a foreigner!' Then she asked if I was all right? I expressed surprise that she and Peter had not followed us up to the gallery of the theatre; this sent her into a flurry of explanations. She kept on repeating that they had waited and waited for us. Presumably they were waiting for their secret police contact. I rang off coldly wondering if even now I should not make a fuss about the fact that she and Peter had been with us at the theatre? But how could I be dead sure that all three were equally 'in it'? Also, I was overcome by a curious paralysis induced by feeling that probably everyone was in bad faith and that any protest one made would be no more than a formality.

At the airport the guide left me in a palatial waiting-room with a restaurant next door where I had a leisurely lunch. By three o'clock there was still no sign of the plane – 'owing to the weather' said an Intourist girl who had arrived to keep me company. I began to wonder what the Rostov Hotel would do if no plane arrived that day, but in fact we got off at five.

KRASNODAR

When we landed at Krasnodar in an Arctic gale, Tanya, a plump Intourist guide, accompanied by a boy-friend-guide, met me at the foot of the steps; they were dressed in light coats and had waited all through the cold afternoon. Tanya was disappointed at my talking Russian. She had been a school teacher, and had only started her present job in the late summer and so, as in winter there were not many tourists, she had had few opportunities to practise her English. I therefore obligingly stopped speaking Russian, which cheered her up.

The hotel was newer but had less style than the one in Rostov. I was given two rooms, complete with the usual crushed velvet and a radio, which I mistrusted.

After I had unpacked, Tanya hurried me protectively through a restaurant with a loud band and loud clients to a quieter one. Here I could sit where I liked and was not pursued by a flag.

A technician, he looked about forty-five, came to share my table. I asked him about present conditions. He said there were shortages and that prices were high. Then he winked cynically as he said, 'Everything will be OK in five years' time.' We talked about the threat of war. He thought things unlikely to come to that. China might be feeling aggressive but everyone was afraid of the destruction that a nuclear war would bring. On the other hand, he was very proud of 'our technology'; 'it is tremendous, you just push a button and everything goes up in the air.' He seemed to have no fear that more countries would get the bomb (I think he had China and Albania in mind) because 'our Security Organs are busier than ever.' As to the tests, the Soviet Union was too big for the fall-out to reach all of it.

We discussed the exposure of Stalin's crimes and he assured me that a big clean-up was now going on and that fifteen hundred Stalinists had been picked up. They would not be shot, he said, but made to work. As for the Anti-Party group,[2] he thought they were just out for themselves.

Next morning, Tanya took me for a sightseeing tour; Krasnodar is a charming town with tree-lined streets, small pink, Regency-looking houses and new suburbs with austere blocks of flats and institutes.

Though proud of Krasnodar's history, she seemed rather ashamed of so much surviving pink and Regency and insisted that these buildings would soon be replaced.

We drove along Red Street, the principal thoroughfare. It is not named for Red[3] Revolutionaries but was so named by the Cossacks who came here to fight the Turks when this area lay on the frontier. Krasnodar means 'beautiful gift'. Catherine the Great gave the Cossacks land and, in 1794, they built a fortress; then, emerging from it, to the sound of a salvo of gun-fire, six oxen ploughed a long straight furrow, this is where Red Street now runs. The log hut of their Hetman Chapygin is still standing.

Soon we came to an old barrier through which the Decembrists passed on their way to exile in the Caucasus, then up a hill where, in 1918, The Workers' Artillery defeated the Whites, and a stray bullet killed General Kornilov.[4] There is a monument here to the 2,500 men who were killed in the battle; next we went on to The Park of Culture where the Germans massacred the Jews; there is no monument.

Krasnodar now has 371,000 inhabitants and many new industries such as vegetable oil, fruit canning, textiles. Its tobacco research institute, under the direction of a well-known scientist, is, according to Tanya, world famous. Indeed the region's agricultural development seems to be very successful, for the winter wheat is selected and gives the highest yield of any in Russia, while the sunflower seed, selected by another scientist, has a fifty-two per cent oil content.

Back in the centre of the town, Tanya pointed out a board of honour set up in the Municipal Garden on which were inscribed the names of the best kolkhozes; they are changed monthly. After this I was shown the imposing building of the City Soviet, and Tanya proudly told me that out of two hundred and ten deputies half were women and forty per cent non-Party. I inquired about an almost grimly grand building opposite; this proved to be the Party HQ.

In the afternoon I asked if I could have a look at the Steppe. We drove out of the town into a landscape that was unbelievably flat and endless-looking with strips of black *chernoziom*, the richest soil in Russia, showing between the winter wheat. Tanya thought the Steppe melancholy at this time of the year though, even so, it had a curious fascination; in summer, she said it was lovely, which I could well believe.

Before the war Krasnodar used to live off its orchards but many were destroyed in the fighting. Now they have been replanted and soon, said Tanya, there would be more orchards than ever before and she added hopefully that one day there would be no uncultivated land left. At the end of our expedition, as we stood looking at the River Kuban, its muddy waters reflecting the sunset, Tanya made tantalising references to Cossacks, Armenians and Circassians still living in the area. The Cossacks, she said, lived in their own villages and had kept to their way of life; they gave displays of dancing which the people of Krasnodar went to watch. Unfortunately these did not take place in the winter.

The Armenians and the Circassians, it seemed, also had their own quarters in the town but they were said to have mixed with the local population and lost most of their character.

On the following day, I was to visit a factory at eleven. This left me some time to put in so I went out with my camera. First I sat in the Municipal Garden looking at the pink houses showing through the bare trees and took some photos, then I went to the market.

As soon as I reached the street leading to it I found myself in a different world, with horse carts rattling on cobbles and drivers in wadded jackets.

In the middle of a big square there were pavilions for meat, dairy produce and vegetables, surrounded by open stalls. I photographed a woman in a grey wadded coat and shawl selling brilliant autumn flowers, and the crowd sitting or standing around. One woman posed for me, then a handsome old man in a fur hat and wadded coat asked, 'Where can we get the prints?' A babushka remarked 'It must be for the newspaper,' adding mysteriously, 'Probably it is about the cabbages.'

At this moment a severe young woman in a town coat and a silk scarf, her lips daubed with lipstick, asked me who I was, fired off a lecture on taking pictures of 'the dark side of Soviet life' and informed me that there was no cabbage shortage – the crowd was only waiting for another load to arrive and as for the old man, though he was a pensioner, he had a better coat at home. If I wanted to photograph representative Soviet types why had I not taken her picture? Comparing her smug face and hideous outfit with the peasant faces and the clothes of the crowd, I found this too difficult to explain, so I replied that markets were always picturesque and liked by all photographers and added that Soviet visitors to London often took pictures of our markets. Since however my taking such pictures seemed to offend her I promised not to take any more and put my camera in my handbag.

A few minutes later I had to take it out to get at my handkerchief and notebook, after which I put it back again, and went into the dairy pavilion.

When I came out four people in town clothes surrounded me, and said I must come to the militia post for an identity check. I replied that if they wanted a check it would surely be better to go to the hotel which held my passport and where I was known. But the two men and the two women insisted that I must go to the militia post and as they looked as though they were prepared to carry me off bodily I stopped arguing.

I wondered if they were *druzhinniki*,[5] or if the severe young woman had followed me from the hotel, or if perhaps they were simply eager beavers?

This time I was less interested at being taken away for interrogation than I had been in Rostov, the novelty had worn off, all the same I felt that some expression of annoyance was called for and would seem natural, so I said it was shocking manners to treat a visitor like this. In spite of my protest they marched me off.

At the militia post all four said, 'This woman was taking photos in the market.' After a longish wait I was escorted upstairs by a policeman. I asked him what all the fuss was about? He said 'popular indignation' at my taking photographs of the market. I pointed out that the old man had actually asked me for prints. The policeman replied, too quickly, 'That was a joke, he told me so.'

We entered a spacious office in which a handsome Police Superintendent sat at a desk with a shield of honour behind him indicating that he was the best Police Officer in the town. There were comings and goings, a man in mufti came in and asked the policeman a few questions and then went out again. I had another long wait during which the policeman kept a silent watch over me, then the man-in-mufti returned and said they would have to take and develop my film but if it was all right I would get it back. Soon the photographer arrived and removed the film under a black cloth.

I continued to wait; meanwhile the Superintendent conducted other business. He answered the telephone and said he was sorry, it was too late, Citizen Sedin, though a candidate for Party membership, had already been tried. Then he rang off and told the policeman to go to the Court where Sedin was being tried. Next he made another call and told whoever answered that Sedin was to be given fifteen days.

Interested, I asked what this meant. The Superintendent replied that if a comrade, who might in other respects be a decent fellow, misbehaved, e.g. was drunk and disorderly: 'We don't now as a rule try him, but give him fifteen days during which time he will not be in prison but employed in the nastiest job we can find for him, unpaid and in public, street sweeping, for example. This will shame him before his comrades who will afterwards take a hand in persuading him not to repeat his offence. He will remember the episode for the rest of his life. If the offender is not a man but a *damochka*[6] the impression made on her will be still deeper.' All this was said in a tough but hearty scoutmasterly tone.

I asked about 'Comrades' Courts'. The Superintendent said that initiative was now passing to the collective. Comrades knew the accused better than anyone else and were therefore well fitted to judge him. At this moment the man-in-mufti came back and the Superintendent told him in a sour-amused voice that I was asking questions about 'our Comrades' Courts'. I told them that in England it was thought fairer to the accused that no member of the jury should know him. Both men looked genuinely surprised and commented that 'the Comrades' were apt to be, if anything, too lenient.

In spite of his polite attitude towards a foreigner-who-might-even-be-a-journalist, I suspected him of longing to put me, as a damochka, to street cleaning, if the telephone calls to Rostov and Moscow, which had presumably been put through downstairs, didn't allow for something worse.

The man-in-mufti said that a statement would now be drawn up and he summoned the witnesses.

The severe young woman said I had been taking tendentious photographs. She and her two friends had stalked me without my noticing them. ('You didn't notice us, did you?') I had kept on vanishing, then I spoke to someone (this was presumably when I had asked which pavilion was which), and they had seen me taking photos secretly after she had warned me not to do so. Also, they had seen me writing in a notebook. The other witnesses confirmed her statement. Then the old man, a Tartar, was produced and said, in broken Russian, that he had a better coat at home and even money in the bank. Upon which the man-in-mufti asked, nastily, if I would like to see his other coat and added that presumably I expected to sell my photographs at a good price.

The statement was then produced, ready for my signature. I said I would not sign it as I hadn't taken tendentious photographs and had not taken any after I had said I would not do so, and since they had the film they could check this. One of the witnesses began to look rather embarrassed but persisted in saying that I had gone on taking photographs. The man-in-mufti remarked that if I would not sign he would have to go further into the matter.

'What was your father's occupation?'

'Banker.'

'Ah,' exclaimed the witnesses, and the interrogator went on,

'Then you had no reason to love us. What was his name?'

'Benenson.'

'What is your nationality?'[7]

'British.'

'That's your citizenship, not your nationality. What is that?'

'In the Soviet Union it would be Jewish, but not in England.'

One witness gave the others a satisfied glance.

'We thought so from the name.'

I felt sure that the Superintendent would never believe that Jewish 'nationality' did not exist in England, so it seemed hardly worth while arguing the point, but I was annoyed at their behaving as though I had at last 'come clean'.

'When did you leave Russia?'

'Nineteen-fourteen.'

There was a pause while the man-in-mufti was writing all this down.

'Well, you slithered away just in time, didn't you?' said one of the male witnesses.

I gave him a withering glance and said he had no business to use such an expression.

One of the girls suggested that perhaps the statement should include the fact that I didn't want to come to the police station. At this I suddenly got cross and said 'Certainly I was indignant, and I want that included in the statement.' The girl insisted that I had 'begged' to be taken to the hotel and had said that it was the right place for an identity check.

The man-in-mufti remarked sententiously that it was the business of the collective to decide where I should go.

Ideas about the rights of the individual swarmed in my head – what kind of a law was this if, on the one hand, the Superintendent gave Sedin fifteen days, and on the other hand it was the collective who decided? One of the witnesses said I had complained that it was shocking manners to treat a foreigner like this.

'And,' interposed the man-in-mufti, 'Didn't you say that foreigners in England could go freely to markets?'

'Certainly!'

The girl said: 'That is different; they come to look at your prosperity.'

So there it was, the heart of the matter perhaps, but she went on about the unfairness of photographing people in 'working clothes'.

'Why should working clothes be shameful?' I asked.

'These weren't representative of Soviet workers,' she replied.

The man-in-mufti read out the statement in which my 'version' went down as 'in spite of the evidence of citizens given in her presence ('You admit that, don't you?' he asked, proud of this evidence of keeping to the rules) Englishwoman Harari claimed that her photographs were not tendentious and that she stopped taking them when warned.' I signed the statement, though I was not sure if I were giving in to a sort of paralysis induced by the sense of general conspiracy. The witnesses were dismissed. The man-in-mufti and the Superintendent said they hoped I understood. I said I did now – 'Russians are evidently morbidly sensitive about things taken for granted everywhere else,' but they warned me to take the incident seriously into account and said I could go now, but a report was being sent to Moscow and perhaps also to my 'superiors'.

A little surprised at being free I took a tram to the hotel. I had left the market at 9.45 and it was now 1.30 and we had missed the visit to the factory. I felt more tired than in Rostov. Getting cross is not a good idea, both because it makes you feel less dignified and because it involves you in exhausting indignation. I went on wondering who was who – the 'witnesses' *could* have been just vigilant citizens, but the police were surely carrying out orders. Was I going to be arrested every two days until I gave up and went home, or they got me?

At the hotel Tanya said, reproachfully, they had waited for me at the factory all morning. That afternoon she saw me off to Yalta with her usual friendliness and conscientious fluster. I told her about the market incident and she looked upset and claimed she knew nothing of it. I asked her if she had been with me would she have stopped me from taking photographs in the market; she said 'No' and that anything could be photographed except military objects and there weren't any in Krasnodar.

YALTA

When I landed at Simferopol, the Intourist girl who met me proved to be a second generation émigré, who had returned from France. She still looked smarter than the rest. The weather was mild but it was drizzling. Outside the airport there were the usual new blocks as well as some small houses. The road to Yalta ran across mountains, with views of the sea; the driver was proud of their beauty and said the coast was like that near Naples.

There are two Intourist hotels in Yalta. I stayed at the Ukraina which seemed to be the second best; it was not on the sea front. I was given a largish room with a bathroom, but no alcove; again there was a suspicious radio.

A soft looking middle-aged type joined me at lunch. He had a job as a grape selector at a local research institute. He had lived in Leningrad till '51 and was still nostalgic for it. He suggested we should meet again and have a 'philosophical talk.'

'Everyone seeks his truth,' he said.

'Hard to find,' someone at the next table called out.

'Always was hard, still harder now,' said the soft type.

I asked if they could tell me where the Post Office was as I wanted to send a cable. The soft type offered to show me the way. I went up to get my coat but when I came down he had fled.

I walked along the front, to a square with a statue of Lenin, and sat down on a bench next to two men; one turned out to be a foreman in a carpet workshop, the other a war invalid. The invalid said Stalin had been the 'greatest of all Socialists'; now he had been demoted – it was a shame. The foreman told me there were many statues of Lenin in the region and also of Stalin, but that a night or two ago Stalin's statue had been removed from the main square. 'We were surprised,' he remarked, 'by the anti-Stalin statements at the Congress.' I asked him more about the Congress.

'He'll tell you,' said the foreman, pointing to the invalid. 'He's a Communist.' The man responded by asserting that 'By 1980 the plan will have been achieved, there will be prosperity throughout the country and as a result everyone will be good.' Then he mentioned, as a new trend, the growing importance of the collectives illustrated by the Comrades' Courts. He did not think Russians were afraid of war, but, of course, they would fight if they had to, meanwhile it was bad that the West was encouraging the Germans.

Both these men listened to The Voice of America, the BBC and the Munich and Deutsche Welle broadcasts, which are easy to hear on the coast.

The foreman had been in Austria in the army of occupation and

changing world

ENGLAND

as a little world by itself by the side of the greater, for the diversion of mankind

David Jones' cover design for an
issue of 'The Changing World'

had found it interesting. He asked me if there were more goods in English shops than in Russian shops? I hesitated politely, but no doubt taking my answer for granted, he went on to remark that Austrian shops were better stocked and that Russian prices were higher and had risen since the currency change.

He believed that Stalin had done some good but things were better now, for example people could talk freely, within certain limits, also contacts with foreigners were now possible, though again only within certain limits. He showed me where to have tea and then left me in front of the café; perhaps he was making his point about meetings with foreigners needing to be conducted prudently? That night the hotel restaurant was closed, so I dined elsewhere. A reporter from Moscow shared my table. He put on a man-about-town act and talked about a friend of his, of his own age (late twenties) who was actually a believer, and went to church; for that matter, his father was a believer, but at least he prayed only at home, and that was all right.

After he had left, a man whom I had noticed listening to our conversation came and sat down at my table. I wondered then if he were a 'follower' and I was never able to make up my mind. I thought he looked Jewish, so I asked him about anti-semitism; he said it had been bad under Stalin but wasn't now, and he assured me that he did not think being a Jew would prevent him from rising in his profession. He was married and had a son, and hoped he would become a technician like himself, but his wife wanted him to be a lawyer or a diplomat. The boy, he said, spoke good English, adding that languages were very well taught at school.

The conversation turned to the subject of war; he believed that the Russians and the Chinese were the world's toughest fighters. During the war his unit had been surrounded and they had been without food for days, but all the same they had eventually succeeded in breaking out. Towards the end of the fighting he had been taken prisoner but had been freed by the men of his own company. Speaking of the Crimean Tartars he said they had been deported and forbidden to return because they had collaborated with the Germans. Now they were living on the Volga. He and his wife had spent a year near the Chinese border among deported Bulgarians. They worked in the mines and were paid the same wages as Russian miners but had to register with the police to prove they had not moved.

Describing Stalin's visit to Yalta he said that he had been guarded by soldiers who not only surrounded the villa but were posted on the mountains all round. 'Khrushchev,' he added, 'may also be guarded but at least the guards are kept out of sight and he has won the people's hearts by his accessibility.'

As to the plan which the invalid had assured me would bring prosperity by the eighties, my new friend considered it foolishness to imagine that it would be fulfilled. After all, it had been based on people's estimates of how much more they could produce. 'Can you see anyone telling the truth about that? If a man says he can produce X amount more than he has been producing up till then, this can only mean that he has been lazy or in fact producing X plus Y and keeping the difference for himself as a reserve for the next period or selling it to his friends.' This attitude, he commented, was as common among the highest operatives as amongst the lowest paid workers. The big shots, he assured me, earned ten thousand new roubles a month and 'if your wage is above that figure, then they don't pay you in money, you just say what you want and they get it for you.'

When the restaurant closed we walked along the sea front but I wondered if while I collected my coat from the hotel someone had warned the man for now he was both cautious and aggressive. This seemed to contradict my earlier suspicion that he might be a 'follower'. But perhaps he was just a neurotic type (very common today in the USSR) his two psyches alternating from one moment to another.

When I finally returned to the hotel the Intourist woman at the desk said, rather reproachfully, that it was usual for foreigners to go on expeditions which had been arranged for them by the Intourist office at the Oreanda Hotel, so next day I duly went there and saw a dear old gentleman. He said that obviously I did not need an interpreter and that I should go to The Chekhov House and ask to see the curator. In spite of this Marianna Kuzminishna, a smart and pretty guide, came up saying she was my interpreter. I pointed out that I did not need one. 'We don't foist ourselves on people,' she replied; but firmly did so.

We drove through the usual new suburbs, up to a restaurant on a hill with fine views visible through rain. Here I got my own back on Marianna, who thought we should stay indoors, by saying that I was used to rain and keeping her out in it in her light mackintosh, which she assured me was 'of excellent quality'. After she had told me that everything could be photographed, including the port, I took out my camera.

Yalta, founded by the Greeks, became fashionable in the nineteenth century, but it was Lenin who turned it into a health centre.

There is a legend about the neighbouring resort of Gurzuf where there is a rock which looks like a stooping bear. The story goes that a baby girl was stolen by bears and brought up by them; then, one day, while the bears were out hunting, a Prince Charming turned up and carried her off. When the bears returned they pursued the couple up to the moment in which they were boarding the Prince's ship. Then, discouraged, all went off except for one bear who tried to drink up the sea. Seeing this the girl called out a magical word and turned him into a rock.

During most of our sightseeing expedition Marianna nearly killed herself trying to explain Soviet achievements. There was a 'wonderful' Pioneer camp at Gurzuf and 'wonderful' sanatoria and 'wonderful' rest houses at which a stay of twenty-four days cost only seventy roubles, two thirds of which was paid by the Trades Union and there was a 'wonderful' projected law which would make the journey to the resort free of charge. She seemed convinced that only in the Soviet Union was there any kind of Health Service. I said we have one too, but she didn't appear to hear me and went straight on.

I had lunch at the Oreanda where the cloakroom girls inquired about the price of my Greek shirt and the waiter asked if he could buy my ball-point pen.

An old Bolshevik schoolmaster, on holiday, came to share my table and at once went into the attack. 'London slums, beggars,' etc. After my morning with Marianna I was feeling rather fed up so, a little rudely, I told him to 'come off it'. Instead he started on 'our technology and how many bombs would be needed to wipe out England?' Then he remarked that 'when a number of countries had begged Khrushchev not to explode the fifty-megaton bomb he had not done so.' The schoolmaster's attitude seemed to me to illustrate the ambivalence, so often observable here, that appears to come from wanting to be feared as strong while at the same time being respected as 'cultured'. Finally he reverted to social conditions, taxation, etc. I tried to explain the social and economic changes that had taken place in England since the war and the new face these had given to capitalism. When I stopped he said, 'All the same capitalism exists with you? The Welfare State doesn't alter that.' But clearly he suspected that what had taken place had altered the situation and that we were achieving the real aims of the Revolution more quickly than the USSR was. This attitude is very general and has the effect of making people cling to abstract differences.

Later I went to a church where there was to be a service at six. I waited for the doors to open. In the yard a man was standing quite still. I wondered what he could be. A watchman? A 'follower'? A lunatic? Soon the usual woman came along, looking important, unlocked the door, tidied up and took charge of the candle stand. Then the church began to fill with old women, sitting at the back, and a sprinkling of men and girls in front. A youngish priest whom, after the service I asked to see, said I should come back on Tuesday but looked distrustful.

I walked out of the church next to a respectably dressed man in his fifties, and when we reached the street I talked to him. He said that both his parents had been believers and he had always been one; he found it 'good to go to church in times of both sorrow and joy.' His wife was neutral, his children did not believe and his brothers and sisters laughed at him. Science, he said, did not conflict with religion. 'Look at Pavlov, officially described as an atheist but well known as a believer; a church in Leningrad which was to be destroyed was preserved till after he died because of his influence.' This reminded me that in '56, when I was in Pavlov's native town of Ryazan, I had heard a story about a church there which had been saved thanks to him. The man then told me about Archbishop Luke, who had died recently. Before he took orders, he had been a surgeon and during the war told Stalin that he wanted to use his skill and went back to surgery. And then there was the Metropolitan Alexis who had three learned degrees. All of which proved that religion was not just for the simple.

At dinner that night I shared a table with an elderly woman, a postmistress who had retired four years ago. She was friendly, bright, down-to-earth and wilful, in an old-ladyish way. Her daughter, also a post office employee, was working in the Arctic where the pay was very good. But Murmansk was, the old lady said, a fearful place:

barren, 'lacking oxygen' and enveloped in the polar night. Her little grandson lived with her but she took him to visit his mother in the winter.

'Why in the winter?' I asked.

'Well, I'm not going to do without my summer,' she replied.

'We've lived through terrible times,' she went on.

She had been in Kiev during the Revolution and described the dreadful street fighting. The years of the NEP had been good but then came the famine. In '33 she had had an abortion, though the doctor had told her 'You'll be ruining your health.' But how could she bear to give birth to a child who would inevitably starve? Then there had been the war and after it more terror.

'We knew,' she said, 'that people vanished, but we didn't know why. Now we know that there were criminals in the Kremlin. Why didn't they tell us then? We'd have done something.'

'But, could you have done anything?' I asked.

'Perhaps not, people who have suffered too much become too patient!'

She said that things were better now, but not all that much. She had 7,500 roubles in savings, now Khrushchev had put off repayment for twenty years, for her that meant that her savings were as good as lost 'even if ever they do repay them'. Like others she complained that the shortages of meat and butter and the high prices were due to food being exported 'to the Congo and other places of that sort'. 'As patriots, we are supposed to understand; but when will the Russians live well?' Then she told me an old joke:

Peter the Great to Stalin: 'I opened a window on Europe, you banged it shut.'

Catherine the Great to Stalin: 'I corrupted a palace, you corrupted a country.'

At this point a friend put her head round the door and called her out. She returned looking worried and saying she must go. I tried to reassure her but still evidently upset she went off.

Next morning, after going to a crowded service, I went to Chekhov's house where the Curator kept me for two hours helping him to translate a Chekhov bibliography he had been sent from the United States. He was a nice old boy, half deaf and half blind, which seemed symbolical. He works in a semi-basement study unchanged since Chekhov's day and is nannied by a kind, middle-aged assistant. Delightedly he corresponds with Chekhov experts all over the world and is oblivious to everything else. He dug up a *Times* cutting about the translation of *The Cherry Orchard* I made for the BBC, and told me that the play had been translated thirty-four times into English (that included American as well as English texts), and that a girl in Tbilisi was writing a thesis on this remarkable fact.

Afterwards I sat on the quay with a middle-aged Ukrainian couple. Talking of recent events, he said 'Fancy Beria having been an agent all along, right since the twenties.' (!) Unlike most of the other people I had talked to, his wife said that people were worried by the tests and afraid of war. Two or three promenaders stood round listening to us; then one of them, a sombre-looking youth, sat down next to me and announced importantly that he was writing a poem on Lenin. He made much of his writing, and said he had recited verse with Paustovsky at a local poetry reading. He then showed me his poem as well as one by Bedny[8] pointing out that he, unlike Bedny, did not use angry clichés.

By this time the Ukrainian couple had gone off and the poet asked me to go with him to the restaurant at the Yuzhny Hotel; I went and had tea while he drank 150 grams of vodka.

He wanted me to give him topographical details about London to use to complete his poem on Lenin. I asked why there were so many new poems on Lenin? He replied 'That's how it has to be.' He assured me, proudly, that some of his poems had appeared in *Novy Mir*, and asked me if there were censorship in England, adding 'Here you can write what you like, but it is not always published.' Then, obviously thinking he had gone too far, he claimed that a writer could always defend his work. He knew that there were clandestine writers but said that there were none of them among his circle. Amongst other odd things, he insisted, evidently in good faith, that Pasternak was living, rich and happy in Moscow.

When I returned to the hotel, Marianna bore me off on a slow drive to the Vorontsov Palace where Churchill stayed 'and felt at home'. There we saw an alabaster ceiling, made to look like wood, and plaster flowers covering cerulean walls and many other marvels, 'all made by the hands of serfs', Marianna commented. In the winter garden there were busts of Vorontsova, Catherine the Second, and, improbably, one of Pitt. With Marianna still going on about tyrants and slaves, we made our way to the Tsar's Summer Palace, now a sanatorium. The Emperors, she said, had had to take fantastic precautions to ensure their safety. 'Like Stalin,' I suggested. She looked hurt and said the stories about Stalin were exaggerated. While she went to wash her hands an attendant came in and, taking me for a guide, asked me where my tourist was?

On the drive back the chauffeur told me that the people of Yalta were passionate fishermen, and indeed I had seen many fishing with a line from the shore, using feather baits. Marianna improved the occasion by telling me that fishing in the Soviet Union was scientifically organised for the citizens' welfare; for instance, Intourist had recently bought a cutter for its staff which proved how much they cared for their employees.

A retired librarian, with whom I had breakfast next morning, came, to my surprise, as arranged, to my room at three o'clock. A widow, sixtyish and childless, she had lived in Moscow till the war. She proved to be lonely, civilised, knowledgeable about 'abroad' and open-minded, except where national pride was involved.

Talking of English books she said that Galsworthy was good, but not considered distinguished; Somerset Maugham was stimulating; Graham Greene was popular with many readers though *Our Man in Havana* was too complicated for some tastes, while others thought him a little journalistic. She was well aware of his Catholicism (noted in the Soviet Introductions to his books) but found this no more odd than the religious views expressed by the authors of the Russian classics. I asked her what she thought of Pasternak and she said Ehrenburg, whose judgment she respected, must have given a fair description in his *Memoirs*. 'It is probably true that Pasternak misjudged opinion at home and alienated it by publishing abroad.' She asked a lot about English publishing, then picked herself up, a compact little bun, and firmly went off.

Next day I went to the market at 8.30. The weather had cleared and a cold wind was blowing off the mountains, snow-covered and topped with a pink cloud. I saw the usual old woman grumbling in a corner as she waited for the Co-op stalls to open. Kolkhozniks were selling fruit and vegetables grown on their private plots – melon, passion fruit, strings of small green peppers, saucers of salted cabbage and beetroot. I bought some tiny, green, but sweet tangerines, from a gay young woman who had brought them from the Caucasus, 'forty-eight hours away', because she could sell them at a better price in Yalta. I also bought some small sweet grapes from two jolly girls who said four of them had hired a car which cost forty roubles, to bring them the two hundred and sixteen kilometres from a Crimean kolkhoz to Yalta, 'not exactly because prices are high here but because everyone around us grows the same things as we do'.

I breakfasted in the cafeteria with schoolchildren and people going off to work: coffee, bread, butter, cheese cakes, for fifty kopeck. Then I went to church where the liturgy was just beginning.

When I came out I saw a gaunt young woman with a child of two, begging for 'money for a journey'. I asked her if she were a widow; she said, no, her husband had left her stranded in Yalta. I went outside with her and asked more. Galya came from a kolkhoz in the Krasnodar region and had another child whom she had parked in a crèche there. She had consulted the *prokuror* (public prosecutor) who had told her to go to Simferopol where the regional Trade Union would help her – no help was available in Yalta because it is a resort. She said she had no money and felt ill. I asked her about her health and she obviously got tied up in lies, saying she had just had a third child who had been adopted by a doctor. The rest sounded true and the Trade Union in Simferopol was perhaps the best place for her to try to find help, but she looked quite unable to get there or to argue with officials if she did, so I offered to take her; I also felt it would be interesting. Galya went to consult another beggar – a jolly looking girl with a baby – who was sitting in the porch. Then she went back into the church and I talked to the second beggar, Tanya, who seemed thoroughly sensible.

According to her, Galya was her cousin; she was twenty-seven and had lived for seven years with a man in her kolkhoz without the marriage being 'registered'. She had had two children, had worked as a cleaning woman and as a dairymaid. Then she had become pregnant again and the man had taken up with their landlady and the two of them had thrown her out. She had 'slept in the stables' all summer, had an abortion and had been ill ever since.

248

Tanya was twenty-five; she came from a kolkhoz near Chelyabinsk where her father lived. She had a nine-year-old son by her first husband who had been killed in an accident, and an eight-month-old baby by her second husband and was now again pregnant. Her second husband left her because she wouldn't send the boy to an orphanage, but later he had written from Leningrad asking her to join him. She went there, but he left her again and the Housing Department helped her to get home. Eventually her husband came back to her, but then went off to Yalta to find a better job and a flat. From here he wrote and wired that he had been successful and that she was to come. She said she had 'tempted' Galya to travel with her 'for company, and because Galya was miserable', but when they arrived Tanya's husband was away on official business, and his flat was occupied by his 'new wife'.

This had happened two days ago. The women had been to the public prosecutor who told them that Galya had no case against her husband because she wasn't registered, but that Tanya had one, only it would take time to sort it out. He told them they couldn't sleep at the Yalta station because the place was a resort; they should go, he suggested, to Simferopol where they would probably be allowed to sleep in the station and where the Trade Union would help them. The most that could be done for them in Yalta was to take Galya's small child into the crêche. Neither girl had money and both were sure the Trade Union would not give them more than five roubles, whereas the journey to Chelyabinsk (to which Tanya firmly said Galya must come with her, as her father would help both of them and certainly Galya mustn't go back to 'hell in her kolkhoz') would cost a lot more. In spite of what the public prosecutor said, they had been to the harbour station and got the attendant to let them sleep in a corner. Now they intended to beg at the church door until they had enough money to get them to Chelyabinsk.

I contributed to their fund and went off saying I'd see them later in the day. I had coffee in an open-air café where a stern miner from the Donbas[9] joined me. He was square-faced, about forty and said he had met 'many foreigners' as they visited the Donbas. He told me he 'knew' rationing was still in force in England and that Russian émigrés were persecuted by the police. On the other hand, he neither knew nor wished to know anything about foreign politics (including bombs) as all that was 'the business of the authorities'. I got fed up with him so I told him about my photographing episode in Krasnodar. His comment was that I had got what I deserved and he went off in a huff.

I walked along the front; it was sunny but with fine snow blowing, so fine in fact that I first took it for the seeds of some plant. I watched fishermen winding in their lines and talked to a young man in a splendid check coat. He said he'd bought it at the market – unfortunately clothes were no longer allowed to be sold there, only in the shops where 'you can't make a profitable deal'. He was not pleased.

Fat, jolly women in white aprons were selling ices to men in fur hats. I went to eat in the *Pelmennaya*[10] with the Communist brigade staff. With broth or sour cream *pelmein* cost about fifty kopeck. The room was steamy and pleasantly warm but people were not allowed to sit on after they had finished eating. Though he assured me he always came here for lunch I was annoyed and suspicious when I saw the Intourist porter from the hotel come to sit at my table. He told me he earned sixty roubles at the hotel and twenty-five roubles for teaching English in school. God help his pupils! His English was awful.

I went back to the church and found it closed. But the mysterious man in the wadded coat and cap was, as usual, standing in the yard. I asked him if he came there often? He told me he was always there and added that he came from far off but he would say no more – and when I spoke to him he just turned his face away and was silent.

During another walk I bought a printed scarf in a gift shop, saying to the shopgirl that it was for a present to take abroad. She looked surprised because 'abroad' things are supposed to be better. Then I went back to the church which was now open, and I found Tanya and Galya sitting in the porch. Tanya repeated parts of her story, interrupting it to ask kind 'Uncles' and 'Aunts' for 'journey money'. She said that at home she would have collected the sum she needed in no time, but in town there were fewer kind people and when she had tried going from house to house some of the front doors had actually been banged in her face. All the same, she was sure that she and Galya would be all right. By last night they had already collected three roubles then, 'feeling weak', they had tried to get a room in a hotel but none would have them.

As people went into the church some stopped and listened and asked the women to tell their story. One old lady rebuked Tanya for mentioning the devil so near the church; (the devil is always at our back and shouldn't be given a chance). Others gathered round and said: 'And we calling ourselves Christians and not helping the homeless.' One remarked that if she had the key to her barn she would let the girls sleep in it, but getting hold of the key was a problem. Another said crossly that the girls shouldn't have come without being sent for; Tanya pointed out with a kind of patient dignity that she had been told to come. Everybody seemed to find the situation interesting but not surprising. Several women gave Tanya coins and, much to Tanya's amusement, one gave some to me as I sat next to her in my plain black coat and shawl.

I said I didn't understand why not one of the Yalta authorities had offered them effective help. Tanya assured me they had tried all of them, but that they had simply been scolded for leaving their kolkhoz and told they'd be lucky if they didn't get into more trouble for that. I wondered if this were true or if fear of just this happening hadn't made them shy of applying for official help, though Galya insisted that they had tried to spend the night at the 'kolkhoznik house' but either there was no room there or they wouldn't have them.

I had a curious feeling of this world at the church door being parallel with the official one, but a different world; here people might scold but they also understood.

I went in to keep my appointment with the priest. I thought him too smooth at first and a bit elegant as he took up his stance by the candle stall, then I decided this impression came from the fact that he was half-Polish, half-Ukrainian and rather civilised. He had studied at the Leningrad theological academy before the war, then fought in the army, afterwards he had continued his studies by correspondence and was still doing so and also going to Leningrad three times a year. He told me that the monastery of Zagorsk also had a correspondence course; both these two were seminaries. I asked him about other seminaries, but he was vague about numbers. He told me that at Yalta an average of fifteen babies were christened on Sundays. While he talked, nervous watchdog-women vergers and candle sellers were kept at bay by his commanding gestures.

The evening was getting very cold, there was a snowy wind blowing from the mountains and Tanya's baby was wrapped in only a cotton square, so I went to buy a blanket. First I visited a children's shop but it had no blanket, shawl or even any sort of baby clothes; nothing for a child of less than about three. Then I tried all the other shops along the front for any usable woollen clothes; finally I came to the Ukrainian souvenir shop and found one small semi-woollen shawl for five roubles; the other shoppers ogled me with envy as I snatched it. I was much relieved for as I chased around in the wind, I had developed the nasty feeling of being identified with the local shoppers in a domestic crisis and especially I felt that I must get Tanya into shelter before the baby caught pneumonia.

I went back determined to find a warm place for the night for both women and then send them home next day. I collected them and took them to the Yalta Hotel nearby and told them to ask for a room. They advanced on the administrator in their 'other-tribe' clothes, with their children. She stopped gossiping and said sarcastically, her fist on her haunch: 'Where do you think you are?' Bolstered up by the fact that the girls had already assumed that I was 'someone from Moscow', I joined them and said in an official and sententious voice: 'Have you a room for these comrades?' At this the administrator became all smiles and replied:

'Yes, number 7, a nice warm room.' Would they register?

Floored by forms they asked my help: name, age, where born, residence, work, what authority had issued their identity cards (they each had one with all the details).

No. 7 turned out to be a summer annexe, not warm but better than the street or the station, with four beds at sixty kopecks each, a couple of kitchen chairs and a small chest of drawers, all crowded together but fairly clean. A middle-aged woman was already there; she at once became interested in the girls' story of which Tanya gave her an outline. Galya went to buy food; I gave Tanya money which, with what they had collected, would be enough to pay for their journey. She was pleasantly grateful, not in the least overcome, just surprised: 'never seen such a person' – and returning at once to her natural cheerful self, left the baby in charge of the lodger and went back to church where a woman had offered her a *baikovoye*[11] dress. She made me promise to come next morning; they wouldn't leave till ten o'clock.

I had dinner at the Oreanda, where a large, blonde 'lovely' in pale blue – really beautiful and representing confidently a style and fashion to be found in no other country – was leading on a Southerner with a flashing eye and a curly moustache; besides them there were two or three lonely, pale, young men, each sitting at a separate table.

As soon as I had breakfasted I called Intourist to ask the time of the plane to Odessa. Then, at 9.30 I went to the hotel where I had left the girls, but when I looked through the glass top of their locked door I saw that the room was empty. I asked the administrator about them. With a treacly smile, she called last night's administrator who, with the same treacly smile, said that the girls were at breakfast and had asked me to wait. In ten minutes she came back saying they had gone, leaving a message for me to say that if I came after 9.30 they couldn't wait, as they must catch the trolleybus to the bus station. I looked for them at the trolleybus stop and in the cafeteria where they had eaten yesterday, but there was no sign of them.

After that I left for Simferopol (thank goodness Marianna did not accompany me), the good old Intourist chauffeur told me that he and his colleagues were made to learn English during the non-tourist season. He said he earned ninety roubles and was given one suit of 'representative clothes' a year; lorry drivers earned a hundred and twenty, but their work was harder.

Speaking about the Tartars he said they had betrayed partisans and given stocks of arms to the Germans and that they had killed Jews and gipsies. In his opinion gipsies were a thieving lot; no wonder the Germans wouldn't put up with them, but not all Jews were bad. The Tartars, according to him, had also wanted to kill Russians and Ukrainians but the Germans prevented them from doing so. Even so, not all the Tartars were bad; he knew this because he had three Tartar friends who had fought with him all through the war; they too had been deported. The good ones, such as they, had been told: 'Go and teach your nation.' He said, nowadays, there were many German tourists in Yalta, some had come to see where their sons had fallen in war. He added that there was no general hatred towards them among Russians, only war veterans with special grievances detested them; this was because most of the population were too young to have war memories.

At the airport, which had a smart new glass and steel annexe, I was told that the plane might be late. I hung around, looked at a bookstall where Lenin's and Khrushchev's works were displayed at the sides, and papers including the *Daily Worker* and *Humanité* in front.

When I went to lunch in the restaurant, Boria, an engineer, joined my table, though told by the head waitress not to do so as my waitress was 'inexperienced and slow'. In fact she was very quick, and we pulled her leg about her 'testimonial' from her boss. Later, in the plane the engineer sat next to me and we talked except when the hostess sat in the third seat.

He seemed to be a man-about-town type with a European outlook and manner; possibly he was Jewish? After the war he had been in Hungary and had learned Hungarian. He liked the life. Now he was due for leave. 'Where will you go?' I asked.

'Evidently not to Paris.' He said he would probably stay at home.

ODESSA

As we were landing he suggested ringing me up; since there are only two Intourist hotels it would be easy to discover where I was. I said it wasn't certain I'd get the message. 'Was it awkward for me to be rung up?' he asked.

I answered, 'No, but mightn't it be awkward for you to ring me up?'

'Well, they can't throw me out of the Party, I don't belong.'

Svetlana, a pretty guide, self-contained and unsavage (unlike some I've met) saw me to my hotel which was on the front. While my room was being vacated I lunched in a palatial restaurant which was most un-cosy. A few 'lost' couples were eating there.

My room, which looked on to a desolate promenade, had a huge bathroom and a remarkable piece of furniture; a tallboy with bronze cut-outs of cherubs with bunches of grapes, the grapes being made of glass knobs. I wondered if they could possibly be peepholes, but the tallboy was not attached to the wall or to the floor, so I suppose it was just in the local style.

I went out for a walk (conscious as I passed through the hall of more than the usual number of dark eyes glinting at me over newspapers) past handsome, unwashed façades along a promenade ending in the old Stock Exchange which has a classical façade.

Wandering on I stopped to look at the entrance to a sordid yard, from which a distinguished-looking old gentleman was coming out, and we got into conversation. He was a seventy-year-old Jew, born in Odessa. He had fought on the famous steps in 1905,[12] had been in the Merchant Navy and had spent three years in the USA. He spoke French and English. His children were married and one son was a 'writer in Moscow'. He and his wife had a nice flat before the war, but had been evacuated and came back to one small room in this slummy yard. By now both had given up hope of ever getting better lodgings. Two of his seven brothers were abroad; he too could have stayed out but he came back. Was he glad he had done so, I asked? 'Well . . . I'm fond of Odessa.' A cheerful old fellow.

Later, I drove around the town with Svetlana; she is the daughter of a journalist who worked in Riga but had recently moved to Odessa – 'as journalists will', she said. This was annoying to her because she had to leave Riga University where she had been studying languages for two years. Now she is continuing with a correspondence course, because if she studied in Odessa she would have to learn Ukrainian. For two months a year she goes back to Riga to attend lectures and exams. When she gets a diploma she will be allowed to teach, but would prefer to be an industrial interpreter.

Odessa is built on Greek catacombs, or perhaps smugglers' caves or quarries; these were used by the Partisans during the war but are now closed as unsafe. The city was founded by Greeks. Slav tribes and Greek colonists lived here until the thirteenth century, when it was taken by the Turks and occupied by them until the time of Catherine I. The town has many historical associations: the handsome Potemkin Steps are the place where fighting took place in 1905; they are topped by a statue of Armand-Emmanuel, Duc de Richelieu[13] who founded the university. During the war the Opera House was saved by the Partisans from destruction by the fleeing enemy. Tchaikovsky conducted there, and there is a monument to Pushkin who wrote part of *Evgeny Onegin* while in Odessa.

The University has eight thousand students; as they come from other towns, many live in. Svetlana told me there is an internationally famous eye clinic, where all the treatment is free, even for foreigners. But there are also five or six private clinics, 'mostly for foreigners or people out of town who are not registered with a local doctor.' We saw a handsome sanatorium with gardens.

I then told Svetlana I wished to go to a 'working' church. Several were closed or used for other purposes. She took me to one near the station. It was open but almost empty. I bought a candle and prayed for a little while, Svetlana standing by politely. I asked her if many Russians went to church; she said (but again politely) that very old people did and those mostly from the country. Did English people go to church every Sunday, she asked, adding that Tolstoy in his books mentioned this habit as existing in the Russia of his day.

Back at the hotel the maid said someone had rung up; he had travelled with me from Simferopol and would ring again next day – presumably the man was determined to be as daring as he had promised to be. And he did ring again and said he'd come at twelve o'clock next day.

I went out early for a walk and looked at the fruit stalls. Women asked the prices; the sales girl, plaintively rather than rudely, replied: 'They're all written up'; this caused a storm.

Customer: 'When we were your age we could see.' (Implying that the sales girl should have read out her prices.)

Girl: 'It's not my duty.' But the row went on. I've noticed that in the Soviet Union older people seem always to be educating the young and they are expected to 'take it' and mostly they do, except for the occasional perky one and a few who are brutally insolent.

At lunchtime Boria came. He had a lot of complaints. Housing was difficult now, 'it might improve in twenty years' time – but that is a long way off', and meanwhile he had no bath.

Clothes, he says, are few and bad and all those who, like himself, want to be elegant wear foreign clothes: he had a foreign raincoat and a suit made of Hungarian cloth and Arab socks bought from government stores which sell confiscated smugglers' goods.

Plainly Boria is an altogether frivolous character who believes that if you drive nature out through the door it comes back through the window. He says that films attract an audience if they are known to be for adults only. His seven-year-old son wanted to go to one with his parents but they said 'No' and sent him to the circus from which he came back saying he'd enjoyed it very much, especially the 'naked aunties'!

Boria is not interested in politics. However, he remarked that

Manya with Robin in South Uist

Manya in Samothrace

Khrushchev must have been 'in it' under Stalin as well as the rest of the gang – but added 'who can blame them?' He thinks the Russians are afraid of war but are not worried by the tests which they believe to be only an answer to the French open and the Anglo-Saxon secret tests. However, he did ask me about the development abroad of cures for cancer, and said people wondered if the incidence of cancer hadn't been increased by the fall-out.

He told me that anti-semitism had increased since the war and the occupation; for instance, he wanted to be a journalist but didn't think he'd get far as a Jew. He said however that he didn't, in fact, himself often meet with anti-semitism but probably that was because he doesn't look particularly Jewish and has no Jewish accent. As a child he had an accent but went to a speech specialist who cured it; his son has an accent, and he too will have to go to a specialist. Boria didn't think there were many Orthodox Jews left in Yalta. One synagogue remained open – in a workers' quarter, 'the most anti-semitic in town'. He found it difficult to define the present state of anti-semitism. There are few Jews left at the top ('Kaganovich is the worst anti-semite of the lot'), and there are many Jewish scientists, writers, etc., yet it is harder for Jews to get on in their studies and in many professions. He feels particularly aggrieved about this because the Jews fought so well in the war.

Odessa is, he says, doing well out of its reprobate ways. Plenty of speculation and blackmarket, and the doctors thriving on all the people who come for cures. It is the only place where you can get English cigarettes – and with this he presented me with a hundred.

Boria then asked me for fashion papers for his wife, and particularly for magazines showing the lay-out of shops abroad, as he was keen to suggest improvements.

Before going he suddenly became microphone-conscious and inspected the inside of the cupboard, even though he had said he thought not much attention was paid to foreigners now as there were too many of them around and the Security Organs couldn't keep up. I suspected his naiveté, but gave him the benefit of the doubt.

In the evening I went to *The Red Flower* (formerly *The Red Poppy*) ballet in the handsome Opera House. The dancing was good and zestful and the blonde beauty who had been dining with the curly moustached man at the Oreanda in Yalta was taking one of the principal parts. The theme described the oppression of the Chinese in the twenties by cowardly British bullies, and showed how China had been championed by Russian heroes, who could do everything better than the cruel and effete Imperialists (e.g., dancing, winning fair ladies, unloading ships when the Chinese dockers turned against the Imperialist supervisor-with-his-whip). It was such a disgusting piece of chauvinism that I felt perhaps I ought to walk out. In the interval my neighbour commented on the unseasonably warm, wet weather in Odessa now and the change of climate generally. Was it the inland seas,[14] I asked, remembering that this had been the Rostov Intourist guide's explanation.

'That, and something else,' she said. She hinted it was the tests and said about the rain: 'Let's hope it's only rain.' I then realised that this had been hinted at by several other people.

I went to the synagogue in the slummy quarter. There I found some sixty men, some young, some old, and thirty women in the women's gallery. I got into conversation with a woman of about fifty. She whispered: 'You're from there?' and then passed the information on to the woman behind her in a low voice and told me to sit next to her and wait till she had a chance to talk to me. She opened her prayer book, chanted from it in Hebrew and, to the same tune, lamented, for my benefit, in Russian. Young Jews were being 'got at' to give up their religion. Judaism was dying out through the fault of the Jews who allowed themselves to be influenced; there were also vague hints about persecution. Later she whispered that synagogues were being closed: a friend of hers had just come back from Kherson, and told her that the synagogue there had recently been shut down. Things like this were always made to appear as if they were done with the consent of the Jews, for there were always some collaborators to be found to say that there were not enough Orthodox Jews left to keep the synagogue open. At the end of the service she came down with me and asked me, half frightened, half devil-may-care, to come to tea with her in the afternoon.

After the service, Svetlana took me to the museum; the house had belonged in former times to the Potockis. The collection included paintings by Breughel, Correggio, Rubens, Rembrandt and Millais; also Chinese paintings and French and English porcelain, and much junk as well. It was hard to see anything because of the bad lighting and the Chinese paintings were probably being ruined by exposure; but the total effect was of remarkable richness for a provincial museum. This and the Opera House recalled the city's civilised tradition, but perhaps I was moving in the wrong circles to see its living survival – while its reprobate tradition was clearly alive and robust. In general, Odessa looks like a bedraggled great lady in a gone-to-seed palace with a staff of crooks.

I had a snack in a café with a flashy character who said that under Stalin one piece of gossip about a person was enough to finish him; now three or four were needed plus a generally subversive air. The rehabilitation of Stalin's victims he thought right, but said bitterly that it couldn't bring back the dead or the lost years. Then, with pride, he drew my attention to his blackmarket Chinese sweater which he had bought for fifty roubles.

On my way home the taxi driver remarked to me: 'Foreigners can demonstrate against bombs, we can't.'

At tea time I walked to the door in the yard where the Jewish woman had said I was to ring three times, which I did. She had spoken as though the flat belonged to a dvornik but I wondered if she herself were not the dvornik. She opened the door which led to a passage in which she was cooking; then we walked along a smaller pitch-black passage to a dank but biggish semi-basement room which she shared with her two children and also, it seemed, with another woman who wasn't there at this moment. There was another guest, however, a dear old gentleman.

I was pressed to eat *gefilte fisch*, made of something frightful. Sabbath prayers were read at intervals. The old man said it was rare for a woman to be so learnedly Orthodox as our hostess. She told me that, to her grief, her two children had stopped practising when they married, though they still kept the big feasts.

Both the woman and the old man talked darkly about 'bad times for Jews' but neither would give any details: 'Such things are not good to talk about.'

He – little, neat, oldish with a small beard – had charming manners and only occasionally a wild gleam in his eye. He told me he was anxious to meet me because he needed to publish a manuscript abroad. It was some time before I realised that he was as mad as a coot. He said he had had a good job as a scientist until he was locked up in '45 and 'kept in' until after Stalin's death. While 'there' he discovered that the earth was flat with a knob on top – 'the knob is all we have explored' – and he had also discovered that all the distances between the heavenly bodies had been miscalculated, as well as their sizes and densities. As a result there was now a great danger of rockets, etc., stumbling into the sun and blowing it up with disastrous consequences to the earth. He had sent his conclusions to the Academy of Sciences and had written a book on the subject, but they refused to publish it though their replies were polite; he showed me one of them. Then he said would I get in touch with the Academy of Sciences in Moscow and ask them to get his MS published in England: this would be quite legal so long as the Academy was first approached. Also, when I returned to England, would I enlist the interest of Bernal whom he had read and admired. Later, he saw me to the tram, talking on and on – but so patient and civil, poor fellow, with hardly a sign of lunacy in his kind, harassed, intellectual face! He got into the tram with me and implored me to meet him again the next morning at the inter-town telephone office near the hotel, so that he could show me his papers.

At seven o'clock I went to the Cathedral and found a crowded service going on in the crypt; among the congregation were some men and some young women. A young priest gave a good simple sermon on looking after the soul rather than the body 'though we're none of us rich we must live for others'; in fact, putting 'Communist' ethics into their Christian setting. About thirty people went to communion and I saw a well-dressed man going from ikon to ikon with a small child.

I walked from the church to the market, passing a long queue for paraffin, which was being sold from a van, as was milk.

Later I met my poor old madman and we sat at a crowded table, he explaining his discovery. An officer sitting opposite us began to look more and more disturbed until I smiled, winked and touched my head while the old man was absorbed in leafing through correspondence with the Academy of Sciences.

I 'dined' at four with a blackmarketeer who entertained me lavishly at the station restaurant but was cagey about his identity, though not about details of the blackmarket. The most desirable commodity was gold; there was always a market for it. But the pound sterling (bank note) was now down to 5r50k owing to a vast racket having been uncovered in Moscow through the fault of some Poles and an indiscreet woman. As a result trade was very unsafe at the moment. The prices varied according to conditions and went up with the arrival of foreign shipping. The pound had been up as high as twenty roubles; the dollar varied from four to nine roubles. Gold and jewels were collected, particularly by watchmakers and wine merchants who had made vast fortunes (a friend of his had made 700,000 roubles). Big speculators, he said, travelled on business from town to town, but the gold was carried by insignificant subordinates. Foreign currency was wanted by people who go, or hope to go, abroad as tourists or on a 'one way journey'. Gold was kept 'against eventualities' – there was, he said, 'no confidence in the Soviet currency and a vague feeling that anything might happen to it, but gold was always reliable.' Sometimes it could be bought cheap from Arab sailors. The first principle of the trade was, if caught, to say nothing: confessing did no good and not confessing meant that you kept your friends and, on coming out, there was money waiting for you. Clever people, he assured me, did well in Odessa, and also in other ports. But it was essential to hide all signs of one's wealth, e.g., not wear expensive Swiss watches (three thousand of these had been imported and sold at 700 roubles each) and to keep your cars out of town.

The blackmarketeer did not take a gloomy view of the chances of escape by ship, though he was obviously doing much too well to be tempted. He told stories of graft throughout trade and industry: perfect goods marked defective and sold on the side, or a part of production held back as a reserve or sold privately, etc. 'Even officials in *sovnarkhozey*[15] have to live,' he commented. The Chinese, he told me, sold currency stolen from the Bank of Shanghai. The blackmarketeer was evidently comfortably off but insisted that conditions in Odessa were bad. For instance, housing was rotten; ninety per cent of people in the town had no hot water; gas had been promised three years ago, but the pipes were still being laid. New flats went to Managers who gave their old flats to their friends. There were shortages of all kinds. On the other hand, there was, in some ways, more freedom but relations with foreigners were still a sticky affair. At the time of the U2 and the failed summit they had become very dangerous, but had varied since then.

Jews, he assured me, could get high up in certain fields, e.g., science, but all the same a VIP Jewish scientist usually had a gentile administrator above him, and so had important Jewish engineers. After the war very few Jews were left in Odessa, but some had come to live there since then. He said there was a general feeling of instability in the Soviet Union and a change was expected, but whether for better or worse, who could tell.

I went back to the hotel to pack up; Boria dropped in to say goodbye and to remind me to send magazines, also an 'automatic' for his boy (toy shops have other weapons but no automatics). We had a long talk; among the things he said were that there were still many Jews in the Party, also in the security services. He also told some jokes: Can Communism be built in America? Yes, but why? Can Communism be built in one country? Yes, but better live in another. Can Communism be built in Armenia? Yes, but better start in Georgia.

He said that he and others thought too much money was being spent on space flights and that this was one reason for the shortages. He also complained bitterly of the rudeness of the sales assistants, but believed that an effort was being made to train them, e.g. notices were put up in shops (I saw one in a food store) saying 'You are being served by So-and-So' and this made for more personal relations between customers and assistants and gave the assistants a sense of responsibility.

He told me he had bought a radiogram on HP for 320 roubles. HP terms were $\frac{1}{2}\%$ added to the cash price. Delay on paying instalments meant forfeiture of the object and of the earlier instalments.

Finally, he went off proudly displaying his foreign raincoat, with a check lining, bought for 110 roubles.

MOSCOW

I flew to Moscow by TU 104 which had a more streamlined and less cosy atmosphere than the inland planes I'd been in so far.

While looking for a taxi I was accosted by a drunken officer.

'Stop,' he said. 'Must tell you I've been to church and forgiven everyone.' When I went on he stopped me again to apologise for being a little tipsy and insisted that 'holy prayers exist all the same'. At this point a passer-by joined in the conversation, saying he did not believe the drunk was an officer, and I left them to it.

I found a taxi and talked to the driver, who told me he used to be chauffeur to a General who worked in a Ministry and had a 'personal' car. As a result he had got a flat with twenty-five metres for himself, wife and child. He works on alternate days, eight or nine hours with an hour's break, and has to fulfil his plan (which he usually finds easy); taxi drivers who are graded 'first class' can make 120 roubles.

Ira (my guide), had made an appointment for me with the 'Foreign Section' of the Writers' Union, and insisted on coming with me, saying she was interested in literature; so she firmly sat in on my meeting with a dim, youngish man and a sharpish woman of about thirty-five, who knew an astonishing amount about English literature and still more about books from Australia and New Zealand, this because they were preparing an anthology of Australian and New Zealand verse. She told me these were easier for their readers to understand than modern English poetry. She also said that C. P. Snow was being translated, and that books by Graham Greene had been so successful that they were now bringing out his *Heart of the Matter*.

Then she asked me which writer I wanted to meet and I gave her a list which included two young men. When I came to their names she made a face and said English reviewers kept taking up Soviet writers whom they thought – quite wrongly – to be critical of the régime. I said a critical tendency existed also with us.

Since I now had a little time to spare I thought that in the afternoon I would take a short trip outside Moscow and wander about the countryside. I got out at a chance station, actually before the one to which I had taken my ticket, simply because the surrounding country looked attractive. After a long walk I went back to the station waiting-room. No train back to Moscow was due for a long time.

Here I found an old woman, Anna, a couple of men, Andrei and Pavel, and a girl Moura. As usual, they at first took me for an important Soviet representative on an official journey but they were so friendly that I felt it would be wrong for me not to tell them that I was a foreigner and English. They were greatly interested, and did not seem in the least frozen by the information. All were obviously friends. They asked question after question aimed at being told of better conditions in England than in Russia.

'And how is it with your land reform?' I said that we have done it mostly through taxation. 'Who owns land and how are agricultural workers paid?' I did my best for them. 'And how is it with the Party in England?' I said the Communist Party was small, but then realised that by Party they meant the Government. I explained that we had several parties.

'Yes,' they shook their heads after every answer, 'It's all different, all better than with us.' For a moment I wondered if this were a trap.

The men had their reasonable male way of talking while Anna broke in with illogical female exclamations, and the girl nodded her head.

'Are there many Russians in England?' Anna asked. 'Some,' I said, 'but more Poles.' She sighed. 'If only our Antonina might be there.' Her daughter had been deported to Danzig by the Germans in 1942. Anna had applied to the Red Crescent and the Red Cross after the war, but they hadn't traced her. All at once Anna became real to me. I offered to try the British Red Cross when I got back and she let me write down her address and the name and details of her daughter.

'Perhaps our Boria is there too,' said the girl. Her brother had disappeared. He was a soldier; the last she heard of him was in '42. He might have been killed; they would not have known. I put down his name as well.

'And yet, it doesn't make sense,' she went on. 'Why wouldn't they have written to us after the war?' The men shook their heads.

'Why would they let anybody know where they were – to get twenty years?'[16]

We had made another step in intimacy. 'You don't know how it is with us,' said Andrei. 'We could tell you.'

'Tell me.'

'Take the four of us here.' I took a look at the four of them in this dark cosy cell.

'Do you think any one of us would go on to a collective farm? We'd sooner do anything than that. Am I saying the truth?' he asked each of the others, and they agreed.

'Why wouldn't you?'

'It's the hunger, the insecurity. In a collective farm you have thirty sotniks, that's a hundredth of a hectare, to yourself, but apart from that you might get nothing. You work all the year round, then the Government takes so much, and so much is put aside for seed, what's left is shared out. But there may be nothing left – it depends on the year and the land. Perhaps you get a hundred grams of bread and perhaps now-a-days a rouble or two a day. It used to be even worse. A State farm is a bit better: there you get a wage, it's very little but you do get it whatever the harvest. In a collective farm there's no security. That's why people leave the country for the town. Yes, it's a bad life, and ours is not much better. Not that we would have talked so openly a year or two ago.'

'How is it you talk now?'

'We don't, except among a few people we trust. We four know each other.'

Andrei's 'old woman' is a member of a collective farm and this gives her a house and thirty sotniks. That helps them out, 'if it weren't for the taxation.'

'Those taxes,' Anna broke in. 'You tell her about the fifteen hundred they taxed you,' but Andrei shook his head: 'Another time.'

'Still it isn't fair,' Anna protested.

'And is it fair that a poor woman in the village who's too old for regular work should have to pay 150 roubles for doing a little sewing; the village is small, if she gets a dress to do for fifteen roubles she's lucky.'

The conversation got lost in memories of the war but after a time they again talked about conditions, the low pay and the way one is 'hunted'.

'It's the Party members,' they said. 'A kolkhoz of five hundred people is run by five of them.'

'What are your relations with the Party?' I asked, meaning how much do they have to do with it.

'Even among us five I wouldn't tell you what I think of it,' said Andrei. 'But I'd tell you if we were alone. All I'll say is it's no good.' The others nodded, a little nervously but with enjoyment.

'Anyway, what does a man need? Do you know? Socialism, Communism, Capitalism, what does all that matter? A man needs to live, that's all. We can't live on what we earn.'

'That's right,' said Pavel. I asked him what his wage was? 'All I'll tell you is that I can buy bread, and I have bought a suit but I now can't buy a pair of boots' and he thrust out his feet in their shoddy, broken-down boots.

'Now I want to ask a question,' said Andrei. 'How is it with your churches? Are they working?'

'Yes, they're working.'

'Not like with us; our churches are shut down. Not that they're shutting them down now, that's past.'

'All the same,' said Moura, 'When they restored the church after the war they re-opened it as a club.'

'You're believers?' I asked.

Andrei answered: 'I have been a believer all my life. Not when I was in the Komsomol, but before and after.' Anna and Pavel approved.

The girl said shyly: 'My father used to say, whether there is God or not, act well and you'll be all right.'

Andrei went on: 'Perhaps to an educated, clever person like yourself it seems absurd. But to us, simple people, it means everything. You go to church. You beg of God. You pray, that's the only thing that makes life bearable.' I said I was a believer and they were pleased. They all agreed there ought to be churches and freedom of conscience.

'Still, things are not so bad now, a church is open in the next village and there is a priest whom we know, he is a good man.'

'Are there many believers?' I asked.

'Most people are believers.'

'Even Party members?'

'Well, no, they can't very well, though how does one know?'

Moura said: 'Even among Party members, there are plenty who, I know, go to church, get married in church and have their children baptised.'

'What about the children?'

'Schoolchildren can't.'

'But do their parents teach them religion?'

'It's difficult. The teachers ask the children and the children have to tell the truth, then the parents get into trouble.'

'What kind of trouble?'

'It's difficult to explain,' they said. 'Anyway, a child who says he's a believer can't get into the Komsomol, and that's very bad for him. That stops many parents. It's all right until they're seven, after that they go to school, and then it's finished till they've left the Komsomol.'

'Yes, that's how it was with me when I was in the Komsomol,' said Andrei, 'but when I came out I changed.'

'What made you change?'

'A man needs faith. He needs to pray. Do you understand?'

'Yes, I understand.'

Andrei smiled. 'I had an argument with a Communist once, an atheist. I said: "You're so clever you've thought of everything and you've discovered that there is no God. But I'm cleverer still. I've discovered that God exists." As to which of us is right, only God can judge.' They told me of a young 'atheist' who gives his parents money to put up candles.

Our conversation had lasted a long time and I thought my companions must wish to go home, but they looked at each other in embarrassment when I suggested it. They said they wouldn't leave me alone for the several hours before the train was due. Andrei invited me to go and see his 'old woman', but Anna lived nearer and insisted that I should go with her. Outside the snow had stopped falling, but we walked through deep slush.

Anna said: 'That's the house.' But I couldn't see anything. Then, when we were at the door she said, 'Perhaps you would like to use the lavatory?' and when I answered yes: 'Please piss on that side of the yard.' This was said with the utmost naturalness and politeness.

Afterwards, I followed Anna up some steps, through a dark porch into a narrow passage used as tool and woodshed. I opened a door on the right into the living-room – perhaps eight foot by ten foot, the wall on the left was taken up by a combined stove and range, there was a window on the right with a table and four stools under it; the walls were covered with a faded paper, a few nails were stuck into them; a bare board floor, but not just mud as it would have been in my time.

'Would you like some tea?' Anna asked, but she would evidently not have made it for herself, so I refused. We talked and talked, and suddenly I looked at my watch and realised with horror that I had missed the train and that there wouldn't be another till late the next morning. Anna too was appalled, but determined I should stay. 'You're tired, you must go straight to bed,' she said. 'Take off your clothes.' I took off my coat and boots; she wanted me to take off my suit too but I didn't want to make a night of it. She showed me through a curtain to a narrow cubicle with just room for a bed, a tiny window and a small table covered with lino, and nails in the wall for hanging things.

'It's a good, clean bed,' she said. 'You needn't be afraid.'

'Where will you sleep?'

'I'll be all right. I don't want to sleep. I can't.' She sat down and rubbed her head. 'Such a headache I have these days.'

I insisted that she must sleep. Finally I said I would lie down if she got into bed with me – it seemed quite natural.

But she answered, 'I know what it is, you are afraid, you don't trust us.' So I took off my jacket and skirt, hung them on a hook and got into bed. It really was a good feather bed with clean rough sheets and two pillows.

Anna bustled about: 'A fool I am, I forgot to give you water to wash. Get up!' She went out and came back after a time with a small jug of water and an enamel basin with dark dregs in it. She apologised for the dregs: the potatoes had been washed in the basin. Then she hunted up a piece of soap, warmed the jug on the stove and poured water over my hands while I washed them in the basin. Finally she sent me back to bed.

'But where will *you* sleep?'

'With my daughter-in-law. She and my son and their little boy live with me.' I settled down and heard her groaning and getting into bed behind the partition.

I lay in bed comfortable and drowsy but did not go to sleep. A little grey light came through the casement by the bed. In spite of the feather bed I was very cold. Soon, it was five and I heard people moving – it must have been the daughter-in-law and son getting up. I heard them dressing and washing in the living-room and decided not to get up until they had eaten, but I didn't hear any sound of tea-making. Finally, I put on my clothes and came out through the curtain. A young woman, Masha, was there, and a shy-looking man, her husband Alexei. Valery, six years old, stood on one unshod foot. I realised they must all have come out of the other cubicle, the same size as the one I had rested in, and that Anna was still in it. The two cubicles made up the other half of the cottage, separated from the kitchen-living-room by two curtains and from each other by a wooden partition which ran half way down the middle of what must have been one room.

I made friends with Valery, a fair, ugly, nice little boy, not shy and showing off a little. He would go to school next year. We discussed schools with Alexei – education in Russia and England. He had meant to be a technician, but within a week of leaving school the war had broken out. He didn't have to work today because he was having his annual fortnight's holiday. We sat down at the table and talked, Valery clambering over us. The women did a little cleaning – by now Anna had got up. I asked Masha how Anna's headache was; she said she was always ailing. Alexei was nice looking; I thought he must be in his early twenties but, in fact, he was thirty. He and his wife were shy at first but soon they relaxed and he settled down for a good talk.

We compared their revolution and our social changes. Alexei took it for granted that things were well with us. I said comfortingly: 'England is a small country, industrialised long ago. Naturally things are easier.'

Suddenly he asked: 'What do they say in your country about NATO?'

'Just what do you mean?'

'The grouping the West has made against us.'

'Well, you know, our impression is that it is the Soviet Union that made a grouping first – immediately after the war.'

He smiled. 'Yes, that was Churchill's excuse.' I tried to create a diversion, saying 'Anyway, things are much better now internationally.'

'That's good,' Anna broke in, 'They don't want war, do they?'

'Nobody wants war; it's a great pity countries don't know more about each other. It is because they don't that they get frightened of one another.'

'Yes,' exclaimed Alexei, 'It's true, the West must be frightened of us. They know how strong we are. But it's also true, there is a relaxation now. One must give the Western countries their due, they've opened up.'

'Yes, there's a change,' I said. 'See how I can travel here now. I hope you'll come and see us one day.'

'Would the Western countries let us in?' They don't know, or Alexei pretended not to know, that it is their own government that doesn't let them out. He scratched his head thoughtfully.

'All the same, you know, it isn't good that they don't want Communism in the West. So long as they don't want it, things can't be really peaceful.'

'Why not? You and we have different problems. You agreed that things were better with us economically. Communism is an answer to your problems, not to ours. We don't want Communism at home. But we don't interfere with you having it.'

'All the same, it's bad. They recognise us as a country but not as Communists. I've read that in the paper.'

'We only don't want it for ourselves. Why should we?'

'Well, it's natural you should fear it if you don't want it.'

To get out of the impasse I attacked politely. 'You spoke of groupings. It wasn't just Churchill's excuse. After the war you occupied one country after another. How could we know where you would stop if we didn't protect ourselves?'

He smiled. 'You're right there. We did occupy those countries and they certainly wouldn't have had Communism without us.'

'You imposed it on them by force.'

'Yes, that has to be admitted. Why should they have had it but for us? We know what workers and peasants are like. Why should they set up Communism?'

Anna sat down at the table and said slyly: 'In England sugar is very cheap.' We talked again about conditions and wages.

Alexei squirmed a little. Then he came back to politics. 'What is it they reproach us with in the West?'

'I can only give you my own opinions. Before I came here, I thought you were not so badly off economically, but I didn't think you had much freedom.'

Alexei got excited. 'Why should they think that? It's true there was no freedom of the Press under Beria. But look at it now. There's criticism everywhere. The papers criticise, they show up people. That goes on at all levels. Even when Malenkov and Khrushchev talk together, they criticise each other.'

'That's a very good thing. But suppose now you, yourself, didn't want Khrushchev to rule you? Could you say so openly or print it in a paper?'

He looked bewildered and mumbled: 'What do you mean?'

I felt I had gone too far and explained: 'Well, you know, we have a different system, several parties, so that when the people get fed up with one they put in the other.'

Alexei was silent, but his wife who had been listening, standing with her back to the stove, suddenly turned on him: 'Well, tell her, could you say you didn't want Khrushchev?'

Suddenly Alexei collapsed. 'Yes, of course you're right . . . It must be admitted . . . It's not good with us. We don't have any say.'

Anna said, 'Everything was better under Malenkov. It's a shame they got rid of him.'

'What was so much better?' asked Alexei. 'Things are getting better all the time. Anyway, you don't understand. You think of Malenkov as a Tsar. It wasn't just Malenkov; the whole party was behind him, they talked things over, they knew what he was doing.'

'Then why are things worse since he's gone? Under him there was the amnesty, and our living standard was going up.'

'You're always looking back,' said Alexei.

'Well, I've got a long time to remember. I'm fifty-five now.'

'I'm fifty,' I said, for no particular reason.

She looked at me disbelievingly and enviously: 'You see how they look at fifty in England.' Indeed, she looked at least fifteen years older than I did.

Now they insisted that, as I had not eaten last night, I should have an enormous breakfast and they'd make their dinner of it: cabbage, fried potatoes, black bread, very weak tea and jam to put in it. There was a little butter for Valery, and for me three fried eggs. I was horrified, but they insisted it cost them nothing, they had chickens. Anna stood and served us while we sat on the four stools, anything else was unthinkable. Suddenly she got upset because she had not remembered to put a hot brick in my bed. I must have been cold – I couldn't have slept.

Alexei had been in the siege of Leningrad and he really hated the Germans; he began to talk. 'The West may be right about a lot of things but not about the Germans. The best thing we could have done would have been to exterminate them. Strutting about they were, laughing at starving people, saying how the ring was drawing closer and closer round Leningrad till it would be crushed.

'Two years the siege lasted,' he went on, 'but the first winter was the worst. During the second year provisions began to come across Lake Ladoga. But that first winter . . . Black frost, no light, no fuel, no water – the pipes frozen and the shelling . . . And so many people died of starvation, I can't tell you how many. The rest were too weak to bury them. You'd walk along a street, quite empty they were; suddenly from a balcony above your head something crashed down – a corpse – that was all they could do with it. I'd try to drag it in under the stairs. I'm strong enough, that's how I survived, but then I was too weak. I could only drag the corpse a little out of the way. That's how the dead bodies lay all the winter. Then in spring we went and dug trenches and the corpses were wheeled along, still frozen stiff, and dropped into the trenches in rows.

'There's nothing bad enough to say about the Germans,' he concluded. 'Those camps. And now they accuse us of having camps. Don't you believe what they say. Ours are nothing like theirs. Of course conditions are hard in them, why shouldn't they be? But nobody is permitted to lift a finger against a prisoner. I don't say it doesn't happen but if it gets back to the authorities, they're sure to be punished.'

Then, after a pause, inexplicably, Alexei qualified his statement and said 'Things are better now but it must be admitted they were bad at one time. Many people disappeared. It was happening all round and for no reason. It was very bad under Beria.' He looked puzzled as he added, 'But why they were so bad under Stalin, it's hard to understand.'

As it was still not time for the train and I was afraid of immobilising the household, I said I would go for a walk. When I was outside, Anna came after me and asked if perhaps I had gone out to look for the 'lavatory' – if so I could use the cow shed.

The house was built of logs and painted green; it looked like the old *khata*[17] but with a roof of wooden slats instead of thatch. The private plot – fifteen sotniks (the amount of land a worker who did not belong to a collective farm was allowed to have) was planted with vegetables but now it was a patch of snow and mud. The sky was grey and the ground deeply muddy.

I had left my bag behind, with all my money in it and my jewels; it would have looked distrustful to take it; but now I was worried at the temptation put in their way and also that they might be shocked at finding so much in it. They could hardly fail to see the contents because Valery had been busy with the fastening, and had examined everything on me. Is this a watch? he had asked of my gold bangle. Then he was puzzled over my two rings – only then I realised that I had kept on my emerald ring on top of my wedding ring; with my watch and bangle I must have looked like a Christmas tree.

When I came back my bag had been put out of Valery's reach, and everything was in it. I asked Anna, who was alone, to let me pay for

Manya on the tiles while
'The Flying Poodle' is being photographed

my meal; she was horrified. I began to take my leave, and promised I'd do what I could to trace her daughter but she held me back. 'If only I could know she was alive. Even if I were never to see her again. War is terrible.' Suddenly her voice changed and she lamented – for herself and for the whole people. If her daughter were here life would be different for her. Her other daughter had not so kind a heart. Not that she could do much anyway, she had her own troubles. If only Anna had worked when her husband was alive. If she had worked for twenty-five years she would have a pension. But her husband used to say: 'Don't worry while I'm here to take care of you. You'll have worries enough when I am gone.' So she had only been working since her husband had been killed in the war.

She might have had a little personal pension all the same, but she had a daughter, 'so they said, she must feed you, why should you get anything, go and live with her'. But what could her daughter give her? Fifty roubles a month at most. So she had to work. Everything had gone in the war – her husband, her daughter, all her relations – eighteen of them! Who knew what had happened to them? They had been scattered in occupied territory and had never been heard of again. Her house had gone, and all her things. Last year she had bought her bed. Four years she had saved up for it, that was all she had. She still wore the clothes she had in the war; I could see what they were like, they had burned up on her. But nothing would matter if she heard from her daughter. And so long as there was not another war. 'Tell them, darling, go back and tell them, there mustn't be another war. Anything rather than that.'

I was crying, I think, more than she was. The sound of her voice would have been enough, this ancient stylised voice of lament. Perhaps she was only a silly old woman and without dignity, but it was like hearing the whole people.

We kissed and I left. Alexei, who had just turned up, took me to the station. He pointed to the houses being built and said anyone could build a house. They were lent money and got the materials on credit from the building trust. That was how he had built his. It had some disadvantages, for instance, the well was two hundred yards away, but that would be put right. 'You'll have water laid on?' I asked.

'Well, no, but I'll get around to digging a well near the house.'

I thought he was happier talking without his women. Perhaps also anxious to give me a better view than I might have formed from the general conversation. 'Women don't understand. And people like Pavel don't either.' Certainly he, Alexei, understood things differently and he had reason to feel cheerful. When we got to the station I found that the train was due in a few minutes.

After this adventure I went to see a friend who lived in Moscow. She had been going regularly to the Mayakovsky Square meetings,[18] though her husband was increasingly nervous and said that the poetry read there was bad and that there were too many hooligans, but probably he was afraid of her getting into trouble. Before the closing down of *Syntaxis*,[19] Ginsburg[20] read the same poem every week, a *Manifesto of Man* not particularly subversive but pessimistic. When Ginsburg was arrested another young man took over, and when he was arrested two girls took over. My friend saw them removed but they reappeared at the next meeting. She asked them what had happened. They said they were taken to the police station where one of them argued that the poem wasn't anti-Soviet, only pro-peace; while the other asserted it was a nonsense poem such as Blok used to write, and she started reciting reams of Blok. In the end the police had enough and evidently thought the girls too silly to be worth troubling about, so let them go. My friend thought there would be no more meetings after the most recent row. She said her generation were 'not normal' because they had been through Stalin's Terror but that their children were growing up 'normal' and the Government might feel they had 'to put them through it' because they can't cope with normal people. She herself tried to behave 'normally', come what may, i.e. to think and talk freely – the country was not free but she tried to act 'as though it were'. She ended up by saying 'We are doomed', meaning her generation, or possibly her set. She felt passionately about ethics, and was proud of having preserved her 'inner' freedom throughout, but nevertheless said 'we are all corroded by lies', i.e. the lies heard and spoken; she believed that even the official lies are told without much scruple because 'everybody knows one doesn't mean what one says and one only says it under unbearable compulsion, but this leaves its mark.'

As an example of such lies I asked what she thought of Pasternak's letter of apology to Khrushchev and *Pravda* in connection with the Nobel Prize. She said she saw it as an act of great courage, considering how much more was demanded of him and how much he risked, but she felt deeply the humiliation caused by such situations and was sure that in general they help to disintegrate personality.

'Propaganda,' she continued, 'has distorted all terms' and she personally avoided everything 'highfalutin' – saying 'I am too lazy to lie; all one can teach one's children is to be honest and kind.' All causes, she believed, were discredited and artists could only keep their integrity by being wholly unpolitical.

She didn't hold with defectors; saying that those who defect, after going out as tourists, only cause trouble to others and discourage the authorities from relaxing travel restrictions. She also seemed to beileve that many defectors were 'ex-policemen who had got into trouble.'

She assured me that she spoke freely in front of her children; she refused to lie to them as she didn't want them to have illusions.

Talking of schools, she told me that every class is divided into two – the *otlichniki*[21] and the Komsomol on the one side, and the 'others'. (The 'others' are more numerous.) It is the same throughout the country. The 'others' are peasants, workers, ordinary people, 'all of us'. The otlichniki are the careerists. The children are frank about it; e.g. three little girls talking at school: the eldest said 'I won't join the Komsomol, it's boring, will you?'

'No.'

'And you?'

'Certainly I will.'

'Why?'

'I want a good job.'

The 'others' are seething with discontent; peasants and workers are angry because of economic conditions and talk like the taxi driver who had driven me to the hotel, saying 'there's discontent everywhere. That's why the Government is frightened and will have to do something; things must get better or worse – they can't stay put. Meanwhile no one feels any ground under his feet.'

We discussed the tests: my friend thought that one reason for them, and also for spy-scares and even the working up of international tension, was to have a pretext for tightening things at home in case of need.

Another reason for the tests was fear of what China might do. China was aggressive and careless of lives – didn't care how many people were killed so long as five million Communists were left. So Khrushchev may have wanted to show the Chinese that even they would lose more than they liked in a nuclear war. The time might come she thought, and this had been said to me before, when Russia and the West would be linked together against China. At present 'we think of China as you think of us, or as you used to think of us.'

Simple people, she said, were shocked by the removal of Stalin's body from the Mausoleum and regarded it as an insult to the dead. Indeed some young people, who didn't remember the Terror now, posed as Stalinists to look subversive.

The driver of the taxi I took to go back to the hotel pointed to a house saying 'That's Beria's house.'

'Not a nice man,' I remarked.

She shrugged. 'Who knows? We don't. We're just told things. Now we're told several other people are criminals and they'll find a few more, but where were *they* at the time?' She turned and winked. 'In our country, it's the people who decide everything.'

Later I went to see the poet Robert Rozhdestvensky with an interpreter. First she had said she wasn't coming as I didn't need her, then she told Rozhdestvensky she would leave us together, but in the end she sat in throughout. Rozhdestvensky lives with his wife Ala, his small daughter Katya and his mother-in-law in a modern flat in a modern block opposite the Ukraine Hotel. They occupy several small rooms, with Swedish furniture and cactus plants.

Rozhdestvensky was born in 1932 in Altai. He went to the Gorky Institute (where he met his wife who is a literary critic) and stayed on in Moscow but now he only lives there four months in the year; the rest of the time he travels in Russia and abroad – he has been to Vienna, Poland, Roumania, Czechoslovakia, Bulgaria.

I asked him, with apologies for such a crude journalistic question, how far poetry still had to be didactic. He said, with obvious Victorian sincerity, that he wanted his readers to become better people through reading his verse. Also that poetry must be many-sided and have a philosophical content. Nature poetry was good, love poetry was very important, but if Shakespeare had written nothing but his sonnets he would have been only a virtuoso of genius and those with less genius must take even more care not to be one-sided.

He spoke of the enormous interest in poetry among young people and advised me to go to the Mayakovsky Square meetings which, he said, were still being held. Yevtushenko and his group (of whom R.R. was one) were immensely popular.

When I left, the interpreter went off and I got a taxi and had the usual talkative driver. 'Nothing has changed except that more houses have been built and you can talk more.' He told me he earned sixty-five roubles if he fulfilled the plan and could make up to a hundred as he was '1st Class'. His wife worked but, even so, with two children they couldn't make ends meet. He was anxious that his daughter should go to the Institute as otherwise she wouldn't get a good job. But he said it was difficult to get into the Institute 'because of all those foreigners'. Besides this, it was hard to get a job in Moscow, even for Institute graduates – because they all wanted to be there but instead got sent to the periphery. He wished he owned his taxi. He did own a car (a Moskvich, which cost 2,500 roubles; a Volga costs 4,000) but if you were caught using your car as a taxi you would get fined and the car would be confiscated. He wished there were private property here 'like there is abroad where things must go swimmingly because of it'. He ended up with: 'Well, we're alone and I won't see you again and as there's no witness, if you reported me I could deny what you said. So I'll tell you: if I had my way I'd dissolve all the kolkhozes. What can you expect of such a system? The kolkhozniks are miserable, they all flock to town.'

'Do they still?' I asked.

'Now they won't let them in.'

'But surely they're a little better off than they were considering all that's been done for them?'

'I can't keep up with all those politics . . . They say Communism is coming, but I don't care one way or the other about that. Things will still be the same; you can't change human nature.'

That evening I went to see a friend at the National and found him being interviewed for the radio. The interviewer asked if I wouldn't speak for Moscow Radio – he thought it would be a good idea. I said I found it difficult enough in English, and doubted if my Russian were up to it.

Next day, in the Kremlin garden, I met an agreeable woman and lunched with her at the Prague. Evidently it was her day for getting things off her chest. We took a liking to each other but agreed she should keep her identity to herself. She was about fifty, slight, dark, with a thin, intelligent 'former-person'[22] face. Married to a professor, they had no children.

She said de-Stalinisation was good, but that both the Twentieth and the Twenty-Second Congresses were a shock: 'People had died for Russia and for Stalin during the war; they couldn't believe he was responsible for all those crimes.' As a girl she knew Postyshev[23] and others close to him. She said he was charming, 'talked like a writer, loved Beethoven, was intelligent about films'; true when they went to see him they didn't know if they'd come back but they were charmed all the same.

The Government's prestige had been shaken by the recent revelations. People said: 'What's been going on inside the Kremlin for thirty years?' or 'Who'll be accused next?' Even workmen were shocked by the 'bad manners' shown at the Congress and by Khrushchev banging the table with his shoe at UNO. Simple people who felt Stalin was 'a mountain at their back' now said 'the cult exists, personality doesn't'. But Khrushchev is trusted not to make war, approved for working for co-existence and because there is no terror at home. '*Khrushchev ne krovozhaden*' ('Khrushchev is not bloodthirsty') people say – all the same he is hated by workers and peasants because of the bad economic conditions.

Poverty and shortages are acute in the countryside. And a sense of insecurity has been caused by the repayment of a State loan being put off for twenty years. People feel that all their savings have gone – twenty years is too long to wait, and that there is no certainty of repayment even then. This echoed what the retired postmistress had told me in Yalta.

Housing was the only field in which there was an improvement. She and her husband had moved two years ago to a one-room self-contained flat in a new suburb. At first the streets were unsafe because of hooligans, but there are fewer now though her husband still carries a *finka*[24] 'just in case'. Their neighbours are workers who turn flats into slums; one-room flats meant for a couple soon swarm with babies and relations from the country, and the mothers, while doing their housework, turn their children out on the stairs which they use as a WC. The building is shoddy, and the steps and plaster are already cracking though this block is only two years old. All the same, housing is better than it was and new houses are going up.

The woman told me that she and her husband liked being on the outskirts of the city, close to the country, and being surrounded by simple people who paid no attention to them. Her husband had assembled a good radio set and they listened in from the 'zone of silence' (where there is less jamming) outside Moscow to which they go in the summer.

Meeting foreigners was still difficult, though easier than it used to be. In any case, her work put her in touch with them. The staff used to be briefed about which of them was to meet which foreigner. Now there was less briefing, but she was still chaperoned when foreigners came, and if a foreigner asked her out the chaperone said at once that unfortunately she would be busy at that time. Most 'ordinary' people felt that meeting foreigners was unsafe and therefore avoided them. She and her husband used to have one or two foreign friends but they had left. The friends would ring up before coming (they had a telephone in their old flat) and her husband would go out before they arrived and make sure they weren't being followed; if today he had a telephone and foreign friends, he would still do this.

She complained of a feeling of political uncertainty, of having 'no ground under one's feet'. Some intellectuals, she said, were cynical; some tried to get out of practical work and go into research. There was seething discontent and no guarantee that the Terror would not come back. Certainly, freedom would not be possible until economic conditions improved. But 'our people love their country and their work and are infinitely patient, and this may see the country through.'

She herself felt doomed – 'it's only a question of time.' But she pinned her hope of things getting better on the young people, who are 'normal because they haven't seen the Terror'; also they are getting educated and therefore learning to think. Then she told me more about her own reactions. She felt the only thing was to hang on to honesty and was proud of having kept her integrity through the bad times. She was religious and believed it was her religion that had seen her through – that and her interest in her work. She is a fighter and now was joining her colleagues in a protest which she thought might cost her her job, if not worse.

At dinner a middle-aged engineer shared my table. He was a war veteran who had later done six years at the Moscow Institute of which he proudly wore the badge; afterwards he had rejoined the army for a time, but got out because 'I prefer building to destroying'. Now he had settled and married, but he travelled all over the country on official business. Early in the meal I had mentioned England and assumed he realised I was a foreigner. But when I mentioned England again he asked me why I kept on talking about it, and blankly disbelieved me when I said I was Russian-born, but had lived in England since the age of nine. He insisted I couldn't possibly have kept my Russian if I'd lived abroad for so long and to my amusement apparently suspected me of being a Russian pro-Western snob. He asked me in what way England was different from Russia and grilled me on English books about which he knew little and therefore suspected I was inventing. Suddenly, with a malicious gleam he announced 'England can't be outstripped – she's chasing too fast after her colonies . . . And what about the Americans – they can't even manage to keep their monkey in space.' I told him off for his chauvinism. He replied 'the truth is one and the Soviet Union have it. You can keep your comforts – we have what matters.' I replied that truth was many-sided. He said science had shown it was not. I answered that all men wanted the same things, 'Justice and happiness for all.'

'Not for *all*,' he said. 'Not for the wicked,' adding that this was what foreigners didn't understand. I pointed out that the English too had fought the Nazis.

'Did they?' he remarked nastily, after which we had a polite but furious row. Finally, in explanation of his lack of manners, he said he had meant to provoke me to see if really I were English and (with an air of making a patronising concession) went on to remark that England must have had a bad time before the Soviet Union came into the war. At this I got up and walked off as a demonstration (fortunately I had paid my bill), only to be grabbed by a drunken officer on my way out of the cloakroom; he clung to my arm and tried to get into a taxi with me. I appealed to 'the comrade taxi driver' who gallantly threw the man out. A disagreeable evening!

The next day I spent seeing friends and in the evening dined at the Metropole, sharing a table with a nice *petit bourgeois* couple who lived eighty kilometres outside Moscow. He was a school teacher and so was she. They hadn't been to the Metropole for ten years – rarely came to Moscow and were having a spree. They were delighted to meet a foreigner as none came to their town. Both wanted to travel but said that no doubt the Western countries didn't give visas to Soviet citizens and that was why no *putyovki*[25] were handed out. He had been abroad only once, in the Far East, during the war. He had a lot to say about Stalin; he thought de-Stalinisation a good thing, though Stalin had done some good and didn't know all the evil that was done in his name. People trusted him, and even wrote him letters, but they got no reply. 'He didn't know the country's need.' In Stalin's time there were no open meetings (i.e. Party meetings to which non-Party people could come). Now the Party in his town held an open and a closed one alternately. Non-Party people like himself went to the open meetings and were invited to criticise. The Party then discussed the criticisms at a closed meeting and decided what was to be done. Officials who were much criticised were now apt to be dismissed. The advantage of not being in the Party was that one was less criticised and could criticise others more. But he believed that today everyone could be criticised, all the way up to the top.

He thought there was no fear of war because all countries were too much afraid of destruction. For that matter, the Soviet Union had had an atom bomb at the time of Hiroshima – perhaps only a small one, but anyway they had refrained from using it.

If conditions improved, that is if the plan were fulfilled, his wages would go up in three years' time. That would be wonderful; he counted on it. 'Not so good if it doesn't happen,' he added, as though to himself. He seemed eager to believe but suspected an abyss of disillusionment.

A few years ago, he said, they couldn't have been seen talking to me. Now they could almost invite me to their home. (They obviously weren't going to do so.) I asked if contacts with foreigners were still pretty difficult? 'Unfortunately, so many tourists turn out to be spies,' he said, and went on 'Does that happen in England?' I said Soviet spies were the best in the world, but all the same some did get caught. He listened to the BBC and also got unpublished news from friends in the Party who heard things at Party meetings and passed on the information.

281

He had fond memories of United States' aid in war and also of British greatcoats.

The following morning at about eleven o'clock I went to Mayakovsky Square, where I found a crowd of three to four hundred breaking into shifting groups which coalesced and then broke up again. Someone said, '*Druzhinniki razgonyayut.*'[26] I joined a group to which a young man was reading poetry, and asked a girl what was being read; then I realised she herself was a druzhinnik.

'Nothing's being read,' she said, 'It's just a pretext for filth.' Druzhinniks were in every group, shouting, laughing, arguing. Most of the men and girls were respectably dressed, in fact some of the men were elegant in Western-style coats and beautiful fur hats. But there were also some rough-looking types, and one who, I thought, appeared sophisticated and degenerate.

Two older men were talking, one about poets, the other about druzhinniks: 'They read much. Why don't they read Mayakovsky?'

'They do.'

'They choose only the bad bits.'

'Why not let young people get on with what they want to read?'

'They can read what they like but it must be good, representative stuff.'

Loud guffaws from the bystanders. An educated druzhinnik, seemingly a student, was arguing with a poet who was not a student.

'Why do you have to read there, when plenty of nice clubs are provided?'

'I can't go into them without a student ticket.'

'I'll send you a ticket to a reading next Saturday.'

More laughter around. 'It's to get us off the square.'

'No,' said the poet firmly, 'here we meet, it's our custom, here we shall go on meeting.'

Two young men were led off by druzhinniks who suddenly produced their arm bands; one of the prisoners struggled and kicked; a girl druzhinnik tripped after them. A few people left at this moment, but a biggish group stayed on to listen to a handsome young poet reading, first Esenin,[27] with much expression, then his own verse. As soon as he had finished he went off with his friends, but a young couple ran after him, shook his hand and thanked him emotionally; others asked him about himself. He said he worked as a male nurse in a hospital.

By then only four young men were left. One asked me if I was interested in poetry? I said yes, but when he wanted to know which poets I liked, I foresaw embarrassment due to my ignorance and said I was a foreigner interested in both poetry and lively discussion among the Soviet young.

Another said 'Everyone must look at things through his own eyes, poets too.'

'Yes, but we must look at things in the right way, poets particularly, since they have a greater responsibility than the rest.' I said perhaps things weren't just black or white, different people saw different aspects. One agreed; the other didn't. All four were science students. I thought at first they were druzhinniks but I hadn't seen them taking part in a row and came to the conclusion they were fairly neutral observers. We stood for an hour in a blizzard, arguing amiably.

They said they weren't worried by bombs because they were unafraid of war. The Russians were tough and had suffered more than anyone in the last war and could face it again. But Soviet citizens were so vital that they turned their backs on the past and looked to a peaceful future. No one in the Soviet Union wanted war. I said no one did in England either, but they were quite sure Western capitalists did because they wanted to fill their pockets. One said:

'They'll only just put up with peace if their profits can be guaranteed without war.'

I said nobody could think they'd make anything out of a nuclear war, and they agreed the destruction would be terrible. Since by now there seemed to be some measure of agreement in the air, I suggested there were common values deeper than structural differences, such as having one instead of several parties. They agreed, but said several parties showed disunity. I argued that competition was for the good of the people. This ghastly phrase went down well, though the fact was doubted. They were convinced that competition was only for votes. I said all the same, it could benefit the people; we didn't assume perfection. The woman said, neither did they; the men disagreed.

Then one inquired, 'What do foreigners think of our Party now? Look at how it has admitted Stalin's mistakes. Would your Western parties have had such courage, such unity?'

I said, 'Ours wouldn't have stood for Stalin.'

They thought this over: 'You mean several parties are a safeguard against despotism?'

Then they began arguing among themselves about what had made Stalin's despotism possible: 'He had persecution mania,' said one.

'He wouldn't let the Party control him. Khrushchev does,' suggested another.

The argument went on 'It's all very well saying we should have controlled them "up there" but how could we if they didn't want to be controlled?'

'All the same he couldn't have set up the cult of personality by himself; it must have been everybody's fault.'

'Up to us now to sweep away the remnants of Stalinism.'

They assured me again that Russians didn't want war with the West. I asked, 'What about China?'

'That's different,' they said.

Finally they took me politely back to the hotel; by then my teeth were chattering.

Today is Constitution Day. After overcoming many doubts, a friend said she'd take me to see some painters who would be entertaining because of the holiday; we could always decide to turn back if we were followed. She asked me to meet her at eleven o'clock at Oktyabr station.

I arrived a few minutes early and noticed a man in a grey military-looking coat and a brown fur hat, he had a portfolio under his arm. He got out of the train after me, spoke to two girls and went on. I thought if he were following me he would probably be looking less conspicuous. However, I walked down the street, so as not to hang about at the station, and went into a small side street which turned out to be a cul-de-sac, so I turned back and bumped into 'Grey-coat', who looked embarrassed and apologised.

I went back to the station and when my friend came, told her about Grey-coat, but she said we'd see on the way to the other station from which we were to take the train. Grey-coat turned up in the ticket queue, though there had been no sign of him till then. My friend could not at first believe he was a 'tail' – she thought, as I had, that he was too unsuitable and too smartly dressed, but after seeing him look furtively at us and go up to the platform keeping us in sight, she agreed that that was what he was doing.

We felt it was no good going back now, probably he knew where we were going; so it would look worse if we went home. We proceeded, Grey-coat got into another carriage, disembarked when we did, saw us take the country bus and vanished.

After we had paid our visits we took the train home. At the station in Moscow, Grey-coat reappeared, spoke to someone and joined the taxi queue behind us; meanwhile two cars drove up and followed our taxi; when I dropped my friend at her home they separated, one following me.

Later, I went to see a dear old lady of eighty. She came of a good family and was evidently proud of it. She had eloped with a Jew whom she was only able to marry after the Revolution as, she said, it was 'forbidden' before then. She had lived with him abroad, 'not as an émigré,' from '24 to '40, then came back. She avoided other aristocratic émigrés as she didn't like 'former-people ways' and thought a woman who hadn't worked all her life had something missing in her.

She congratulated me on the translation of *Zhivago*. She liked the book and liked Pasternak, but didn't seem to have known him well.

She thought Stalin's era was as inexplicable as Hitler's except in terms of pathology – not only the tyrants but their subjects were insane at the time! Stalin could not have set up the personality cult without support. Russian people were at bottom anarchic but so patient and obedient. There had been a great change for the better since Stalin's death.

She was surrounded by theosophical books including all those by Krishnamurti, and was delighted to learn I had once met him in Egypt. She found theosophy a great comfort. She was very friendly in a warm Old-Régime manner and implored me to come again for a long talk. Perhaps she managed never to see the whole horrible reality.

LENINGRAD

That evening I took a plane to Leningrad. An engineer sat next to me. He had about him an air of wealth and privilege; he lived in Leningrad but dashed up to Moscow for a day or a weekend, staying with an old friend of his mother's. He also travelled around Russia by car or motorbike with his wife and golden-youth friends. His mother, aged seventy-five, had studied at the Sorbonne and travelled a great deal before the Revolution.

He said de-Stalinisation was a good thing. As a child, he knew of arrests but didn't understand much about it. 'I knew the truth without knowing it,' he explained. He understood it in '48 – 'a terrible year'. His mother knew Krestinsky[28] and Kirov. 'If people like Kirov had lived, things would have changed sooner,' he said.

I suggested that the Lenin party organisation was now playing a more important role than before. He thought the effects of the Congress were 'complex' and it was better not to talk about it. He was in China in '58; now this would be 'more difficult'.

When I arrived, the Intourist guide who took me to the Europa Hotel was a middle-aged man, an old Leningradian; he taught English, was proud of his city and of Russia rather than of the USSR and, I thought, he seemed less brash, than the Muscovite variety. Perhaps I was influenced by feeling myself a Petersburgian.

A chatty maid who brought my breakfast had been born in Leningrad in '20, she had trained as an X-ray nurse and worked as such in Finland in the war. She changed to being a maid because nurses get 'very little more pay' and a maid's work is 'more companionable'. She considered bombs terrible; something that should be given up by all. She was a widow and had a son of thirteen.

My window faced a closed church and the Gostiny Dvor. It was decorated with Christmas stars on its windows and Christmas trees on the pavement outside and reminded me of that evening's Christmas shopping with my mother in 1912 (church, beggars in the square and the arcade, glamour in the shop) when I lost my mother's huge muff. Now there were no beggars but a queue outside a vegetable stall, and little glamour in Gostiny Dvor where I went to try to get a fur hat for Billy Collins. There were, however, some astonishingly pretty Christmas tree decorations – plenty of tinsel – strings of glass bubbles and other bubbles; glass vegetables including very fine cobs of corn (in honour of *Kukuruznik?*[29]), glass Grandfather Frosts, old peasants, knights and their glamorous *boyariny*[30]; all expensive and no queues for them. I bought some. A gramophone was playing dance music and there was a typed list of records in stock, but the most popular ones were sold out.

A well-dressed young-middle-aged woman stopped me to ask where I had bought my bag.

'Abroad.'

'That explains it. Would you sell it?'

I said I was a foreigner and couldn't sell it as that would be illegal.

She said 'But I know foreigners sell their things. I'd give you literally anything for it.'

I sympathised but felt a little suspicious of provocation. We had the usual conversation about why, if I were a foreigner, my Russian was so good – what was shopping like abroad, etc. Would I like to come back to Russia for good? I said I had a family in England. Wouldn't I sell her the bag after all – I could get another abroad. I finally offered to send her one as a present from England, but she said that would place her under suspicion of having foreign contacts. I said that was the sort of thing that would make me hesitate to settle in Russia. She looked startled.

I went in the direction of the Moika to see my old home but lost my way and sat down on a bench in Mikhailovsky Park next to an old gentleman. I asked him the way to the Moika and we began to talk. Soon a young woman sat down on the same bench, lit a cigarette and read her paper. All the other benches around were empty – but perhaps she was just Russian-sociable, and not a druzhinnik?

My old gentleman was joined by his wife who said it was time to go home, and they suggested I should go with them as their house was on the way to the Moika. The old man seemed to have had a stroke and limped but, all the same, hobbled ahead at an astonishing speed; we followed. His wife told me he was a retired army officer and she a retired teacher of French, both old Leningradians though she was born and brought up in Kronstadt. They had a son. During the war her husband had served in the south. She had lost touch with him and the boy whom he had taken with him and placed with friends. Then she went to Moscow where she got news of him, found her boy and took him to the Urals where they starved until they were put on army rations. After the war they went back to their flat which they'd had since '37. It had been robbed and was dilapidated but they had managed to keep it. Did we have communal flats in England? Most people here lived in them, but the disadvantage was that the residents came from such different backgrounds.

When we got to their house they insisted on my going in and having lunch with them – 'only their usual light midday meal' as she had no time to cook the chicken she had bought in the market.

Two biggish rooms were cluttered with heavy furniture but they had a nice view in which they took a proper Leningradian pride. The old lady gave me soap and a towel to wash in the communal bathroom – she said they couldn't keep them there as they got stolen. I helped her to get food from the kitchen where two other women were cooking.

They had seen the film *Two Lives*, which I had heard praised by the unsophisticated: a story of a Greek revolutionary about to be executed by 'the Americans' and of other revolutionaries seizing an American boy as a hostage which led to a moving scene between the mothers of the two boys. What had struck my hostess was an émigré waiter who sees he has been mistaken in emigrating. She told me this with the usual candour and disregard for my being myself an émigré, though perhaps half consciously comparing my fate with hers and hoping she, not I, was right.

Over the 'simple meal' – mainly porridge – her husband said he was content with his lot except that they were both getting old and he was now dependent on her help (she had stopped working after his stroke to look after him). So the future looked a bit bleak – all this was described with a mixture of despair and amusement. They had enough to live on – he got a pension of two hundred roubles, she of eighty roubles and there would soon be more and more material things available according to the Plan, but what then? Hunger would soon be lacking in the Soviet Union (not like in the West) and what would one do then, 'because one can't enjoy one's food without it?' But what did man live by? What did I believe was the purpose of man's life? I said to love God and one's neighbour. This led to a discussion on religion. Both had been religious but she had lost her faith, as had all her school friends, though her school chaplain in Kronstadt had been 'a wonderful man, a revolutionary anti-clerical.' He had vanished after the Kronstadt rising of 1921[31] when the rebels were defeated by Trotsky's army and 'a cloud of them' fled across the ice to Finland, the chaplain among them. Her father had been 'saved by his sailors'. Her

Manya at Sagres

husband too had been an atheist for a long time, and to support this he asked provocatively what was truth and why should one love one's neighbour? But we agreed that for the moment the neighbour was still hungry in the Soviet Union and had better be fed, and that without truth people felt strangled. 'Though not all truth is good to tell,' he said, referring to truths told at Congress.

Still, de-Stalinisation was a good thing, they said, as the Stalin era had been terrible.

The old man told me he had heard Kerensky[32] make speeches; he was a wonderful orator, and the soldiers had wanted to go on with the war so long as he spoke to them. It was a hard choice, he said reflectively.

'But in the end the men found it an easy one,' his wife protested.

'Naturally,' he replied.

Before I left we got back to philosophy. Communism, he asserted, was something that had never existed and could never exist.

'They say that when there's enough of everything, everyone will be good. Can you believe that?'

That evening I dined in a restaurant where, except for one blonde accompanied by an officer, I was the only woman. I thought I had put my foot in it by coming on my own, and I felt obliged to explain to the waiter that I was a foreigner so I didn't know better. He said that since I was a foreigner it was all right. The company consisted of lonely drunks, cheerful blackmarketeers, Finnish sailors and waiters cosily smoking with them. I offered a 'Players' to my waiter and he hinted that he would like to buy the box but I said it was my last.

While I was eating, a chubby waiter, pink and white with thick black hair, was introduced to me as a man who knew foreign languages. He proved to be French. He mentioned that life was hard – I sympathised – then without a change of expression or voice, he said 'You don't know how hard, Madame, you can't know.'

He had worked in Paris as a hôtelier, married a Russian émigré whose parents were living in the Soviet Union. She had wanted to return and he had agreed and come with her. Before he had realised what he was in for, and not knowing Russian, he had signed a paper and found himself a Soviet citizen. After that no one could help him. Moreover his wife found that her parents were dead, and after a few years she, too, had died. He had married again and had a little boy by his second wife. He asked me if I would come to his flat on his day off and meet his wife? I said I would.

When the day came, I went to the appointed place and after a time the man sauntered up. He was wearing a beret and a high-necked sweater; his face was expressionless.

He asked me if I thought I had been followed? I was reasonably sure I hadn't been. There was no dvornik in sight. His flat consisted of two rooms at the back of a yard, but with their own entrance. The rooms measured twenty-five metres overall and had no running water, WC or kitchen except for an oven for cooking and heating which used wood, coal or scraps. They drew their water from a well in the yard.

The place was stuffed with furniture, including a television set. They had had a radio but although jamming could be avoided and reception was pretty good they had sold it because he had got fed up with politics. Materially he said he was all right, but miserable because he couldn't talk and he was very nostalgic for Paris. He complained that Russia was helping to feed Indo-China in spite of shortages at home. There had been little meat or butter in the shops recently; maize and rice too were short, and there was no wool either. His daughter's pretty knitted coat had cost him forty roubles on the blackmarket.

He had tried to go to France after his first wife had died, but was told he couldn't as he had no hostages to leave behind him. His second wife would have been willing to leave but they had no putyovkas. He had the impression that most Russians were miserable but that some of the young people believed in Communism, whereas the older generation knew the facts and didn't. Most kolkhozniks, he said, were wretched, though there were some 'millionaire' kolkhozes which were shown to foreign visitors.

He himself escaped from despair into the pleasures of materialism and the delights of 'fiddling', enjoying a sort of desperate pleasure in the risk combined with a French belief that he was being practical and prudent.

He had now almost ceased to correspond with his relations in France because his uncles sent him fashion magazines for his wife and he had nothing to send them in return. About her, he said he was lucky to have found such a nice girl but he did not talk freely in front of her and she didn't know all his thoughts. After a while she came in in her curlers, shy and silent, but soon returned to the other room where she was cooking.

Walking back along Nevsky to my hotel I saw a crowd in a semi-circle round a drunk who was being held up by two toughs. The people in the crowd said: 'We should call the militia. Fancy undressing a poor drunk . . . They only started putting his clothes back on him when we came.' And, in fact, the toughs were dressing the drunk whose coat and shirt they had taken off despite the frost. No militiaman was about and the crowd gradually dispersed.

Later that day I set out to see a friend; a young man behind me in the taxi queue asked where I was going as he wanted to share my taxi. I inquired where he wished to go. He said, unwillingly, 'Labour Square'. I replied that I'd drop him, but then he became cross saying he didn't want to be dropped without knowing where I was going. Meanwhile, a woman at the head of the queue drove off without telling the queue where she was going and they commented that this was very ill-mannered because it showed she was unwilling to share her taxi. So when my turn came I was careful to say 'Warsaw Station' adding that the young man, who got in with me after all, was to be dropped at Labour Square. When we reached it he exclaimed that he had no change and went into a shop, ostensibly to get some. We duly went on to the station but when we drew out of it, a car (19-28) started up after us then dropped out of sight. When the taxi left me several blocks away from the house to which I was going I walked through some back yards and returned to the street I'd just left to see 19-28 coasting slowly along. At this, feeling a fool, I decided to go back to the hotel. Presumably the young man had telephoned from the shop.

As I could not discover a Catholic church, though a mosque built by Tartars was repeatedly pointed out to me, I went to an Orthodox one, then I took some photographs along the Moika and the quay. A group of street cleaners along the Moika insisted on being photographed. A man who had been sitting by the canal, seeing this came up to me and asked me who I was and why I was taking photographs? I said I was taking pictures of a street I had lived in forty-five years ago – the actual house was just opposite. And who was he, I inquired?

'Just a moment,' he replied. 'Has your identity been checked this morning?'

'No.'

'Then what about telling me who you are?'

'Why?'

'Well, would you just wait a moment?' he begged, and crossed the narrow street to talk to a passing militiaman. The militiaman said loudly:

'Why should the citizeness's identity be checked?' and the man came back discomfited, gave me an oily smile and said I could proceed.

'All the same, who are you?' I asked. 'Just an ordinary citizen?'

'Not quite.'

'A druzhinnik?'

'Not quite. My function is somewhat different.'

I gave it up, suspecting he was just an eager beaver.

MOSCOW

On my return to Moscow I went to tea with Ehrenburg. He was more cheerful than I had ever seen him.

De-Stalinisation, he said, was a splendid thing. No one regretted Stalin except those who wore his medals. True that re-naming Stalingrad was an exaggeration. 'But that is the only thing we regret.'

History still had to reveal Stalin's 'greatness', i.e. his genius for intrigue and his talent for creating confusion and covering up his tracks. He, Ehrenburg, knew what terrible things went on but even he did not suspect the extent of Stalin's responsibility until after the war, and only knew it for certain 'two months before his death'. Stalin spoke 'little and wisely'. In 1937 and during the war, simple people looked on him as their saviour – the strong, wise man who knew what the country needed and what dangers threatened it. When the campaign against the Jews began he would send for Jews and ask them what the Press was up to: 'It smells of anti-semitism,' he would say.

What had helped to confuse people was his unpredictability. Not only did Litvinov[33] 'die in his bed' – which was surprising enough – but when he was demoted Stalin gave instructions that he should keep his flat and his car.

When, in 1937, Ehrenburg came back from Paris, he found all hell let loose, and wrote to Stalin asking for permission to emigrate. He received no answer but an official saw him and said as there was danger of war he was needed at home, but his wife would be allowed to go to Paris to fetch his things. Ehrenburg thought it over and decided this was not good enough so he wrote again to Stalin asking him to reconsider his decision and actually saying 'I can't write in the Soviet Union.' A week later he got permission to return to Paris.

Now the whole truth about the Terror would gradually come out. Ehrenburg had written in *Pravda* that in the remaining part of his memoirs he would deal with 1937 and 1949. These were, as everyone knew, the peaks of the Terror; the fact that *Pravda* published his statement meant that the truth about that time could now be written. Since then he had received letters from victims offering material – not just the VIPs mentioned at the Congress but ordinary workers and peasants who had suffered equally, a fact which could now gradually be admitted.

The effect of the Congress would result in more freedom for writers.

The post-war Terror affected fewer people than did the Terror of 1937. It involved 'only the massacre' of Jewish writers and the repression of those who had been repressed before.

De-Stalinisation and the revelation of the facts were guarantees against the Terror coming back. De-Stalinisation had been held up by the Hungarian revolt and 'perhaps because there was too much pressure from the Western Communists and from China'.

There would be no mass repression of Stalinists. The anti-Party group would be pensioned off 'on the same scale as engineers'. Molotov was a *chinovnik*;[34] Kaganovich a scoundrel; Voroshilov[35] was generally pitied because of his age. A few of Beria's men might be repressed.

Stalin's removal from the Mausoleum was awaited all through the Congress. But it was done tactfully – after the Congress was over and by night.

Of the foreign delegations, most brought only a wreath for Lenin; but some Far Eastern delegations, other than the Chinese, brought as well one wreath without a name.

It was on the last day before I was due to leave Russia that in the morning I had a call from Babkin (Head of the Intourist organisation) asking me to go at once to his office. I could not imagine what this could be about. When I arrived he told me that I had behaved very badly. I asked him what he meant. 'Well, you got picked up by the police in

Rostov, didn't you?' I replied that I had been extremely shocked by the incident and couldn't imagine what the fuss had been about.

He answered, 'For one thing, it is not etiquette for a woman to be alone with a man.'

I said 'Rubbish', and that in any case I had started off with two men and a girl and that their sliding off had greatly surprised me. I could think of no regulation, let alone law, that I had broken.

'If you had, you would have been arrested and expelled, or tried and put in prison. *Do tovo ne doshlo – poka.*'[36] And would I take his warning seriously into account.

Next morning I went to the airport where the plane was held up for half an hour while six men feverishly searched my luggage – but not my handbag. A fantastic touch was given to the proceedings by a boy going through my face cream and breaking open some of my cigarettes; while another told a slow-witted colleague that they were searching for anti-Soviet literature. I protested furiously against the confiscation of two large tins of caviar which the hotel had exchanged for my many unused coupons. They said only four hundred grams could be taken out of the country but, in fact, allowed me to take eight hundred which were in glass jars of a hundred grams each and were clearly not anti-Soviet manuscripts in disguise.

The Author

The Russian writer Babel is known to have made twenty-two drafts of a short story before he considered it fit to send to the printers. Manya's way of writing was hardly less meticulous. Every fact was checked and rechecked, every phrase polished and repolished. Finally came a close scrutiny to ensure that a normal number of articles and auxiliary verbs were present – in fact, that no Russianisms remained.

When she was in the Foreign Office, where deadlines were strict, her meticulousness obliged her to work not only during the long office hours but through most of the night as well: fortunately she seemed to need less sleep than most people. Later, when she became a publisher, her insistence on a very high standard made her decide that she must try to understand every side of the business. She attended courses on design, she bought paper, she visited printers and binderies and when, at last, there were books to be sold she decided to travel them herself in London.

With unabashed optimism she offered her highbrow volumes not only to the big bookshops, whose buyers might perhaps be expected to place an order, but to any small shopkeeper who happened to have a bookstall and she was not in the least discouraged when she was met by the remark: 'Books is dead since sweets came off the rations.'

More serious was the fact that some of the big buyers felt obliged to offer her cocoa and drink it with her instead of consuming gin in their beer, which might have led to a more convivial atmosphere and consequently to larger orders. Travelling books was not one of Manya's most successful ventures; she gave it up and Harvill acquired a very efficient Sales Manager.

There was a strong contrast between the way in which she carried out her creative work – slowly and with infinite patience – and her extrovert activities, in which she operated with so much rapidity that colleagues sometimes referred to her as 'having passed through our office on her broomstick'. But one characteristic was common to everything she undertook: her determination to achieve what she wanted.

Manya Harari Memoirs 1906–1969

If Harvill ran into financial difficulties before it became associated with William Collins this was not due to any vagueness on Manya's part, nor to a tendency to overlook the hard, practical side of publishing: it came from her sense of priorities. Regardless of missed deadlines or expensive resettings in proof, every book had to come out just as she had visualised it. Besides this, her decision to publish any text which seemed to her to be of value in its own field, however small that field might be in terms of readership, was not designed to keep the firm in good financial standing, even though it contributed to the prestige of the imprint. Those who said of her: 'What's the matter with you is that you really hate money' should have qualified their statement. It was true solely of her personal life, in which a pair of slacks or a skirt, a shirt, shoes, a typewriter, a very large handbag and an enormous box of cigarettes were her only needs and sometimes, when she had given everything else away, her only possessions.

At various times Manya embarked on a number of enterprises which might at first sight appear disparate, but which, on closer examination, prove to have a common factor.

Above all else she was a bridge builder. She found expression for this in her periodical *The Changing World*[1] which, during the first years of the war, supplied English readers with facts about Russia, the United States, France and other countries. The Sword of the Spirit, in its earliest days, those in which she was associated with it, was a precursor of the Ecumenical Movement. Finally, Harvill provided a focus for an exchange of ideas between intellectuals who had been cut off from each other by six years of war. In this connection it is relevant that its first publications came from authors living respectively in Egypt, France, Germany, Greece, Italy, Kurdistan, Palestine and Spain.

Manya was particularly fitted to the task of bridge building because of her exceptional capacity for identifying herself with the hopes and fears of individuals and peoples and with different climates of thought and of culture. She also had a great talent for vividly communicating her impressions and convictions.

Probably her greatest achievement in bridge building was the one to which she devoted the last fifteen years of her life, introducing contemporary Russian writers to English readers. It was through her work as a publisher and a translator, or a co-translator, that Pasternak's *Doctor Zhivago*, Solzhenitsyn's *First Circle* and the works of such writers as Andrey Sinyavsky, Evgenia Ginzburg, Andrei Amalrik, none of whom could publish their books in their own country, came to be widely appreciated in the West.

It would, however, be wrong to draw the conclusion that she restricted her Russian list to writers who were in trouble in the USSR. Her first important publication was Ehrenburg's *The Thaw* (which she translated). Later came Bulgakov's *The Master and Margarita*, Yevtushenko's *Poems* and many volumes of Paustovsky's autobiography. What a manuscript required to qualify for Harvill's imprint was literary quality and a humane outlook.

Often the publication of Russian books caused Manya grave heart searching for, as one Sovietologist wrote of her, 'she was always deeply concerned about the safety of her authors'. There was no doubt that the Russian list was produced in an atmosphere of crisis – sometimes quite fortuitously: even so harmless a book as Tatiana Tolstoy's *Memoirs* was not immune. Jean-Jacques Kean, who had been helping in the translation, had not finished his revision when he had to go to the States. He flew out in 'The Bermuda Sky Queen' which developed engine trouble and landed in the ocean. Among the last to leave the plane was Jean-Jacques who was seen swimming to the rescue ship, holding the MS high above the waves.

The atmosphere in which she worked was very characteristic. For many years Harvill operated from Dickensian quarters in Lower Belgrave Street, where the staircase was so rickety that the visitors' necks were prudently insured. Very soon the office took on the air of a club. Here, at all hours, Manya was to be found, barely visible through a cloud of cigarette smoke, sitting on a floor knee high in proofs. Often she would be listening intently to some exile propounding his views on the best way to restore good government to his distant homeland. The door would open to admit a student come to borrow a book or to get advice on his thesis, or to let in a clergyman or a priest who wanted to discuss ecumenism, psychology or the worker priests' movement. If sometimes the company looked shabby or drab, this would soon be relieved by the arrival of an African or an Afghan in splendid robes or an elegant Sinhalese friend. The venue was not luxurious, nor was it functional, but it was friendly and its hospitality so warm that even Simon, Manya's poodle, caught the spirit of the place and was once seen entering the office via the kitchen, carrying a small glass of vodka in his mouth.

Later, when she came to devote most of her time to translation, Manya found that she could not concentrate adequately in the bustle of Harvill's small office, so she transferred herself to a room at the top of her home in Catherine Place. Here, surrounded by bookcases filled with Russian publications, she recreated her familiar atmosphere, the proofs cascading from the table, the smoke-laden air, the devoted poodle, no longer Simon but Robin, and the endless flow of visitors. Many of these were friends belonging to the fascinating world of Sovietology; others came simply because they were unhappy or worried. With inexhaustible generosity she always had time for them. Her family and friends, alarmed by the fact that, owing to the number of her callers, she had to reduce her sleep still further to get through her work, pointed out that among her visitors some had troubles which seemed to be self-invented and others were plainly impostors. So far as the first were concerned, it was enough for Manya that they were unhappy, whatever the cause, and as far as the crooks were concerned, she recognised them for what they were – rascals – and rather enjoyed their company. In any case she was too humble to demand excellence of her friends and acquaintances. Besides offering her ears and her intelligent advice, she had a curious capacity for making her visitors feel that they were, after all, a little better than they sometimes feared – perhaps even the crooks appreciated this.

In 1932 Manya's early attraction to Christianity had found fulfilment when she was received into the Catholic church. Her conversion never had the effect of making her feel one whit less Jewish or less interested in Israel. As she wrote earlier in this book, she found it most appropriate to be a Christian Jew in the Holy Land. To quote Charles Péguy – she was not one of those who love one entity *against* another.

Her interest in religion was reflected in the Harvill list. Father Victor White's books were among the first to discuss the relationship of religion to psychiatry, Gabriel Marcel's to offer a Christian approach to existentialism, while Roy Campbell's translation of the poems of St John of the Cross became a classic.

What has so far been written may have given the impression that Manya's life was entirely devoted to work and to very serious matters. This would be false. She had an immense capacity for fun and for relaxation. She loved the ballet, the theatre and the cinema: her consumption of detective stories may well have established a record and it only needed the excuse of a festival for her to become absorbed in decorating fantastic Easter eggs, making a Crib or decorating one of the Christmas trees which will live in the memory of her friends as a very personal expression of joy.

She went on painting holidays to the Greek Islands and the Outer Hebrides. These wild places held elemental and magical qualities that moved her, but to the run-of-the-mill countryside her reaction was very unlike that of most English people who, however long they may have lived in a town, usually retain the feeling that life in the country is 'the better', indeed, 'the good' life. So far as Manya was concerned, civilisation and 'the good life' were closely associated with pavements and city lights. She never entirely rejected the Russian view that the country was 'dark and deaf'.

In 1964 Manya, who had always been very short-sighted, developed cataracts in both eyes. Recalling that someone had once told her that the operation to remove cataracts was much more difficult in the case of short-sighted people and not knowing much about the advance in eye surgery, she thought it likely that she would go blind. She faced the prospect stoically and made practical arrangements for organising her life should this disaster befall her. Fortunately the operations were entirely successful. She could hardly believe her luck. Driving away from the hospital she gazed out of the window of the car, declared that never before had she seen the world so well and added that after such a good look round she would not mind dying. She still had five years before her but by 1967 she was far from well and in January 1968 she went into a hospital for tests. The diagnosis was a severe form of cancer. On learning this she wrote the following letter to her son.

'I am writing because I want you to know what I feel about being ill.

'Firstly, as I told you, it is in no way a shocking surprise, because I have half known it for a long time; not, of course, in any clear way but so well, however unclearly, that I would have been more surprised to find that there was nothing the matter with me. This has spared me the difficulty of sudden adjustment. It also means that what I now think has not been thought up on the spur of the moment.

'Secondly, I do not think death a desirable thing, so you can be quite sure that I'll do everything I can to put it off. I know that, as you say, there are various things nowadays one can do and I had a good practical talk with Gordon Bourne. He told me that in my particular case there is a very good chance of the ray treatment not only arresting the spread of the disease but actually dissolving (whatever the word is) this particular lump, and also that there are other chemical methods of treatment as well, if this one fails. Naturally, he did not pretend that any of it was a panacea, or that one could say with certainty what would succeed or for how long. I am telling you this not out of a morbid rejection of optimism but because it is obviously true, and also because of what I want to say next.

'There are two things that help me to see things in proportion. One is that being ill and dying is a job, in a sense like any other, but of course an important one. The important thing is to do it as well as one can. I find that knowing about it in advance, however uncertain the date, but with a knowledge more precise than one has when one is well is something so real, factual and also demanding, that it leaves one hardly any room for nostalgia or sadness for oneself, or even for re-gretting what one hasn't managed to get done in life. I feel this has become entirely God's business to look after: all there is to do is to get on with making good sense of what there is ahead. When I talk of "making as good a job of it as one can" I don't of course mean doing anything special like, say, withdrawing mentally into some special place. I only mean living more attentively than I have been in the habit of doing. This at present seems to me to be something very simple – I don't mean easy, but uncomplicated. In this sense, having some advance knowledge makes things simpler because it brings them into focus, and is therefore a considerable help – at least I feel it is to me.

'The other thing, which is very closely linked up with this is my view of death in general. I don't think the difference between your philosophy and mine need make it difficult for us to understand each other about it. The relevant point about mine is that death is a mystery at least as great as life. As I am sure you will understand, what I mean is that, for me, death has none of the element of tragic futility which it has for many other people. It is not somewhere "out there" – it is properly within the same order as life and (however little enthusiasm one may have for it) to be viewed as eminently normal and, like life, with a certain piety. Further than that, the "consolations of religion" are very solid and very great. The reason I talk so much about what I feel is that I think it will help us both if we know it. But, of course, I have said nothing about my distress for others. I know, darling, that you do and will feel sad, and that nothing I can say will prevent this. Only do remember that it is normal for one to survive one's parents; and I do know from experience that when it happens, one does accept it – one's whole nature is geared to accepting it – and somehow one feels more, not less rooted in life because one is more strongly linked to the generation before one. This is no disrespect to one's parents; on the contrary, it is simply in the nature of things.

'I needn't tell you that the real problem for me is Ralph. The doctor has promised not to tell him sooner than is necessary. Then, we'll see: I can only hope for some miracle to make it more acceptable to him than it would be now. Anyhow, one can't work everything out in advance.'

At all times Manya wished to know the truth about the progress of her illness and indeed equipped herself with medical books to ensure that nothing was being hidden from her. In order to spare Ralph the unhappiness of knowing that she was in danger, she continued to live as nearly normal a life as was possible. In spite of increasing pain she worked up to eight hours a day at her translating. When willpower alone could not achieve this she had to resort to painkillers.

Eventually she entered a clinic for treatment but had only been there a few days when Ralph became seriously ill. She at once came out and nursed him for the few days he still had to live.

When later, after a period when she seemed better, alarming symptoms developed and she was told that she had only a few weeks before her, she made no mention of this or of the fact that she had received the Last Sacraments, but ordered champagne all round. She continued working until she was too weak to do so. Even if she had not told a friend 'I am infinitely happy and only sad that I am too weak to share my happiness' it was plain that she was at peace. Nor did she lose her sense of humour. To someone who had been praying until recently for her recovery and had now changed her intention, but had certainly never made any mention of this, she remarked: 'Thank goodness you look quite different since you have stopped telling God what to do about me.'

When she first knew she was seriously ill, she had written to her son, 'dying is a job . . . the important thing is to do it as well as one can'. When death was imminent her attitude was the same.

Two days before she died, she looked for the first time troubled and said: 'Until now I have always known what God wanted me to do, but now I feel quite extraordinary, and I am not sure what I should do. Do you think the cancer has reached my brain?'

When told that she was actually dying and that it would not last long, she relaxed and said 'In that case it is very simple, but would it be peculiar if I asked to have the Last Sacraments again?'

*

The author was a meticulous writer and the editors of this volume are painfully aware that, had she lived, the drafts she left would have been revised many times before she would have allowed them to go to press. As they stand they have however a spontaneity which is some compensation for the loss in style.

In order to ensure the complete safety of people who spoke to Manya in confidence it has been necessary to remove any indications which would identify them.

A Letter and some Notes

Index

Letter from Dr Thomson Hancock

I first met Manya Harari in February 1968. She was brought to me by her general practitioner and at that time I had no knowledge of her interesting background and her personal charm.

Her medical problem was resolved and a specific line of therapy decided on which involved treatment with x-rays first to be followed by repeated courses of medicinal treatment. In all stages of her illness Manya gave her medical advisers the greatest possible help in that she showed her trust in them and meticulously followed their advice. She was justly rewarded by achieving a good partial remission of rather more than a year. She would rarely complain about herself and her anxiety was always that she should remain strong enough to look after her husband who, she insisted, must not learn of the serious nature of her illness.

As course succeeded course of drug treatment I came to know Manya well and was constantly surprised at the amount of work this frail-looking woman could achieve. She was a realist and insisted on knowing the truth about her illness but faced the future with steadfast courage.

Manya succeeded miraculously in keeping from her husband all the attendant worries and anxieties he would have felt had he known she was suffering from inoperable cancer. Although she was naturally very upset at his death she was inclined to look on this as an act of God making it easier for her to die peacefully. Prior to the time of her husband's death his health and happiness had been her main concern. Following his death she devoted herself with all her remaining energy to an attempt to complete the book on which she was working.

Manya showed throughout her illness, as indeed she showed in her visits to Russia, a steadfastness of purpose and a complete disregard for danger and discomfort. Only when pain became unbearable would she acknowledge its presence and as soon as means were found to control it she did not need weaning from the painkilling tablets; they were thrown away.

She was always kind and considerate to her nurses and her doctors and never worried or embarrassed them with unnecessary questions. She rightly asked to be told the truth but when satisfied that she understood the position she accepted it and made her plans accordingly.

I have no doubt that her last days were made happier for her by her deep faith in God and by her close community with her son, Michael, which is beautifully brought out in the letter she wrote to him on learning that she had very likely only a short time to live.

Notes to Text

PART I. A RUSSIAN CHILDHOOD

1 Decembrists: liberal aristocrats, mostly young officers, who in 1825 rebelled against Nicholas I. Five were executed, many more sent to Siberia where some wives joined their husbands.
2 In Russian 'dark' is the equivalent of 'ignorant' and is sometimes used of peasants.
3 Glinka's *A Life for the Tsar* is now known in the USSR as *Ivan Susanin*.

PART III. THE MIDDLE EAST

THIS YEAR IN JERUSALEM

1 Groppi is the most fashionable café and pastry shop in Cairo.
2 The Jewish Army, the Hagana, developed with British encouragement during the 1929 Arab rebellion. After 1936 it was trained by Orde Wingate. Later, when British/Jewish relations deteriorated, its members if caught armed were liable to the death sentence, though this was rarely carried out. Eventually nearly all able-bodied men who did not belong to the terrorist Stern or Irgun groups joined the Hagana.
3 Der Yassin: where the Arabs were massacred by terrorists.
4 Sworn in on the previous Monday as the regular army.
5 WIZO: Women's International Zionist Organisation.
6 Forty-eight members of the convoy were killed.

PART IV. RETOUR AUX SOURCES

FIRST JOURNEY TO RUSSIA

1 Malenkov, G. M., b. 1902. After Stalin's death in 1953, he was Chairman of the Council of Ministers. Forced to resign in 1955. Dismissed with Anti-Party group in 1957.
2 Beria, L. P., 1899-1953. Head of NKVD (the then designation of the Secret Police) from 1938. Marshal 1945. Member of the Politbureau and Deputy Chairman of the Council of Ministers. Shot after Stalin's death, allegedly for spying for Britain for over thirty years but more probably suspected of an attempt to seize sole power, with the help of the security apparatus.
3 Molotov, V. M., b. 1890. Commissar then Minister of Foreign Affairs 1939-1949. 1949 signed alliance with Britain. Represented USSR at founding of UNO. Demoted by Khrushchev 1957. Ambassador to Outer Mongolia 1960.
4 Kaganovich, L. M., b. 1893. Head of Party Control Commission in the thirties. First Chairman of Council of Ministers after Stalin's death. Denounced with the Anti-Party group in 1957.

5 Repin, Ilya, 1844-1930. Famous Russian realist painter.

6 *Dvorniki:* Porters. In winter their main task is to clear away the snow.

7 *Gorodovoi:* A pre-Revolutionary term for a policeman.

8 *Fortochka:* Small ventilation window.

9 *Stolovaya:* A cheap restaurant or cafeteria.

10 MID: Ministry of Foreign Affairs.

11 Ehrenburg, Ilya, 1891-1967. The famous novelist. In 1955 Harvill published his novel *The Thaw* translated by Manya Harari.

12 MVD: The Secret Police, now known as the KGB.

13 A *Kremlin,* or *Kreml,* is a fortress. They are to be found in various Russian towns.

14 *Kokoshniki:* High headdresses.

15 *Sarafany:* Long embroidered gowns.

16 Kseshinskaya: Famous pre-Revolutionary ballerina and mistress of Nicholas II before his marriage.

17 Vera Panova. Harvill published two of her books in 1957: *Time Walked* and *Span of the Year.*

18 *Dacha:* Country villa.

19 *Komsomolka:* A member of the Communist Youth League – the Komsomol.

20 *Zhuliki:* Toughs, bandits.

21 *Sovkhoz:* State farm, *Kolkhoz:* Collective farm. Since the collectivisation of the land, peasants are members either of *Kolkhozes,* where they live by the shared profits of the farm and the proceeds of their small individual plots, or of *Sovkhozes,* where they are paid a regular wage.

22 Nekrasov, N. A., 1821-1877. Liberal poet.

23 Yudenich, Nikolai Nikolayevich, 1862-1933. White general who commanded the anti-Bolshevik forces on the North-West front during the Civil War. He nearly recaptured Petrograd before his final defeat in 1919.

24 *Sotnik:* A hundredth part of a hectare.

25 *Ficus:* Little fig trees.

26 Pioneers: Youth organisation for children of pre-Komsomol age.

27 Zhukov, G. K., b. 1896. Marshal of the Soviet Union, Minister of Defence 1955. Dismissed and attacked by Khrushchev 1958.

28 *'Zdravia zhelayem':* 'We wish you health.'

29 NEP: Economic policy introduced by Lenin in 1921. It lasted to 1929 and allowed a certain amount of free enterprise.

30 Obraztsov: In charge of the Puppet Theatre.

31 Zagorsk: Famous monastery and one of the few surviving seminaries.

32 Tretyakov Gallery: The great picture gallery in Moscow founded by a rich merchant, and patron of the arts, of that name.

33 Blok, Alexander, 1880-1921. One of Russia's greatest poets, his influence is still felt today.

34 *Konyok Gorbunok: The Hunch-back Horse.*

SECOND JOURNEY TO RUSSIA

1 Petipa, Marius, 1822-1910. Born in Marseilles. A choreographer who worked with the Imperial Ballet.

2 In fact Vlasov, a Soviet General who collaborated with the Germans in World War II, was executed in 1945.

3 Diamat: Dialectic materialism.

4 *Kulaki:* Rich peasants who were expropriated and either deported or killed.

5 Pavlov, Ivan. Born in Ryazan 1849, died 1936. Russian physicist who won a Nobel Prize in 1904.

6 *Khozyaika:* Mistress of the house.

7 Kirov, S. M., 1886-1934. Member of Politbureau 1930. His murder in 1934 served as a pretext for the Great Purge.

8 Black Marias.

9 The painter and writer, a friend of Manya's.

10 A vegetable oil used in Lent.

11 Razin, Stenka: Cossack leader of a peasant uprising in 1667. Executed in Moscow in 1671.

THIRD JOURNEY TO RUSSIA

1 Although Manya would not have known this at the time, this was the theatre directed by Yuri Zavadsky, which Solzhenitsyn wanted to join as an actor in his student days in Rostov.

2 Anti-Party group: Molotov, Kaganovich and others defeated in 1957 by Khrushchev after a fierce struggle within the Party Praesidium.

3 'Red' – as in Red Square – meant 'beautiful' in Old Russian.

4 General Kornilov was made Commander-in-Chief by Kerensky but broke with him and was killed fighting the Bolsheviks.

5 *Druzhinniki:* Civilian vigilantes.

6 *Damochka:* A disdainful diminutive for 'lady'.

7 Soviet official term for ethnic origin, which has to be entered on everyone's identity card.

8 Bedny, D., 1883-1945. Poet of middling standing, had a strong propaganda line.

9 The Donbas: Steel and coal mining area in the Ukraine.

10 *Pelmennaya:* Eating place specialising in *pelmeni* – Siberian meat balls.

11 *Baikovoye:* Woollen dress.

12 In June 1905 the sailors on board the Battleship *Potemkin* mutinied while in Odessa. They were joined by rioting strikers. The troops fired on the crowd milling on the steps leading to the harbour. Eisenstein's film *Battleship Potemkin* is based on the incident.

13 Armand-Emmanuel Richelieu, Duc de, 1766-1822. Governor of Odessa. Minister during the reign of Louis XVIII.

14 Artificial lakes.

15 *Sovnarkhozy:* Economic Councils.

16 Many Russians who were made prisoners were sent to Siberia on their return.

17 *Khata:* Peasant hut.

18 At which young poets read out their work to large audiences.

19 *Syntaxis:* An underground literary magazine.

20 Ginsburg, Alexander. Poet who was imprisoned in 1968.

21 *Otlichniki:* Star pupils.

22 'Former Person': Soviet term used for members of the dispossessed classes.

Notes to Text

23 Postyshev, P. P. 1880-1940. Secretary of Ukrainian Central Committee, member of Politbureau. Liquidated 1940.

24 *Finka:* Knife.

25 *Putyovki:* Travel Vouchers.

26 The vigilantes are chasing them away.

27 Esenin or Yesenin, S. A., 1895-1925. Lyrical poet of the 'Imagist' school. Married the dancer Isadora Duncan. Went abroad 1923. Returned 1925. Hanged himself.

28 Krestinsky. Commissar of Justice. Liquidated 1938.

29 'Kukuruznik': A nickname for Khrushchev earned because of his passion for maize. *Kukuruza* – Maize.

30 *Boyariny:* Ladies.

31 Kronstadt: Naval base on an island in the Gulf of Finland. In 1921 the sailors there revolted against the Bolsheviks.

32 Kerensky, A. F., 1881-1970. Played a leading role in the February Revolution of 1917. Prime Minister of the Provisional Government. Wanted to go on fighting against the Germans. Deposed November 1917. Fled to France.

33 Litvinov, Maxim (real name Meyer Wallach), 1876-1951. Bolshevik Ambassador to London 1917-18. Commissar of Foreign Affairs 1930-39. Removed from office before the pact with Hitler was made. Ambassador to USA 1941-42. Deputy Commissar for Foreign Affairs 1943-46.

34 *Chinovnik:* Bureaucrat.

35 Voroshilov, K. E., b. 1881. Commissar Ministry of Defence 1929-30. President of the Praesidium of the Supreme Soviet 1953-60.

36 '*Do tovo ne doshlo – poka*': 'It hasn't come to that yet.'

THE AUTHOR

1 *The Changing World:* After the war she co-edited, with Bernard Wall, a second magazine of the same name.

Index

Index

Boni (of Russian Ministry of Culture), 193, 213-14, 224, 225
Boria (Yalta engineer), 254, 256-7, 262
Bourne, Gordon, 300
Braun, Frau (boarding-school headmistress), 16
Brothers Karamazov, The (Dostoevsky), 172
Buber, Martin, 87-9
Buchanan, Sir George, 21
Bulgakov, M. A., 297

Cairo, 50, 69; in the 1920s, 45-9; Jews in, 45-6
Campbell, Roy, 298
Carlsbad, 13
Catherine the Great, 233, 245
Catholic Church, Manya received into, 9, 69
Chamberlain, Sir Austen, 21
Changing World, The, 9, 10, 296
Chekhov, Anton, his house in Yalta, 242, 245-6
Chernyshev (Moscow architect), 166-7
Cherry Orchard, The (Chekhov), 246
Christianity: Manya attracted to, 18-20; and a New Jerusalem, 53, 54; Manya converted to, 69
Churchill, Winston, 246, 269, 270
collective farms – see kolkhozes
Collins, Sir William ('Billy'), 286; in Moscow, 10, 104, 107-33
'Comrades' Courts', Russian, 236-7, 240
Copenhagen, 28
Copts, 44
Culture, Russian Ministry of, 125-6, 183-4, 190, 192

D'Arcy, Father Martin, 9
Dangulov (Foreign Literature editor, Moscow), 166
Dawson, Christopher, 9
Dayan, General Moshe, 95
Decembrists, 14, 233

Der Yassin, 74
Diaghilev, Sergei, 119, 185, 210
Diaspora, 45, 47, 52, 55
Doctor Zhivago (Pasternak), 285, 296
Dom Knigi (House of Books), 139-41, 204
Dora (helper in Geva kibbutz), 60, 61
Dorofeich, Stepan (Redkino agent), 153
Dostoevsky, Fedor, 172
Dublin Review, The, 9

education: difference between English and Russian principles, 35-6; Russian, 187, 268, 275
Egypt: in the 1920s, 44-9; Jews in, 44-8; British management of, 44; landscape, 46; *fellaheen*, 47; ginning factories, 47-8
Ehrenburg, Ilya, 105, 113, 120-1, 140, 171, 172-3, 184, 247, 292-3, 297
Ehrenburg, Mrs, 113, 120-1, 128
Ein Harod, 62, 64, 68
Ein Kerem, 97
El Kantara, 50, 73
Emmaus, Spring of, 86
Esenin, S. A., 282
Evgeny Onegin (Pushkin), 255

Far from Moscow (Azhayev), 199
Fedya (young Rostovian), 229-30
fellaheen, in Egypt, 47
First Circle, The (Solzhenitsyn), 296
Fonteyn, Margot, 211
Foreign Office, Political Intelligence Department of, 9, 104, 295
Fountain of Bakhchisarai, The (ballet), 118, 119-20, 128, 185, 211
Freiburg, 13

Gabovich (Russian writer), 210, 213
Galsworthy, John, 125, 175, 177, 247
Galya (Yalta beggar), 248-9, 250-52, 253
Garona, 95
Gatchina, 134, 141, 142, 144-6, 147
Gerasimov, A. M., 184

Index

Index

Index

Index

Odessa, 254-62; historical associations, 255; university, 255; church, 256; ballet at Opera House, 257-8; synagogue, 258; blackmarketing, 257, 259, 260-1; museum, 258-9; 'bad times for Jews', 258, 259, 262; Cathedral, 260
Ostankino, 169
Our Man in Havana (Greene), 247

painting, Russian, 173-4, 184, 190-2, 214
Palestine: Manya's first visit (1925), 41-3; as Jewish National Home, 42, 52-3, 55, 69; and Zionism, 50-6, 88; kibbutzim, 57-68, 99-100; Manya's 1948 visit, 69, 70-101; increased Jewish immigration to, 70; bi-national state, 70; war of independence, 70-101
Palmach regiment (of Hagana), 84, 86
Panova, Vera, 135, 138, 140, 144, 204, 210
Passover, 18, 20, 52
Pasternak, Boris, 246, 247, 274, 285, 296
Pavel (Russian countryman), 263-7
Pavlov, Ivan, 198, 244
People's Court (Moscow), 200-3
Peter the Great, 245
Peter (Polish orphan in Palestine), 79-80
Peter (young Rostovian), 229-30, 232
Petipa, Marius, 185
Petushki, 222
Pioneers (pre-Komsomol group), 157
Plisetskaya (ballerina), 168
Political Intelligence Department, Foreign Office, 9, 104
Polya (Rostov *provocateur*), 229-30, 231-2
Possessed, The (Dostoevsky), 172
Postyshev, P. P., 278
Pravda, 274, 293
Prince Igor (ballet), 185
Prodigal Son, The (ballet), 210
Prokofiev (Assistant Secretary, Leningrad Writers' Union), 138-9, 140, 142
Prokofievna (Redkino witch), 24
Providence, La (Home for Jewish Orphans), 9, 49

publishing, in Russia, 110, 111-13, 123-6, 138-41, 166-7, 175-6, 183, 192-3, 213, 215, 223-4, 225
Pushkin, Alexander, 255

Rachel (helper in Geva kibbutz), 58-9
rail travel, Russian, 134, 142-9, 159-62, 187-8, 189, 193-5, 197-200, 203-4, 205, 211-13, 215-16, 222-3
Ramat Rahel, 87
Ramleh, 91
Ras el Gin, 92
Razin, Stenka, 219
Red Poppy, The (ballet), 185, 257-8
Redkino (country estate), 9, 22-4; father's purchase of, 22; changing seasons at, 24; Manya's return in 1955, 122, 143-58; rail and bus journey to, 143-50; changes at, 151-3; during Revolution and Second World War, 152, 153, 154; collectivisation, 153; school, 155-8
religion, in Russia, 113-15, 122-3, 154, 163, 168-9, 173, 176, 185, 188, 192, 193, 195, 197, 219, 225, 244, 251, 256, 265-8, 288
Richelieu, Armand-Emmanuel Duc de, 255
Rikarna (governess), 13, 14-15, 18, 19, 22, 23, 28, 30, 33, 129, 131, 132, 147, 149, 162, 174
Rishon Le Zion, 91, 92, 94
ritual murder, Jewish, 19
Roma (helper in Geva kibbutz), 57-9, 60, 61, 62, 63, 100
Romeo and Juliet (ballet), 185, 192
Rostov, 229-32, 293; *provocateur* in, 229, 230, 231
Rothschild, Baron Edmund de, 50
Rozhdestvensky, Robert, 276
Ryazan: Manya's 1956 visit to, 193-200; talk on journey with girl from Siberian camp, 193-5; kremlin, 196; museum, 196; Easter Sunday at

314

Index

Index

WIZO (Women's International Zionist Organization), 75, 85
Wolff, Fräulein (boarding-school head-mistress), 16
Wooden Horse, The (Williams), 125
Workman, The, 108
Writers' Union: Leningrad, 135, 138-9; Moscow, 166-7, 263

Yalta, 239-54; Ukraina Hotel, 240-2; talks on economic plan, Stalin, anti-semitism and war, 240-2; Stalin's visit to (1945), 242; sightseeing tour, 242-3; Bolshevik schoolmaster, 243-4; religion, 244, 250-1; Chekhov's house, 245-6; writer of poem on Lenin, 246; Vorontsov Palace, 246-7; market, 247-8; beggars Galya and Tanya, 248-9, 250-3; anti-semitism, 257
Yevtushenko, Y. A., 277, 297
Yudenich, General Nikolai, 153
Yurik (Redkino boy), 152, 158

Zagorsk monastery, 173, 176, 187-8, 251
Zhukov, Marshal G. K., 170-1, 185
Zmeul (President of Mezhkniga), 112-13, 138, 183
Zoya (girl on Moscow-Ryazan train), 193-5